Mastering French Vocabulary

A THEMATIC APPROACH

D0638290

Mastering French Vocabulary

A THEMATIC APPROACH

Reinhild Herrmann and Rainer Rauch

BARRON'S

Address all inquiries to:
Barron's Educational Series, Inc.
250 Wireless Boulevard
Hauppauge, New York 11788

Photo Credits
The Bettmann Archive, pp. 97, 189, 230. UPI/Bettmann, pp. XV, 28, 125, 277. Reuters/Bettmann, pp. 36, 43, 184, 192.

Library of Congress Catalog Number 95-75990
International Standard Book Number 0-8120-9107-8

Printed in the United States of America

5678 8800 9876

Contents

Foreword

What Is meant by "basic and advanced vocabulary"?

How well we speak French is determined by our knowledge of French grammar and by the number of situations in which we can hold our own. Our performance depends primarily on our knowledge of the vocabulary specific to the situation. In addition, we need a great many set phrases, fixtures of all communicative speech, in order to have a good command of the language. Modern textbooks take these facts into account with increasing frequency, and a modern dictionary should do the same. The present volume, by including basic and advanced terms, attempts to do precisely that. One can identify various levels of competence at which a speaker is able to hold his or her own. The lowest level represents what one could call the survival level. The learner's command of the language is sufficient to get by in the host country to some degree: to go shopping, to ask for directions, and to take part in simple conversations. These are the criteria used to define the elementary vocabulary of a language. Such elementary vocabulary includes about 1200 to 1500 word equations, or verbal equivalents. To enable the learner to handle selected topics well enough to assume active conversational roles, the vocabulary has to be approximately twice that size. A basic vocabulary defined along these lines contains roughly 2500 to 3000 word equations. If the learning objective is moved one notch higher—that is, if the learner is to have an active command of the linguistic situation, with no need to keep asking the meaning of words—then about 5000 to 6000 equivalents are necessary.

This book attempts to meet the second and third of the three educational objectives described above. Knowledge of the 3888 word equations contained in the basic vocabulary will provide the learner with a good and linguistically appropriate command of the subject areas we present. He or she will attain a level somewhat above the one normally described as basic vocabulary. If one takes into account the fact that about 800 French words appear more than once under various headings, the basic vocabulary includes some 3000 French words. In addition, we offer the learner 1943 additional word equations in the advanced vocabulary. Knowledge of that vocabulary will bring the learner to a level at which he or she can claim to have a fairly fluent command of French in the subject areas presented.

Defining "basic and advanced vocabulary"

The words included in the basic vocabulary were selected after intensive examination of the curricula of French and German teaching institutions, and the major textbooks used in schools and adult education programs of these countries. First, all the words that occurred in these sources were placed in the basic vocabulary. That produced a list of about 3500 words. Next, they were assigned to the various subject categories developed at the same time. Then, this rather large basic vocabulary was reduced by about 500 words, on the basis of joint discussions by a number of experts. Some of those words were transferred to the advanced vocabulary, while others were eliminated altogether. The word "allumette," for example, was shifted to the advanced vocabulary; "briquet" was retained; and "lorsque" was eliminated. Next, the remaining vocabulary was checked for consistency, to see, for example, whether all the major colors were included and whether all the major occupations and professions were included.

After the basic vocabulary and all the subject areas had been decided on, the advanced vocabulary was determined. First, about 800 words from the material used in the upper grades of school were obtained and labeled as advanced vocabulary. The final determination of the advanced vocabulary was done in conjunction with the division of the subject areas into smaller parts, known in-house as "bundles," which clearly showed what words had to be added to the advanced vocabulary list under a spcific topic to make the "bundle" rounded—that is, to cover all the major possibilities of speech. The words thus obtained were then presented to other experts. The advanced vocabulary is not based on statistical findings, but everyone who participated in the selection process had a chance to vote on the final selections. At the present time we have to content ourselves with such a rating system, because a body of words organized by topic thus far does not exist, and the available frequency lists are obsolete and not sufficiently indicative.

Defining the themes

This book is divided into 35 subject areas. Each area, or topic, is further broken down into as many as 10 subareas, or bundles. There are several reasons for organizing the book on the basis of subject matter. First, an enormous vocabulary of almost 6000 word equations, whose numbers alone are enough to deter the learner, is divided in this way into small vocabularies with a unifying theme, each containing at most 300 word equations. The amount to be studied and learned thus becomes easier to handle, and the learner quickly becomes able to express himself or herself fully within a thematic context after studying a single topic, which is not the case with an alphabetically organized dictionary. That is a great advantage over the person who is learning all the words beginning with "a," and it offers a less ambitious learner the possibility of learning just one bundle under a single topic—about 30 word equations. In addition, a thematically arranged dictionary also offers the user the possibility of choice: you can begin with a topic that is important to you personally, postponing other, less significant, topics to a later time or omitting them entirely. Arranging the words on the basis of subject matter is done for didactic reasons, but it also has an impact on individual study goals, which each learner has a chance to set for himself or herself.

Once we decided to divide the vocabulary into subject areas, we had to define them. This quite ordinary process, however, in our opinion is extremely difficult and extremely important. Many examples usually begin with the universe and end with the postage stamp. The world view of such models is based on reality, proceeding from things of enormous magnitude through nature and mankind down to the level of truly minor objects. This type of classification, based on natural sciences and philosophy, is seldom suited for languages. Thus, it was felt best to start our thematic classification with the language itself: how does language classify reality, what important things are there in linguistic terms. This method of classification can be compared to the way our sense of touch is organized. If our sense of touch were the sole determining factor, 50 percent of the human body would consist of hands, because the hands are most important for our sense of touch. From a linguistic point of view the most important things are human beings, because only human beings speak. When humans speak, they talk usually about other humans and exclusively with other humans. Thus, human beings are to language what hands are to the sense of touch. Subjectively, human beings are most important. Therefore we begin with the description of human beings and proceed through their more intimate relationships and their external relationships to their activities. Then we take a look at their basic needs and other, more complex, needs. Finally we deal with man's own classification of reality.

In this way we arrived at 35 subject areas which in our opinion are the best possible way to divide the vocabulary. Words that could not be classified—structural words, almost without exception—were given a subject heading of their own; actually they belong to every subject area.

Dividing the subject areas into smaller units—the "bundles"—was quite easy in some cases ("Eating and Drinking," for example), while in others it was heatedly discussed and fairly controversial. These bundles have primarily a didactic function: They break down the material to be learned into extremely small units, which enable the learner to make rapid progress in an objective context. You need to keep in mind that the actual unit of study is the subject area, because your knowledge of French stores and restaurants does not yet enable you to talk about "Eating and Drinking." The topics, therefore, are the real learning objective. Your knowledge will allow you to hold your own in all situations pertaining to the topic.

Naturally the allocation of words to certain subject areas is arbitrary at times: we assigned the parts of the body to the "Illness and Health" category, not to "Appearance," where they also would have had an appropriate place. We proceeded on the assumption that one is more likely to speak about body parts in the context of discussing sickness than in the context of describing a person's looks. "J'ai mal au ventre" surely belongs to the topic "Illness," but "Paul a un gros ventre" falls under "Appearance." In our opinion the first utterance is spontaneous and natural, whereas the second utterance goes beyond the normal description of a person and is slightly malicious: one would be more apt to say "Paul est un peu gros," or "Paul n'est pas maigre." With other parts of the body the situation is even more unambiguous. Faced with this dilemma, we decided to allocate all body parts of the "Illness" category unless they were absolutely indispensable in the "Appearance" chapter.

On choosing the illustrative sentences

In the basic and advanced vocabulary there are 1310 examples, or illustrative sentences, in all. This means that there is one example for every fourth or fifth word equation. The examples are intended to satisfy several criteria. An illustrative sentence is called for when a word equation is not entirely clear, when the grammatical usage of a word in French is not clear, when interesting information about the country can be presented in the example, or when a particular usage or idiomatic use of the French word is possible.

Beyond the aforementioned criteria, we also demanded that every illustrative sentence had to be useful to the learner, and to such an extent that the learner could make almost every example a part of his or her personal vocabulary. That is, we want to provide the learner not only with word equations, but also with sentence equations that can be put to some real use. Naturally, it is easy to find an illustrative sentence for every word equation, for example, "Elle a la taille 36." But we think our example is far more useful: "Vous faites quelle taille?" because one day the learner will hear that very question in France. The examples chosen are very idiomatic, and they usually are formulated in the first or second person, so that they can be borrowed directly, with a minimum of adaptation to the learner's own situation. In the example "Nicolas a trois ans, il est très mignon" only the proper name is variable. By inserting the correct name, you can employ this sentence in a situation in which you are making positive remarks about a small child. When illustrative sentences appear in the third person (i.e., when someone else is being talked about) we usually dispensed with the use of pronouns, which, though practical, are learner-unfriendly, and used the proper names of fictitious persons instead.

One other indispensable requirement for us was the quality of the translation. "Vous êtes libre demain?" usually cannot be translated as "Are you free tomorrow?" In the situation in which the French sentence would be uttered, the English equivalent would have to be "Do you have time tomorrow?" For this reason some of our translations may seem very free; however, we believe that they most closely approximate the French original with regard to usage and content. Where the level of style is concerned, we also tried to employ whatever the corresponding words would be. "Je suis bien avec lui," therefore, we rendered not as "I feel safe and secure with him" but as "We get along well" even though "On s'entend bien" would be a possible retranslation from the English. That means that the retranslation of the English illustrative sentence need not necessarily lead back to the original French sentence.

Some didactic considerations

In this book we have largely dispensed with abbreviations of grammatical and lexicographical terms, and have tried to translate language with language. For this reason the gender of nouns is indicated not by a grammatical abbreviation, but by the definite article; only in cases where the gender cannot be recognized from the article will the learner find the appropriate grammatical abbreviation. The feminine forms of certain nouns and those of the adjectives are given in their entirety. Plurals that deviate from the norm are also indicated. The verbs are given only in the infinitive form, but with the help of the appendix every verb form can be derived. For every lexical entry there is a corresponding phonetic transcription, in accordance with the conventions of the API. The phonetic transcription is based on the so-called "mot phonétique," that is, no word boundaries are marked in the transcription. That should help combat the tendency of English speakers to pronounce the French sentence word by word. The sounds of French, their phonetic patterns, and French graphs are presented in tabular form.

This book is suitable for all learners who want to improve their French. It can be used by beginners who have been studying French for about one year, as well as by very advanced learners, who will find in the basic and advanced vocabulary idiomatic expressions that one otherwise tends to hunt for in vain (we have devoted an entire chapter to fixed expressions). A text that purports to do justice to learners at all levels is automatically suspect. We believe, however, that the present volume succeeds in its effort to do just that. The beginner can study certain subject areas and learn their basic vocabulary; the advanced user will be more interested in special topics and in the advanced vocabulary; and the extremely advanced learner will borrow the idiomatic expressions or add to his or her vocabulary in all the subject areas we present here.

The question about the best method of study is basically unanswerable. One learner will heavily rely on the translations, while another will be able to acquire the thematic vocabulary basically without referring to the English. On the other hand, probably it will be advantageous for all learners to take a fixed amount to study at a time. A beginner can resolve to master a topic in a week's time, while a more advanced learner can do the same amount in a day. Basically, one should study one topic at a time and follow the sequence of the "bundles" within each topic. General topics, such as "Human Activities," are more complex and harder to learn than specialized ones, because the word equations are more complex. "Cake" is almost always "gâteau," and "metteur en scène" is "director," but "penser" can have different meanings in many contexts. It is also important that you check on what you have learned at some later time, to ensure that the French expression has been correctly retained in your long-term memory. The interval between your original acquisition and your review session should not be too brief; that is, you should let at least one week pass before checking on your success. An even longer time lag is preferable, although you run the risk of losing sight of your objective. Very advanced learners may content themselves with first reading through the basic and advanced vocabulary before beginning to focus on particular idiomatic phrases.

La Pyramide de l'architecte Ieoh Ming Pei au Musée du Louvre, Paris.
Ieoh Ming Pei's Pyramid at the Louvre Museum, Paris.

The Sounds of the French Language

Vowels

Symbol	Description	Spelling	Example
[a]	Slightly more open than the **a** in **hat**	a à e	travail voilà femme
[ɑ]	Like **a** in **father**	a â	passer tâche
[ã]	Nasalized [a]	am amp an and ans ant em emps en ent	jambon champ an grand dans restaurant employé temps en argent
[e]	Like **a** in **fate,** but without the glide	ai e é ê ei er es et ez	aider effet blé gêner freiner aimer les et nez
[ɛ]	Like **e** in **met**	ai aî aie ais ait e é è ê ei es(t) et	faire chaîne monnaie français lait cher médecin chèque crêpe peine es, est bonnet

Symbol	Description	Spelling	Example
[ɛ̃]	Nasalized [ɛ]	aim ain ein en im in ingt un	**fa**im m**ain** **pein**dre b**ien** **im**portant **fin** v**ingt** **un**
[ə]	Like **a** in **comma**	e	nous prenons
[i]	Like **i** in **machine**	i î il is it iz y	**il** **î**le gent**il** perm**is** **lit** r**iz** t**y**pe
[o]	Like **o** in **note,** but without the glide	au aud aut aux eau eaux o ô op os ot	**au** ch**aud** il f**aut** f**aux** **eau** Bord**eaux** r**o**se dr**ô**le tr**op** gr**os** coquelic**ot**
[ɔ]	A little more open and rounded than the **aw** in **law**	au o ô u	**au**to **o**ffrir h**ô**pital maxim**u**m
[õ]	Nasalized [o]	om omb on ond ont	**nom** plo**mb** **on** bl**ond** p**ont**

Symbol	Description	Spelling	Example
[ø]	Lips rounded for [o] and held without moving while [e] is pronounced	eu eux œufs	**peu** **yeux** **œufs**
[œ]	Lips rounded for [e] and held without moving while [ɛ] is pronounced	eu œu	meuble **œuf**
[u]	Like **u** in **rude**	ou où oû oût août	**ou** **où** coûter goût **août**
[y]	Lips rounded for [u] and held without moving while [i] is pronounced	eu u û ut	**eu** mur mûr salut

Diphthongs

Symbol	Description	Spelling	Example
[j]	Like **y** in **year** or **y** in **toy**	i il ill ille y	bien travail reveiller feuille yeux
[ɥ]	Like **u** [y] pronounced with consonantal value preceding a vowel	u	huile
[w]	Like **w** in **water**	w ou	week-end jouer
[wa]		oi oie ois oit	avoir voie trois droit
[wɛ̃]		oin	pointure

Consonants

Symbol	Description	Spelling	Example
[b]	Like **b** in **baby**	b	**b**eau ro**b**e
[d]	Like **d** in **dead**	d	**d**ame su**d**
[f]	Like **f** in **face**	f ph	**f**ille **ph**oto
[g]	Like **g** in **go**	g gu gue	**g**arder ba**gu**ette va**gue**
[ʒ]	Like **s** in **pleasure**	j g ge	**j**our **g**ens nous man**ge**ons
[k]	Like **k** in **kill**, but without aspiration	c ch k q qu	**c**ourse or**ch**estre **k**ilo co**q** **qu**alité
[l]	Like **l** in **like** or in **slip**; not like **l** in **old**	l	**l**ivre
[m]	Like **m** in **more**	m	**m**anger
[n]	Like **n** in **nest**	n mn	**n**ord auto**mn**e
[ɲ]	Like **ny** in **canyon** or **ni** in **onion**	gn	a**gn**eau
[ŋ]	Like **ng** in **parking**	ng	campi**ng**
[p]	Like **p** in **pen**, but without aspiration	p b	**p**asser o**b**server

Symbol	Description	Spelling	Example
[r]	Usually a friction **r** with the point of articulation between the rounded back of the tongue and the hard palate	r rc rd rf rps rs rt	**r**ose po**rc** bo**rd** ne**rf** co**rps** deho**rs** po**rt**
[s]	Like **s** in **send**	c ç s sc ss t x	**c**inéma fran**ç**ais **s**avoir **sc**ène pa**ss**er na**t**ional di**x**
[z]	Like **z** in **zeal**	s z	ro**s**e **z**one
[ʃ]	Like **sh** in **shall** or **ch** in **machine**	ch	**ch**ercher
[t]	Like **t** in **tea,** but without aspiration	t th	**t**able **th**é
[v]	Like **v** in **vest**	v w	**v**in **w**agon

List of Abbreviations

adv	adverb
f	feminine noun
fpl	plural feminine noun
inv	invariable
m	masculine noun
mf	masculine and feminine noun
mpl	plural masculine noun
qqc	something; s.th.
qqn	someone; s.o.
s.th.	something
s.o.	someone

The Human Being

as an Individual

Personal Data

l'**adresse** *f* [adrɛs]	address
l'**adulte** *mf* [adylt]	adult
l'**âge** *m* [ɑʒ]	age
aîné, e [ene]	elder, eldest, oldest
C'est mon frère aîné.	That's my elder brother.
l'**an** *m* [ɑ̃]	year
J'ai 19 ans.	I'm 19 years old.
appeler (s') [saple]	be named, be called
Je m'appelle Jasmine.	My name is Jasmine.
l'**avenue** *f* [avny]	avenue
J'habite 3, avenue Foch.	I live at 3 Foch Avenue.
le **boulevard** [bulvar]	boulevard
catholique [katɔlik]	Catholic
chrétien, ne [kretjɛ̃, ɛn]	Christian
le **département** [departəmɑ̃]	department [governmental administrative district]
Nancy se trouve dans le département de la Moselle.	Nancy is located in Moselle Department.
l'**enfant** *mf* [ɑ̃fɑ̃]	child, infant, baby
étranger, -ère [etrɑ̃ʒe, ɛr]	foreign, strange; foreigner, alien
l'**habitant** *m* [abitɑ̃]	inhabitant
habiter [abite]	live in; inhabit
l'**identité** *f* [idɑ̃tite]	identity
J'ai perdu ma carte d'identité.	I have lost my identity card.
l'**individu** *m* [ɛ̃dividy]	individual
madame [madam]	Mrs.
mademoiselle [madmwazɛl]	Miss
majeur, e [maʒœr]	of full age
Je suis majeur, j'ai 18 ans.	I'm of age; I'm 18 years old.
marié, e [marje]	married
le **métier** [metje]	trade, business, calling, occupation
Quel est votre métier?	What is your occupation?
monsieur [məsjø]	Mr.

naître [nɛtr]	be born
Je suis né le 12 mars 1973.	I was born on March 12, 1973.
la **nationalité** [nasjɔnalite]	nationality
Quelle est votre nationalité?	What is your nationality?
le **nom** [nɔ̃]	name
Quel est votre nom?	What is your name?
le **nom de famille** [nɔ̃dəfamij]	family name, surname
le **passeport** [paspɔr]	passport
le **pays** [pei]	country
la **pièce d'identité** [pjɛsdidãtite]	identification papers, documents
la **place** [plas]	place
le **prénom** [prenɔ̃]	Christian name, first name, given name
la **profession** [prɔfɛsjɔ̃]	profession
protestant, e [prɔtɛstã, t]	Protestant
la **religion** [rəliʒjɛ̃]	religion
la **rue** [ry]	street
le **sexe** [sɛks]	sex
la **signature** [siɲatyr]	signature
signer [siɲe]	sign
le **titre** [titr]	title

le, la **célibataire** [selibatɛr]	bachelor/spinster; single man/woman
la **date de naissance** [datdənɛsãs]	date of birth
divorcé, e [divɔrse]	divorced
l'**époux, -ouse** [epu, z]	spouse
être d'origine [ɛtrədɔriʒin]	come from, hail from
Ben est d'origine américaine.	Ben comes from America.
l'**impasse** f [ɛ̃pas]	dead-end street, blind alley
le **lieu de naissance** [ljødnɛsãs]	place of birth
le **nom de jeune fille** [nɔ̃dʒœnfij]	maiden name
personnel, le [pɛrsɔnɛl]	personal
le **signe particulier** [siɲəpartikylje]	distinguishing mark
le **veuf**, la **veuve** [vœf, vœv]	widower, widow

3

Occupations

l'**acteur, -trice** [aktœr, tris]	actor, actress
l'**agent** *m* [aʒã]	policeman
l'**architecte** *m* [arʃitɛkt]	architect
l'**avocat, e** [avɔka, t]	lawyer
le **boulanger,** la **boulangère** [bulãʒe, ɛr]	baker
le **cadre** [kadr]	executive, senior member of staff
le **certificat** [sɛrtifika]	certificate
le **charcutier,** la **charcutière** [ʃarkytje, ɛr]	pork butcher
le **chauffeur** [ʃofœr]	chauffeur, driver
le **chirurgien,** la **chirurgienne** [ʃiryrʒjɛ̃, ɛn]	surgeon
le **commerçant,** la **commerçante** [kɔmɛrsã, t]	merchant, dealer
le, la **concierge** [kõsjɛrʒ]	concierge, building superintendent
le, la **dentiste** [dãtist]	dentist
le **diplôme** [diplom]	diploma
le **directeur,** la **directrice** [dirɛktœr, tris]	director, manager, head
l'**écrivain** *m* [ekrivɛ̃]	writer
l'**élève** *mf* [elɛv] Paul est élève de quatrième au collège.	pupil, student Paul is a student in the fourth year of high school.
l'**employé, e** [ãplwaje]	employee
l'**étudiant, e** [etydjã, t]	student
le **facteur** [faktœr]	mailman, postal carrier
la **femme de ménage** [famdəmenaʒ]	cleaning woman
le, la **fonctionnaire** [fõksjɔnɛr]	official
le, la **garagiste** [garaʒist]	garage mechanic or owner
le **garçon** [garsõ]	waiter

le **gardien, la gardienne**	guard
[gardjɛ̃, ɛn]	
Mon oncle est gardien dans un musée.	My uncle is a museum guard.
l'**infirmier, -ère** *m, f* [ɛ̃firmje, ɛr]	nurse
l'**ingénieur** *m* [ɛ̃ʒenjœr]	engineer
l'**instituteur, -trice**	schoolteacher
[ɛ̃stitytœr, tris]	
l'**interprète** *mf* [ɛ̃tɛrprɛt]	interpreter
le, la **journaliste** [ʒurnalist]	journalist
le **juge** [ʒyʒ]	judge
le **marchand,** la **marchande**	merchant
[marʃã, d]	
le **marin** [marɛ̃]	sailor, seaman
le **médecin** [mɛdsɛ̃]	doctor
le **ministre** [ministr]	minister
le **musicien,** la **musicienne**	musician
[myzisjɛ̃, ɛn]	
l'**ouvrier, -ère** [uvrije, ɛr]	worker, laborer
le **paysan,** la **paysanne**	peasant
[peizã, an]	
le **peintre** [pɛ̃tr]	painter
le **pompier** [pɔ̃pje]	fireman
le **professeur** [prɔfɛsœr]	teacher; professor
la **retraite** [rətrɛt]	retirement, pension
Mon grand-père est en retraite.	My grandfather is retired.
le, la **secrétaire** [səkretɛr]	secretary
le **soldat** [sɔlda]	soldier
le **vendeur,** la **vendeuse**	salesman, saleslady
[vãdœr, øz]	

l'**agriculteur** *m* [agrikyltœr]	farmer, agriculturist
l'**apprenti, e** [aprãti]	apprentice, trainee
l'**artiste** *mf* [artist]	artist
le **bijoutier,** la **bijoutière**	jeweler
[biʒutje, ɛr]	
le **cadre moyen** [kadrəmwajɛ̃]	mid-level executive

le **cadre supérieur** [kadrəsyperjœr]	senior executive
le **chef d'entreprise** [ʃɛfdãtrəpriz]	head of company
le, la **comptable** [kõtabl]	bookkeeper
le **contre-maître** [kõtrəmɛtr]	overseer, foreman
le **contrôleur**, la **contrôleuse** [kõtrolœr, øz]	auditor, comptroller
le **cuisinier**, la **cuisinière** [kɥizinje, ɛr]	cook
l'**électricien** m [elɛktrisjɛ̃]	electrician
l'**électronicien, ne** [elɛktrɔnisjɛ̃, ɛn]	electronic technician
l'**enseignant, e** [ãsɛɲã, t]	teacher
l'**entrepreneur, -euse** [ãtrəprənœr, øz]	contractor
la **femme au foyer** [famofwaje]	housewife
la **garde** [gard]	guard
l'**hôtelier, -ère** [ɔtəlje, ɛr]	hotel manager or owner, innkeeper
l'**hôtesse de l'air** f [ɔtɛsdəlɛr]	stewardess
l'**industriel** m [ɛ̃dystrijɛl]	industrialist
le **jardinier**, la **jardinière** [ʒardinje, ɛr]	gardener
le **juge d'instruction** [ʒyʒdɛ̃stryksjõ]	examining magistrate
le **lycéen**, la **lycéenne** [liseɛ̃, ɛn]	high-school student
le **maçon** [masõ]	mason
le **maire** [mɛr]	mayor
l'**O.S.** m [oɛs]	temporary worker
l'**ouvrier agricole** m [uvrijeagrikɔl]	agricultural laborer, farm worker
l'**ouvrier qualifié** m [uvrijekalifje]	skilled worker
le **pâtissier**, la **pâtissière** [pɑtisje, ɛr]	pastry cook
le **P.D.G.** [pedeʒe]	manager; managing director
le **pêcheur**, la **pêcheuse** [pɛʃœr, øz]	fisherman, fisher, angler

le **pharmacien,** la **pharmacienne** [farmasjɛ̃, ɛn]	pharmacist
le, la **photographe** [fɔtɔgraf]	photographer
le **plombier** [plɔ̃bje]	plumber
le **proviseur** [prɔvizœr]	headmaster
le **rédacteur,** la **rédactrice** [redaktœr, tris]	editor
le **rédacteur en chef** [redaktœrɑ̃ʃɛf]	editor in chief
le **reporter** [rəpɔrtɛr]	reporter
le **retraité,** la **retraitée** [rətrete]	pensioner, retiree
sans profession [sɑ̃prɔfɛsjɔ̃]	without a profession
la **sténodactylo** [stenɔdaktilo]	shorthand typist
le **technicien,** la **technicienne** [tɛknisjɛ̃, ɛn]	technician

▬▬▬▬ Nations and Nationalities ▬▬▬▬

l'**Allemagne** f [almaɲ]	Germany
allemand, e [almɑ̃, d] Je suis allemand.	German I'm German.
américain, e [amerikɛ̃, ɛn]	American
anglais, e [ɑ̃glɛ, z] Je parle aussi anglais.	English I also speak English.
l'**Angleterre** f [ɑ̃glətɛr]	England
l'**Autriche** f [otriʃ]	Austria
autrichien, ne [otriʃjɛ̃, ɛn]	Austrian
belge [bɛlʒ]	Belgian
la **Belgique** [bɛlʒik]	Belgium
le **Danemark** [danmark]	Denmark
danois, e [danwa, z]	Danish
l'**Espagne** f [ɛspaɲ]	Spain
espagnol, e [ɛspaɲɔl]	Spanish
les **Etats-Unis** mpl [etazyni]	United States

7

français, e [frãsε, z]	French
la **France** [frãs]	France
hollandais, e [ˈɔlãdε, z]	Dutch
la **Hollande** [ˈɔlãd]	Holland
l'**Italie** f [itali]	Italy
italien, ne [italjε̃, εn]	Italian
le **Japon** [ʒapɔ̃]	Japan
japonais, e [ʒapɔnε, z]	Japanese
portugais, e [pɔrtygε, z]	Portugese
le **Portugal** [pɔrtygal]	Portugal

l'**Algérie** f [alʒeri]	Algeria
algérien, ne [alʒerjε̃, εn]	Algerian
britannique [britanik]	British
la **Grande-Bretagne** [grãdbrətaɲ]	Great Britain
grec, grecque [grεk]	Greek
la **Grèce** [grεs]	Greece
le **Luxembourg** [lyksãbur]	Luxembourg
luxembourgeois, e [lyksãburʒwa, z]	Luxembourgian
le **Maroc** [marɔk]	Morocco
marocain, e [marɔkε̃, εn]	Moroccan
néerlandais, e [neεrlãdε, z]	Dutch
les **Pays-Bas** mpl [peiba]	Netherlands
la **Suisse** [sɥis]	Switzerland
suisse [sɥis] C'est un passeport suisse.	Swiss It is a Swiss passport.
le **Suisse**, la **Suissesse** [sɥis, sɥisεs]	Swiss (citizen)
la **Russie** f [rys]	Russia

Humans as Intellectual and Physical Beings

General Terms

le **caractère** [karaktɛr]
Paul a bon caractère.

character; nature
Paul is good-natured.

caractéristique [karakteristik]

typical, characteristic

l'**état d'esprit** *m* [etadɛspri]

state of mind, mental condition

la **façon** [fasɔ̃]
Pierre a une drôle de façon de voir
les choses.

way, manner
Pierre has a funny way of looking
at things.

féminin, e [feminɛ̃, in]

feminine

la **femme** [fam]

woman; wife

la **figure** [figyr]

face

l'**homme** *m* [ɔm]

man

masculin, e [mɑskylɛ̃, in]

masculine

passer pour [pasepur]
Marie a 40 ans, mais elle passe
pour une jeune femme.

pass for, be considered
Marie is 40, but she passes
for a young woman.

le **physique** [fizik]
Je n'aime pas son physique.

physique; outward appearance
I don't like her looks.

le **trait** [trɛ]
Le charme est son trait
caractéristique.

trait, feature
Charm is his characteristic
trait.

le **type** [tip]
Quel sale type.

type; fellow
What an unpleasant person.

la **maturité** [matyrite]

maturity

la **mentalité** [mɑ̃talite]
Paul a la mentalité d'un
garçon de 12 ans.

mentality
Paul has the mentality of
a 12-year-old boy.

la **personnalité** [pɛrsɔnalite]

personality

■■■■■ Positive Characteristics ■■■■■

agréable [agreabl]	agreeable, pleasant
aimable [ɛmabl]	kind, likable, amiable
avoir de l'esprit [avwardəlɛspri]	be witty, be intelligent
avoir de l'humour [avwardəlymur]	have a sense of humor
avoir de l'imagination [avwardəlimaʒinɑsjɔ̃]	have imagination
avoir de la volonté [avwardlavɔlɔ̃te]	have will(power)
avoir du cœur [avwardykœr]	be kind-hearted
avoir un faible pour [avwarɛ̃fɛblpur]	have a weakness for
le **bon sens** [bɔ̃sɑ̃s]	good sense
brillant, e [brijɑ̃, t]	brilliant
calme [kalm]	calm, quiet
capable [kapabl]	capable
charmant, e [ʃarmɑ̃, t]	charming
le **charme** [ʃarm]	charm
comique [kɔmik]	comic, funny
commode [kɔmɔd]	easygoing
content, e [kɔ̃tɑ̃, t]	content, satisfied; happy, pleased, glad
Je suis contente de ton succès.	I'm glad about your success.
le **courage** [kuraʒ] Montre du courage.	courage Be courageous.
la **dame** [dam] La mère de Marie est une vraie dame.	lady Marie's mother is a real lady.
décontracté, e [dekɔ̃trakte]	relaxed, at ease
dynamique [dinamik]	dynamic
efficace [efikas]	effective

l'**énergie** f [enɛrʒi]
Ton énergie me dépasse complètement.

energy
You're too energetic for me.

énergique [enɛrʒik]

energetic

être bien vu, e [ɛtrəbjɛ̃vy]

be in favor, be well regarded

être de bonne volonté [ɛtrədbɔnvɔlɔ̃te]

be willing

fidèle [fidɛl]

faithful

fier, fière [fjɛr]

proud; haughty

franc, franche [frã, frãʃ]

frank, sincere

gai, e [gɛ]

gay; lively

généreux, -euse [ʒenerø, z]

generous

gentil, le [ʒãti, j]

nice, kind

habile [abil]

able, clever; skillful

honnête [ɔnɛt]

honest, honorable

humain, e [ymɛ̃, ɛn]

human

innocent, e [inɔsã, t]

innocent

intelligent, e [ɛ̃teliʒã, t]

intelligent

juste [ʒyst]

just, righteous

malin, maligne [malɛ̃, iɲ]
Tu es plus malin que moi.

cunning, sly; mischievous
You're more cunning than I.

mignon, ne [miɲɔ̃, ɔn]
Nicolas a 3 ans, il est très mignon.

sweet, cute, darling
Nicolas is 3; he's really cute.

naturel, le [natyrɛl]

natural

original, e, -aux [ɔriʒinal, o]

eccentric; original

poli, e [pɔli]

polite

prudent, e [prydã, t]

prudent, cautious

raisonnable [rɛzɔnabl]

reasonable

sage [saʒ]

well-behaved, good

sensible [sãsibl]

sensitive; sensible

sérieux, -euse [serjø, z]

serious; sincere; sound, responsible

sincère [sɛ̃sɛr]

sincere

sympa(thique) [sɛ̃pa tik]

likable, attractive

tendre [tãdr]	tender
tranquille [trãkil]	quiet, tranquil
vif, vive [vif, viv]	lively; alive; bright
Mon fils est très vif pour son âge.	My son is very bright for his age.

l'**ambition** *f* [ãbisjɔ̃]	ambition
brave [brav]	brave
la **compétence** [kɔ̃petãs]	competence, proficiency
consciencieux, -euse [kɔ̃sjãsjø, z]	conscientious
l'**optimiste** *mf* [ɔptimist]	optimist
la **sensibilité** [sãsibilite]	sensitivity
la **tendresse** [tãdrɛs]	tenderness

Negative Characteristics

bavard, e [bavar, d]	talkative; gossipy
bête [bɛt]	stupid, foolish
Martine est bête, elle ne comprends rien.	Martine is stupid, she doesn't understand anything.
bizarre [bizar]	bizarre, strange
brutal, e, -aux [brytal, o]	brutal; coarse
la **colère** [kɔlɛr]	anger
Ne te mets pas en colère.	Don't get angry.
compliqué, e [kɔ̃plike]	complicated
curieux, -euse [kyrjø, z]	curious; strange
désagréable, [dezagreabl]	disagreeable
difficile [difisil]	difficult; crotchety
Paul est difficile, il ne mange pas de poisson.	Paul is hard to please; he doesn't eat fish.
égoïste [egɔist]	selfish, egoistic
être mal vu, e [ɛtrəmalvy]	be held in poor esteem, be out of favor
exigeant, e [ɛgziʒã, t]	exacting, exigent

faible [fɛbl]

weak

fatigant, e [fatigã, t]

fatiguing; tiresome

fou, fol, folle [fu, fɔl]
Raymond est fou d'elle.

mad, insane; foolish
Raymond is wild about her.

gâté, e [gɑte]

spoiled

gourmand, e [gurmã, d]

greedy, gluttonous

grossier, -ère [grosje, ɛr]
Quel enfant grossier!

rude, crude; coarse
What a rude child!

hypocrite [ipɔkrit]

hypocritical

idiot, e [idjo, ɔt]

idiotic

impatient, e [ɛ̃pasjã, t]

impatient

incapable [ɛ̃kapabl]
Tu es incapable de faire
quoi qu ce soit.
 Tu es un incapable.

incapable
You're incapable of doing
anything at all.
You're an incompetent!

indifférent, e [ɛ̃diferã, t]
Paul est indifferent à ses enfants.

indifferent
Paul is unconcerned with his
children.

indiscret, -ète [ɛ̃diskrɛ, t]
Tais-toi, tu es indiscret.

indiscreet, tactless
Hush, you're being tactless.

lent, e [lã, t]
Lucie est lente à se décider.

slow; remiss
Lucie is slow to make up her
mind.

méchant, e [meʃã, t]

wicked, evil; naughty

mou, molle [mu, mɔl]
Qu'il est mou, ce garçon.

soft; weak; indolent
What a weakling that boy is.

nerveux, -euse [nɛrvø, z]

nervous

ordinaire [ɔrdinɛr]

ordinary

orgueilleux, -euse [ɔrgœjø, z]

haughty, proud

paresseux, -euse [parɛsø, z]

lazy

sévère [sevɛr]

strict, stern; severe

têtu, e [tɛty]

stubborn

timide [timid]

timid, shy

affolé, e [afɔle]	panic-stricken
l'**audace** f [odas]	audacity
la **brute** [bryt]	brute
l'**indifférence** f [ɛ̃diferɑ̃s]	indifference
ironique [irɔnik]	ironic
passif, -ive [pasif, iv]	passive
rude [ryd]	rude, rough
sentimental, e, -aux [sɑ̃timɑ̃tal, o]	sentimental
snob *unv* [snɔb]	snobbish
Un préjugé courant: Ils sont snob, les gens du seizième.	A current prejudice: People from the 16th District are snobbish.
vulgaire [vylgɛr]	vulgar, common; ordinary

External Features

affreux, -euse [afrø, z]	frightful
Tu es affreux dans ce manteau.	You look frightful in that coat.
âgé, e [aʒe]	old, aged
la **barbe** [barb]	beard
beau, bel, belle, x [bo, bɛl]	beautiful, handsome
Il est vraiment beau garçon.	He is really handsome.
blond, e [blɔ̃, d]	blond
bronzé, e [brɔ̃ze]	tanned
le **cheveu, x** [ʃəvø]	hair
clair, e [klɛr]	light, pale
la **force** [fɔrs]	force, strength
Je ne suis pas grand, mais j'ai de la force.	I'm not tall, but I'm strong.
fort, e [fɔr, t]	strong, powerful
grand, e [grɑ̃, d]	tall; large; big
gras, se [grɑ, s]	fat

gros, se [gro, s]	big, large, bulky
jeune [ʒœn]	young
joli, e [ʒɔli]	pretty; nice
laid, e [lɛ, d]	ugly
les **lunettes** *fpl* [lynɛt]	(eye)glasses
maigre [mɛgr]	lean; thin
mince [mɛ̃s]	thin, slim, slight
moche [mɔʃ]	ugly
pâle [pɑl]	pale
petit, e [pti, t]	small; short
propre [prɔpr]	clean, neat
roux, rousse [ru, rus]	red, auburn (hair)
sale [sal]	dirty
vieux, vieil, vieille [vjø, vjɛj]	old

châtain *inv* [ʃatɛ̃] Marie a les cheveux châtains.	chestnut (hair) Marie has chestnut hair.
d'un certain âge [dɛ̃sɛrtɛ̃nɑʒ]	not so young
élancé, e [elɑ̃se]	slender, slim
informe [ɛ̃fɔrm]	formless, shapeless
svelte [svɛlt]	slender, lithe, willowy

Motion in Space

aller [ale]
Je vais aux toilettes.

go
I'm going to the restroom.

arrêter (s') [sarete]

stop

l'**arrivée** f [arive]

arrival

arriver [arive]
Paul est arrivé à la gare.

arrive
Paul has arrived at the train station.

courir [kurir]

run, race

la **course** [kurs]

running, race; course

danser [dãse]

dance

dépêcher (se) [sədepeʃe]
Dépêche-toi.

hurry
Hurry up.

descendre [desãdr]

descend, go down; stay (at a hotel)

la **descente** [desãt]

descent; stay (at a hotel)

entrer [ãtre]

enter, go in

marcher [marʃe]
Pour aller au Trianon, il faut
marcher.
J'ai marché.

walk; run; go
To get to the Trianon, you have to
walk.
I went.

monter [mõte]
J'ai monté l'escalier.
Je suis monté.

ascend, mount, go up
I climbed the stairs.
I went upstairs.

nager [naʒe]
J'ai nagé longtemps.

swim
I swam a long time.

partir [partir]
Je suis parti à trois heures.

leave, depart
I left at 3 o'clock.

le **pas** [pɑ]

step

la **promenade** [prɔmnad]

walk

promener (se) [səprɔmne]

take a walk or drive

rentrer [rãtre]
Je suis rentrée très tard.

go or come home
I came home very late.

rester [rɛste]
On est restés trop longtemps
à Versailles.

stay, remain
We stayed too long at Versailles.

le **retour** [rətur]

return

retourner [rəturne]
Je n'y retournerai plus.

return, go back
I'll never go back there again.

retourner (se) [sərəturne]

turn around

revenir [rəvnir]

come back

sauter [sote]
J'ai sauté.

jump
I jumped.

sauver (se) [səsove]
Sauve qui peut.

run away; escape
Every man for himself!

sortir [sɔrtir]

go out

suivre [sɥivr]
On a suivi le guide.

follow
We followed the guide.

tomber [tɔ̃be]

fall

trouver (se) [sətruve]

be; be found; find oneself

venir [vənir]

come

voler [vɔle]
L'avion a volé à grande vitesse.
J'ai pris l'avion.

fly
The plane flew at high speed.
I flew.

---

approcher (s') [saprɔʃe]

approach

avancer [avãse]

advance

la **chute** [ʃyt]

fall, drop

le **déplacement** [deplasmã]

movement; travel; transfer

déplacer (se) [sədeplase]

move; be displaced (of things)

diriger (se) [sədiriʒe]
La voiture se dirige vers église.

go
The car is heading for the church.

disparaître [disparɛtr]
Ma voiture a disparu.

disappear
My car has disappeared.

la **disparition** [disparisjɔ̃]

disappearance

échapper [eʃape]	escape
Je l'ai échappé belle.	I had a narrow escape.
éloigner (s') [selwaɲe]	move away
enfuir (s') [sɑ̃fɥir]	run away, escape
la **fuite** [fɥit]	flight, escape
glisser [glise]	slip, slide, glide
J'ai glissé sur la neige.	I slipped on the snow.
précipiter (se) [səpresipite]	hurl oneself; rush
reculer [rəkyle]	move back, draw back
La foule a reculé.	The crowd drew back.
se rendre à [sərɑ̃dra]	go to
réunir (se) [səreynir]	meet, convene
traîner [trene]	drag; straggle

━━━━ Movement of the Body ━━━━

actif, -ive [aktif, iv]	active
l'**activité** *f* [aktivite]	activity
asseoir (s') [saswar]	sit down
baisser (se) [səbese]	bend, stoop
bouger [buʒe]	budge, stir
coucher (se) [sekuʃe]	go to bed
debout [dəbu]	upright; standing; up (out of bed)
Je suis debout.	I'm up.
Je me mets debout.	I'm getting up.
Je reste debout.	I'll remain standing.
exercer (s') [sɛgzɛrse]	exercise; practice, drill
l'**exercice** *m* [ɛgzɛrsis]	exercise; practice
lever (se) [səlve]	get up; stand up; rise
mettre (se) [səmɛtr]	sit down
On se met là?	Shall we sit down there?
le **mouvement** [muvmɑ̃]	movement

agir [aʒir]	act, take action
appuyer (s') [sapɥije]	lean on; be based in; rely on
être à genoux [ɛtraʒnu]	kneel
immobile [imɔbil]	motionless; immobile
redresser (se) [sərədrese]	straighten up
remuer [rəmɥe]	move
surgir [syrʒir] Le piéton a surgi derrière la voiture garée.	spring up; arise, appear The pedestrian suddenly appeared behind the parked car.

■■■ Physical Reactions and Sensory Perceptions ■■■

dormir [dɔrmir]	sleep
endormir (s') [sãdɔrmir]	fall asleep
entendre [ãtãdr]	hear
exister [ɛgziste]	exist
le **geste** [ʒɛst]	gesture
grandir [grãdir] Nicolas a beaucoup grandi.	grow, grow up Nicolas has grown a lot.
gratter (se) [səgrate]	scratch oneself
grossir [grosir] J'ai encore grossi.	get fat, gain weight I've gained more weight.
maigrir [megrir] Tu as encore maigri.	lose weight You've lost even more weight.
la **mort** [mɔr]	death
mourir [murir] Elle est morte d'un cancer.	die She died of cancer.
la **réaction** [reaksjɔ̃]	reaction
réagir [reaʒir]	react
réveiller (se) [səreveje] Je me suis réveillé de bonne heure.	wake up I woke up early.

sentir [sãtir]	feel; smell
toucher [tuʃe]	touch
transpirer [trãspire]	sweat, perspire
la **vie** [vi]	life
La vie est dure.	Life is hard.
C'est la vie.	That's life.
vivre [vivr]	live
voir [vwar]	see
la **vue** [vy]	sight

détendre (se) [sədetãdr]	relax, enjoy oneself
Détendez-vous.	Relax.
développer (se) [sədevlɔpe]	develop
évoluer [evɔlɥe]	evolve
l'**évolution** f [evɔlysjõ]	evolution
l'**existence** f [ɛgzistãs]	existence
le **réflexe** [reflɛks]	reflex
résister [reziste]	resist
rougir [ruʒir]	turn red; blush
J'ai rougi.	I blushed.
le **sommeil** [sɔmɛj]	sleep
survivre [syrvivr]	survive
J'ai survécu à tous mes parents.	I've outlived all my relatives.

Tous les jours je me réveille; donc, tous les jours j'existe.
Every day I wake up; therefore, every day I exist.

Doing Craftwork

bricoler [brikɔle]
Sébastien passe son temps à bricoler sa moto.

putter around, do odds and ends
Sebastian spends his time working on his motorcycle.

coller [kɔle]

glue

construire [kɔ̃strɥir]

build, construct

continuer [kɔ̃tinɥe]
Pierre continue à réparer sa voiture.

continue, keep on
Pierre is continuing to repair his car.

copier [kɔpje]

copy

faire [fɛr]

make, do

faire marcher [fɛrmarʃe]

get to go, get to run

imiter [imite]

imitate

peindre [pɛ̃dr]

paint

produire [prɔdɥir]

produce

le **produit** [prɔdɥi]

product

réaliser [realize]

realize; accomplish

la **réparation** [reparasjɔ̃]

repair

réparer [repare]

repair

effectuer [efɛktɥe]

effect, execute

limer [lime]

file

mesurer [məzyre]

measure

poncer [pɔ̃se]

sandpaper

raboter [rabɔte]

plane

la **réalisation** [realizɑsjɔ̃]

accomplishment; work

scier [sije]

saw

▬▬▬▬ Making Changes in Things ▬▬▬▬

boucher [buʃe]	stop up, plug
Il faut boucher le trou.	The hole has to be plugged.
casser [kɑse]	break
couper [kupe]	cut
couvrir [kuvrir]	cover
Le sol est couvert d'une moquette.	The floor is covered with a pile carpet.
déchirer [deʃire]	tear
envelopper [ãvlɔpe]	envelop; wrap (up)
Christo a enveloppé le Pont Neuf.	Christo wrapped the Pont Neuf.
plier [plije]	fold, bend
remplir [rãplir]	fill; fill up
supprimer [syprime]	cancel, abolish; omit
vider [vide]	empty

briser [brizə]	break
rompre [rõpr]	break
la rupture [ryptyr]	rupture; break

▬▬▬▬ Moving Things ▬▬▬▬

apporter [apɔrte]	bring, bring along
appuyer [apɥije]	push, press
Appuyez sur le bouton.	Press the button.
arracher [araʃe]	tear out, pull out
cacher [kaʃe]	hide, conceal
chercher [ʃɛrʃe]	search for, look for
emporter [ãpɔrte]	take away; carry off
enfermer [ãfɛrme]	enclose; lock up

jeter [ʒəte]	throw; throw away
lâcher [lɑʃe]	let go; turn loose
laisser [lese]	let, allow; leave
J'ai laissé mes papiers dans la voiture.	I left my papers in the car.
lancer [lãse]	throw; launch
lever [ləve]	lift, raise
mettre [mɛtr]	put, lay, place
Mets les fleurs sur la table.	Put the flowers on the table.
Mets la nappe sur la table.	Lay the tablecloth on the table.
perdre [pɛrdr]	lose
placer [plase]	place, lay
porter [pɔrte]	carry; wear
pousser [puse]	push, shove
Poussez	Push
ranger [rãʒe]	put in order
Range tes affaires.	Put your things in order.
recevoir [rəsvwar]	receive; admit
remplacer [rãplase]	replace
J'ai remplacé mon vélo par un vélomoteur.	I replaced my bike with a motorbike.
repousser [rəpuse]	push; repulse; refuse
retirer [rətire]	withdraw
retrouver [rətruve]	find again; recover
tirer [tire]	pull
Tirez	Pull
tourner [turne]	turn; turn over
trouver [truve]	find

acquérir [akerir]	acquire, get
attribuer [atribye]	attribute, ascribe
distribuer [distribye]	distribute
éloigner [elwaɲe]	move away; remove
importer [ɛpɔrte]	import
installer [ɛ̃stale]	install; equip, furnish
la **perte** [pɛrt]	loss
renverser [rãvɛrse]	reverse; overthrow
répartir [repartir]	distribute
la **répartition** [repartisjõ]	distribution

Using Things

charger [ʃarʒe]
Il faut charger la voiture.

load
We have to load the car.

choisir [ʃwazir]

choose

le **choix** [ʃwa]
Au choix

choice
At one's discretion

diriger [diriʒe]

direct, control; steer

donner [dɔne]
Qu'est-ce qu'on t'a donné pour ton
anniversaire?

give
What were you given for your
birthday?

faire voir [fɛrvwar]
Fais voir.

show
Let's see it.

fixer [fikse]

fix, fasten

interrompre [ɛ̃tɛrõpr]

interrupt

monter [mõte]
Qui a monté la tente?

set up; mount
Who set up the tent?

montrer [mõtre]

show

organiser [ɔrganize]

organize

partager [partaʒe]

share; divide

poser [poze]
Pose ça par terre.

place; arrange
Place that on the ground.

présenter [prezãte]   present; introduce

profiter [prɔfite]   profit, benefit
J'ai profité de l'occasion.   I took advantage of the
                                           opportunity.

ramasser [ramase]   gather; pick up
Nous avons ramassé des   We gathered mushrooms.
champignons.

régler [regle]   regulate, put in order; tune
Il est temps de régler cette affaire.   It's time to settle this matter.
Cette télé doit être réglée.   This TV has to be tuned.

rendre [rãdr]   render; yield

salir [salir]   soil

tendre [tãdr]   stretch

tenir [tənir]   hold; keep

utiliser [ytilize]   use, utilize
A utiliser avant le 31 mars 1997.   Usable until March 31, 1997.

voler [vɔle]   steal

---

accumuler [akymyle]   accumulate

appliquer [aplike]   apply

exploiter [ɛksplwate]   exploit; develop

faciliter [fasilite]   facilitate

gâcher [gɑʃe]   spoil

l'**interruption** *f* [ẽtɛrypsjɔ̃]   interruption

le **mode d'emploi** [mɔddãplwa]   directions for use

négliger [negliʒe]   neglect

réclamer [reklame]   demand; claim

secouer [səkwe]   shake

varier [varje]   vary

Pleasant Feelings

aimer [eme]
J'aimerais qu'on aille au cinéma.

love; like
I'd like us to go to the movies.

aimer faire [emefɛr]
J'aimerais aller en vacances.

like to do
I'd like to go on vacation.

l'**amitié** *f* [amitje]

friendship

amuser (s') [samyze]

have a good time

la **confiance** [kɔ̃fjɑ̃s]
J'ai confiance en ma femme.

confidence, trust
I trust my wife.

entendre (s') [sɑ̃tɑ̃dr]
On s'entend bien.

get along; understand one another
We get along well.

espérer [ɛspere]
J'espère que tout ira bien.

hope
I hope that everything will
go well.

gai, e [gɛ]

gay, lively

plaire [plɛr]
Ça me plaît.

please
I like that.

le **plaisir** [plezir]
Avec plaisir.

pleasure
With pleasure.

préférer [prefere]

prefer

réconcilier (se) [sərekɔ̃silje]

reconcile

le **rêve** [rɛv]

dream

rêver [reve]
Je rêve de toi toutes les nuits.

dream
I dream of you every night.

rire [rir]
Nous avons bien ri de ses
plaisanteries.
Il n'y a pas de quoi rire.
J'ai dit ça pour rire.

laugh
We laughed heartily at his jokes.

There's nothing to laugh about.
I said that in jest.

le **sentiment** [sɑ̃timɑ̃]

feeling, sentiment

sourire [surir]

smile

tomber amoureux, -euse
[tɔ̃beamurø, z]

fall in love

aimer mieux [ememiø] J'aimerais mieux que tu ailles lui parler.	prefer I'd prefer that you speak to him.
confier [kɔ̃fje]	confide
le **désespoir** [dezɛspwar]	despair
éprouver [epruve]	feel, experience
faire confiance à [fɛrkɔ̃fjãsa]	trust in
la **gaieté** [gɛte]	gaiety
la **joie** [ʒwa] La joie de vivre.	joy The joy of living.
la **jouissance** [ʒwisãs]	enjoyment
plaire (se) [səplɛr] Je me plais beaucoup à Paris.	enjoy oneself I like Paris very much.
réjouir (se) [səreʒwir]	rejoice, be delighted
rigoler [rigɔle] Qu'est-ce qu'on a rigolé! Tu rigoles!	laugh; joke How we laughed! You're joking!
la **satisfaction** [satisfaksjɔ̃]	satisfaction
sentimental, e, -aux [sãtimãtal, o]	sentimental

Les personnes sont tristes. Elles souffrent et pleurent.
The people are sad. They suffer and cry.

Unpleasant Feelings

avoir honte [avwar'ōt]	be ashamed
avoir peur [avwarpœr]	be afraid
J'ai peur d'être collé.	I'm afraid of getting stuck.
J'ai peur qu'il le sache.	I'm afraid that he knows it.
le **chagrin** [ʃagrɛ̃]	grief, sorrow
détester [detɛste]	detest
l'**embarras** m [ābara]	embarrassment
être obligé, e [ɛtrɔbliʒe]	be obliged
Vous n'êtes pas obligés de prendre le menu.	You're not obliged to take the complete dinner.
C'était obligé.	It had to be.
moquer (se) [səmɔke]	make fun of, laugh at
Janine se moque de tout.	Janine makes fun of everything.
la **peur** [pœr]	fear
la **pitié** [pitje]	pity
Tu me fais pitié.	I feel sorry for you.
pleurer [plœre]	cry, weep
regretter [rəgrete]	regret
Je regrette.	I'm sorry.
se faire des illusions [səfɛrdezilyzjɔ̃]	indulge in wishful thinking
se faire du souci [səfɛrdysusi]	worry
souffrir [sufrir]	suffer
Mémé souffre des dents.	Granny has a toothache.
toucher [tuʃe]	touch
trembler [trāble]	tremble
triste [trist]	sad

craindre [krɛ̃dr] C'est une plante qui craint le froid.	fear; dislike, be unable to bear It's a plant that can't stand the cold.
la **crainte** [krɛ̃t]	fear
désespérer [dezɛspere]	despair
le **deuil** [dœj] Elle est en deuil de son mari.	mourning; grief She's in mourning for her husband.
effondrer (s') [sefɔ̃dre]	collapse
la **haine** ['ɛn]	hate
inquiéter (s') [sɛ̃kjete] Je m'inquiète de sa santé.	worry, be worried I'm worried about his health.
l'**inquiétude** *f* [ɛ̃kjetyd]	uneasiness, worry
la **jalousie** [ʒaluzi]	jealousy
la **méfiance** [mefjãs]	mistrust
méfier (se) [səmefje] Marc se méfie de tout le monde.	mistrust Marc mistrusts everyone.
le **mépris** [mepri]	contempt, scorn
mépriser [meprize]	despise, scorn
pleurnicher [plœrniʃe]	whimper, snivel
s'en prendre à qqn [sãprãdrakɛlkɛ̃]	blame s.o. for s.th.
sangloter [sãglɔte]	sob
la **souffrance** [sufrãs]	suffering
subir [sybir] Caroline a subi un choc.	undergo; feel, experience Caroline has sustained a shock.
la **tristesse** [tristɛs]	sadness
troubler [truble]	upset, trouble; disturb
verser des larmes [vɛrsedelarm]	shed tears

Thinking and Imagining

l'**avis** *m* [avi]	opinion; advice
Quel est ton avis?	What's your opinion?
A mon avis.	In my opinion.
comparer [kɔ̃pare]	compare
comprendre [kɔ̃prɑ̃dr]	understand
Je comprends que tu sois triste.	I understand that you are sad.
la **connaissance** [kɔnɛsɑ̃s]	knowledge; consciousness
connaître [kɔnɛtr]	know, be acquainted with
croire [krwar]	believe, think
Je le crois.	I believe him.
Je le crois.	I believe it.
Je ne crois pas au diable.	I don't believe in the devil.
Je n'en crois rien.	I don't believe a word of it.
Je crois que c'est assez.	I think that's enough.
deviner [dəvine]	guess
Tu devines?	Can you guess?
distinguer [distɛ̃ge]	distinguish
imaginer (s') [simaʒine]	imagine
l'**impression** *f* [ɛpresjɔ̃]	impression
l'**intelligence** *f* [ɛteliʒɑ̃s]	intelligence
inventer [ɛvɑ̃te]	invent
l'**invention** *f* [ɛvɑ̃sjɔ̃]	invention
l'**opinion** *f* [ɔpinjɔ̃]	opinion
oublier [ublije]	forget
la **pensée** [pɑ̃se]	thought; thinking
penser [pɑ̃se]	think
Je pense que tu as tort.	I think you're wrong.
le **point de vue** [pwɛ̃dvy]	point of view
Je partage ton point de vue.	I share your point of view.
prévoir [prevwar]	foresee, anticipate; forecast
la **raison** [rɛzɔ̃]	reason

rappeler (se) [səraple] — remember
Je me rappelle ta jolie figure. — I remember your pretty face.

réfléchir [refleʃir] — reflect; consider
Tu as bien réfléchi? — Have you thought it over well?

retenir [rətnir] — hold or keep back; retain

savoir [savwar] — know
Je sais que tu as raison, mais . . . — I know that you're right, but . . .

se rendre compte de [sərādrəkɔ̃tdə] — realize
Je m'en suis rendu compte. — I realized that.

souvenir (se) [səsuvnir] — remember
L'accusé ne se souvient de rien. — The defendant remembers nothing.

tromper (se) [sətrɔ̃pe] — be wrong

---

apercevoir [apɛrsəvwar] — perceive

concevoir [kɔ̃səvwar] — conceive; compose

confondre [kɔ̃fɔ̃dr] — confuse, mix up

le **doute** [dut] — doubt

douter [dute] — doubt
Je doute de ta sincérité. — I doubt your sincerity.

douter (se) [sədute] — suspect
Il ne se doute de rien. — He doesn't suspect anything.

l'**imagination** f [imaʒinɑsjɔ̃] — imagination, fantasy

intellectuel, le [ɛ̃telɛktɥɛl] — intellectual

la **mémoire** [memwar] — memory
Tu as bonne mémoire. — You have a good memory.

le **raisonnement** [rɛzɔnmɑ̃] — reasoning; argument

raisonner [rɛzɔne] — reason; reason out

reconnaître [rəkɔnɛtr] — recognize

la **réflexion** [reflɛksjɔ̃] — reflection
Réflexion faite . . . — All things considered . . .

résoudre [rezudr] — solve; resolve

se faire une idée [səfɛrynide] — form an idea
Tu ne te fais aucune idée des difficultés. — You have no idea of the difficulties.

supposer [sypoze]	suppose
tenir compte de [tənirkɔ̃tdə]	bear in mind
voir clair [vwarklɛr]	see clearly, understand
Je n'y vois pas clair.	It's Greek to me!

■■■■■■ Wanting and Acting Deliberately ■■■■■■

accepter [aksɛpte]	accept
arranger [arɑ̃ʒe]	arrange
arriver à faire [ariveafɛr]	manage (to do)
Je n'y arrive pas.	I can't manage it.
créer [kree]	create
débrouiller (se) [sədebruje]	extricate oneself, manage
Débrouillez-vous.	Try to get out of your difficulties.
décider [deside]	decide
Le juge décidera du sort de l'accusé.	The judge will decide the defendant's fate.
Le P.D.G. a décidé la poursuite des recherches.	The managing director decided to continue the research.
décider (se) [sədeside]	make up one's mind
Je me suis enfin décidée à acheter cette robe-là.	I've finally made up my mind to buy that dress.
la **décision** [desizjɔ̃]	decision
Nous sommes obligés de prendre une décision.	We have to make a decision.
écouter [ekute]	listen to
J'écoute les informations.	I'm listening to the news.
écrire [ekrir]	write
l'**effort** *m* [efɔr]	effort
engager (s') [sɑ̃gaʒe]	commit oneself
entendre [ɑ̃tɑ̃dr]	hear; understand
Je n'entends rien, il y a trop de bruit.	I don't hear anything; there's too much noise.
espérer [ɛspere]	hope
J'espère qu'il n'a pas tout raconté.	I hope that he hasn't told everything.
essayer [eseje]	try

étudier [etydje]
study

faire attention [fɛratɑ̃sjɔ̃]
pay attention, mind

faire exprès [fɛrɛksprɛ]
Je ne l'ai pas fait exprès.
do on purpose
I didn't do it on purpose.

habituer (s') [sabitɥe]
On s'y habitue vite.
get used, become accustomed
One gets used to it quickly.

l'**intention** f [ɛ̃tɑ̃sjɔ̃]
intention

intéresser (s') [sɛ̃terese]
Je m'intéresse au cinéma.
be interested
I'm interested in movies.

l'**intérêt** m [ɛterɛ]
L'intérêt de la chose . . .
interest
The interesting thing about it . . .

lire [lir]
read

observer [ɔpsɛrve]
observe

opposer (s') [sɔpoze]
be opposed

préférer [prefere]
Je préfère qu'on aille au restaurant.
prefer
I prefer that we go to the restaurant.

prouver [pruve]
Qu'est-ce que ça prouve?
prove
What does that prove?

refuser [rəfyze]
On ne peut rien lui refuser.
refuse
No one can refuse him anything.

regarder [rəgarde]
look at; face

remarquer [rəmarke]
remark, notice

renoncer [rənɔ̃se]
Je ne renonce pas à mes droits.
renounce, give up
I do not renounce my rights.

réussir [reysir]
Il a réussi dans toutes ses entreprises.
succeed
He has succeeded in all his undertakings.

Je n'ai pas réussi à faire fortune.
I have not succeeded in making a fortune.

risquer [riske]
Les gendarmes ont risqué leur vie.
Ça risque de ne pas marcher.
Tu ne risques pas d'avoir froid avec cette fourrure.
risk
The policemen risked their lives.
That has a good chance of failure.
You certainly won't get cold in that fur.

se donner du mal
[sədɔnedymal]
take pains

se donner la peine
[sədɔnelapɛn]

try hard, make a great effort

sentir [sɑ̃tir]
Je sens que ça tourne mal.

feel; smell
I feel that it's going badly.

signer [siɲe]

sign

souhaiter [swete]
Je souhaite que tu viennes avec moi.

wish
I wish that you would come with me.

venger (se) [səvɑ̃ʒe]
Je vais me venger de ce que tu m'as fait.
Je vais me venger de Jean-Marc.

get revenge
I'm going to get my revenge for what you've done to me.
I'm going to get my revenge on Jean-Marc.

vérifier [verifje]

verify; ascertain

vouloir [vulwar]
Je ne veux pas que tu sortes.

want, wish
I don't want you to go out.

vouloir bien [vulwarbjɛ̃]

be glad to, be willing to

la **vue** [vy]
Tu as des drôles de vues.

view
You have some funny views.

---

accomplir [akɔ̃plir]

accomplish

accorder [akɔrde]

grant

céder (à) [sede a]

yield (to)

charger (se) [səʃarʒe]

be loaded

comporter (se) [səkɔ̃pɔrte]

behave

destiner [dɛstine]

destine; set aside, reserve

échouer [eʃwe]
J'ai échoué.

run aground; fail
I have failed.

élaborer [elabɔre]

work out; elaborate

empêcher [ɑ̃peʃe]
Il faut empêcher Paul de faire une bêtise.

hinder
Paul has to be prevented from doing something foolish.

l'**essai** *m* [esɛ]

attempt

éviter [evite]

avoid

faire de son mieux [fɛrdəsɔ̃mjø]

do one's best

faire du tort à qqn
[fɛrdytɔrakɛlkɛ̃]

do wrong to someone

faire semblant [fɛrsãblã] Les enfants font semblant de dormir.	pretend The children are pretending to be asleep.
faire un essai [fɛrɛ̃nesɛ]	try, attempt
forcer (se) [səfɔrse]	force oneself
garder (se) [səgarde]	take care not to
hésiter [ezite] N'hésitez pas à me consulter.	hesitate Don't hesitate to ask my advice.
la **lecture** [lɛktyr]	reading
l'**objectif** *m* [ɔbʒɛktif]	objective, target
oser [oze] Tu oses m'interrompre.	dare You dare to interrupt me.
poursuivre [pursɥivr]	pursue, chase
se tirer d'affaire [sətiredafɛr]	get out of a difficulty
la **tâche** [tɑʃ]	task, job
tenir à ce que [təniraskə] Je tiens à ce que tout le monde comprenne.	insist that I insist that everyone understand.

Il y a peu de monuments si bien connus comme La Tour Eiffel.
Few monuments are so well known as the Eiffel Tower.

Speaking and Informing

s'adresser à [sadresea]
Adressez-vous à la concierge.

speak, address oneself; apply
Speak to the caretaker.

adresser la parole à
[adreselaparɔla]

speak to

ajouter [aʒute]

add

annoncer [anɔ̃se]

announce

appeler [aple]

call

bavarder [bavarde]
J'ai bavardé avec la voisine.

chat; gossip
I chatted with the neighbor.

la **conversation** [kɔ̃vɛrsɑsjɔ̃]

conversation

le **coup de téléphone**
[kudtelefɔn]
Passe-moi un coup de téléphone.

telephone call

Give me a call.

le **cri** [kri]

cry, shout

crier [krije]

cry; cry out; shout

décrire [dekrir]

describe

dire [dir]
Je le dirai à ton père.

say, tell, relate
I'll tell that to your father.

le **discours** [diskur]

discourse, speech

l'**expression** ƒ [ɛkspresjɔ̃]
C'est une expression toute faite.

expression
It is a fixed expression.

exprimer (s') [sɛksprimə]

express oneself

faire une remarque
[fɛrynrəmark]
Il me fait tout le temps des
remarques.

make a remark

He criticizes me all the time.

indiquer [ɛ̃dike]
Pourriez-vous m'indiquer votre
adresse?
Qui t'a indiqué ce restaurant
excellent?

indicate; name
Could you give me your address?

Who told you about this excellent
restaurant?

insister sur qqc [insistesyr]
J'insiste pour que vous veniez
ce soir.

insist on something
I insist that you come this evening.

le **mot** [mo]

word

parler [parle]
J'en ai parlé au patron.
J'ai parlé avec la voisine jusqu'à
midi.
J'ai parlé de mon voyage au Maroc.

speak, talk
I spoke to the boss about it.
I talked with the neighbor until
noon.
I spoke about my trip to Morocco.

la **parole** [parɔl]
J'aime bien les paroles de cette
chanson.
Je donne la parole à notre président.

speech; word
I like the words of this song.

I give the floor to our president.

la **phrase** [fraz]

sentence, phrase

préciser [presize]

specify; be precise

prétendre [pretãdr]

claim

prononcer [prɔnõse]
Le Président a prononcé un discours.

Richard prononce mal, il zézaye.

pronounce; deliver
The President has delivered a
speech.
Richard has bad pronunciation; he
lisps.

raconter [rakõte]
Ne me raconte pas ta vie.

tell, narrate; describe
Don't tell me your life story.

rappeler [raple]
Ça me rappelle ma jeunesse.

remind; recall
That reminds me of my youth.

la **remarque** [rəmark]

remark

remarquer [rəmarke]

remark

répéter [repete]

repeat

taire (se) [sətɛr]
Tais-toi.

be silent
Hush up.

téléphoner [telefɔne]

telephone

l'**appel** *m* [apɛl]	call
chuchoter [ʃyʃɔte]	whisper
constater [kɔ̃state]	certify; establish
la **description** [dɛskripsjɔ̃]	description
le **dialogue** [djalɔg]	dialogue
évoquer [evɔke]	evoke; call to mind
M. Chirac a évoqué les troubles de mai '68.	Chirac recalled the riots of May '68.
proclamer [prɔklame]	proclaim

▬▬▬ **Expressing Judgements** ▬▬▬

l'**accent** *m* [aksɑ̃]	accent; stress
Il parle français avec accent du Midi.	He speaks with the accent of southern France.
l'**avis** *m* [avi]	opinion
la **blague** [blag]	joke, yarn; trick
Quelle bonne blague.	What a good yarn.
disputer (se) [sədispyte]	dispute
l'**excuse** *f* [ɛkskyz]	excuse
excuser (s') [sɛkskyze]	excuse oneself
le **gros mot** [gromo]	foul word
jurer [ʒyre]	swear; curse
Je jure de ma bonne foi.	I give you my word!
Paul a juré entre ses dents.	Paul swore like a trooper.
mentir [mɑ̃tir]	lie
Tu as menti à ton copain.	You lied to your friend.
plaindre (se) [səplɛ̃dr]	complain
Je vais me plaindre au chef de rayon.	I'm going to complain to the head of the department.
plaisanter [plɛzɑ̃te]	joke
la **plaisanterie** [plɛzɑ̃tri]	joke; joking
le **prétexte** [pretɛkst]	pretext
protester [prɔtɛste]	protest

la **dispute** [dispyt]	dispute
le **juron** [ʒyrɔ̃]	curse
le **malentendu** [malãtãdy]	misunderstanding
le **mensonge** [mãsɔ̃ʒ]	lie
la **plainte** [plɛ̃t]	complaint

Exercising Influence

autoriser [ɔtɔrize]	authorize
le **conseil** [kɔ̃sɛj]	advice, counsel
conseiller [kɔ̃seje]	advise, counsel
consoler [kɔ̃sɔle]	console
Comment la consoler de son chagrin d'amour?	How can she be consoled in her lovelorn state?
la **contradiction** [kɔ̃tradiksjɔ̃]	contradiction
convaincre [kɔ̃vɛ̃kr]	convince
la **déclaration** [deklarasjɔ̃]	declaration
déclarer [deklare]	declare
défendre [defãdr]	forbid
Il est défendu de fumer.	No smoking.
demander [dəmãde]	ask; ask for; require
Je te demande si tu es libre.	I'm asking you whether you have time.
Demande-lui de venir.	Ask him to come.
On la demande au téléphone.	She's wanted on the telephone.
la **discussion** [diskysjɔ̃]	discussion
discuter [diskyte]	discuss
On discute de tout et de rien.	We discuss anything and everything.
Discutons politique.	Let's discuss politics.

l'**explication** *f* [ɛksplikɑsjō]   explanation; interpretation

expliquer [ɛksplike]   explain; give an interpretation of

informer [ɛ̃fɔrme]   inform
On a informé de son avancement.   He was informed of his promotion.

interdire [ɛ̃tɛrdir]   forbid, prohibit

interroger [ɛ̃tɛrɔʒe]   interrogate, question

interrompre [ɛ̃tɛrɔ̃pr]   interrupt

menacer [mənase]   threaten

l'**ordre** *m* [ɔrdr]   order

permettre [pɛrmɛtr]   permit, allow
Je ne permets pas que tu sortes.   I don't permit you to leave.

la **permission** [pɛrmisjɔ̃]   permission

persuader [pɛrsɥade]   persuade

présenter [prezɑ̃te]   present; introduce
Jean Marc nous a présenté ses idées politiques.   Jean Marc presented his political ideas to us.

prévenir [prevnir]   warn

prier [prije]   ask, beg; pray
Je vous prie de vouloir me suivre.   Please follow me.

la **promesse** [prɔmɛs]   promise

promettre [prɔmɛtr]   promise

proposer [prɔpose]   propose; recommend
Je propose qu'on aille au cinéma.   I propose going to the movies.

rassurer [rasyre]   reassure

le **renseignement** [rɑ̃sɛɲəmɑ̃]   information

renseigner qqn [rɑ̃seɲe]   inform s.o.

répondre [repɔ̃dr]   answer
J'ai répondu à sa lettre.   I have answered his letter.

la **réponse** [repɔ̃s]   answer

signaler [siɲale]   signal; point out
Rien à signaler.   Nothing to report.

l'**autorisation** *f* [authorization]	authorization
avertir [avɛrtir]	warn
contredire [kɔ̃trədir] Il faut toujours que tu contredises ton père.	contradict You always have to contradict your father!
la **conviction** [kɔ̃viksjɔ̃]	conviction
le **défi** [defi]	challenge
démontrer [demɔ̃tre]	demonstrate, prove
l'**interrogatoire** *m* [ɛ̃tɛrɔgatwar]	examination
l'**interruption** *f* [ɛ̃tɛrypsjɔ̃] Cette dame m'énerve, elle parle sans interruption.	interruption This lady gets on my nerves; she talks without interruption.
la **menace** [mənas]	menace, threat
la **proposition** [prɔpozisjɔ̃]	proposal; proposition

■■■■ Praising and Criticizing ■■■■

accuser [akyze] J'accuse. On m'accuse injustement de vol.	blame; indict; accuse I accuse. I am unjustly accused of theft.
affirmer [afirme] Le témoin affirme avoir vu le vol.	affirm, assert The witness claims to have seen the theft.
approuver [apruve] J'approuve ton choix.	approve, approve of I approve of your choice.
assurer [asyre]	assure
condamner [kɔ̃dane]	condemn
la **critique** [kritik]	criticism; review
critiquer [kritike]	criticize
décourager [dekuraʒe]	discourage, deter
dire du mal de qqn [dirdymaldəkɛlkɛ̃]	speak ill of s.o.

donner raison à qqn [dɔnerɛzɔakɛlkɛ̃]
side with s.o., decide in favor of s.o.

donner tort à qqn [dɔnetɔrakɛlkɛ̃]
decide against s.o.

encourager [ãkuraʒe]
encourage

excuser [ɛkskyze]
excuse

féliciter [felisite]
Je te félicite de ton permis.
congratulate
I congratulate you on getting your driver's license.

insulter [ɛ̃sylte]
insult, affront

pardonner à qqn [pardɔnea]
Je ne lui pardonne rien.
forgive s.o.
I forgive him nothing.

remercier qqn [rəmɛrsje]
thank s.o.

le **reproche** [rəprɔʃ]
reproach

reprocher [rəprɔʃe]
reproach

---

injurier [ɛ̃ʒyrje]
abuse, insult

l'**insulte** *f* [ɛ̃sylt]
insult

recommander [rəkɔmãde]
recommend

vanter (se) [səvãte]
boast, praise oneself

Des personnes politiques au Parlement Français.
French Parliament politicians.

Positive Emotions

admirable [admirabl]
admirable

admirer [admire]
admire

adorer [adɔre]
adore

aimable [ɛmabl]
kind, likable, amiable

amusant, e [amyzã, t]
Je trouve amusant ce que tu dis là.
amusing
I find what you say amusing.

brillant, e [brijã, t]
brilliant

briller [brije]
shine, sparkle

charmant, e [ʃarmã, t]
charming

être de bon goût [ɛtrədəbõgu]
be in good taste

excellent, e [ɛksɛlã, t]
C'est une idée excellente de sortir ensemble.
excellent
It's an excellent idea to go out together.

exceptionnel, le [ɛksɛpsjɔnɛl]
exceptional

extraordinaire [ɛkstraɔrdinɛr]
extraordinary

facile [fasil]
C'est facile à comprendre.
C'est facile de critiquer.
easy; fluent
It's easy to understand.
It's easy to criticize.

fameux, -euse [famø, z]
famous

favorable [favɔrabl]
favorable

formidable [fɔrmidabl]
C'est formidable que tu sois là.
formidable; terrific
It's terrific that you're here.

idéal, e, -aux [ideal, o]
ideal

immense [imãs]
immense

impressionnant, e [ɛ̃prɛsjɔnã, t]
impressive

magnifique [maɲifik]
magnificent

mignon, ne [miɲõ, ɔn]
sweet, cute, darling

parfait, e [parfɛ, t]
perfect

passionnant, e [pasjɔnã, t]
exciting, thrilling

remarquable [rəmarkabl]
C'est un fait remarquable qu'il ait
réussi si vite.

remarkable
It's remarkable that he succeeded
so quickly.

le **succès** [syksɛ]

success

---

capital, e, -aux [kapital, o]
indiscutable [ɛ̃diskytabl]
unique [ynik]

capital, main, chief
incontestable, indisputable
unique

■ Negative Emotions ■

affreux, -euse [afrø, z]

frightful

bête [bɛt]
Qu'il est bête, cet homme.

silly, stupid
What a stupid man he is.

la **bêtise** [betiz]

silliness, stupidity

la **catastrophe** [katastrɔf]

catastrophe

dangereux, -euse [dãʒrø, z]

dangerous

désagréable [dezagreabl]

disagreeable

détester [detɛste]

detest, hate

épouvantable [epuvãtabl]

dreadful, horrible, shocking

la **honte** ['ɔ̃t]

shame; disgrace

honteux, -euse ['ɔ̃tø, z]

ashamed; shameful

insupportable [ɛ̃sypɔrtabl]

insupportable, insufferable

laid, e [lɛ, d]

ugly

moche [mɔʃ]

ugly; shoddy; dowdy

nul, le [nyl]
Pierre est nul en maths.

worthless, of no account
Pierre is no good at math.

pénible [penibl]
Il y a vraiment des gens pénibles.

troublesome, unpleasant
There really are some unpleasant
people.

ridicule [ridikyl]

ridiculous

scandaleux, -euse [skãdalø, z]

scandalous

stupide [stypid]

stupid

terrible [tɛribl]	terrible
triste [trist]	sad

horrible [ɔribl]	horrible
inadmissible [inadmisibl]	inadmissible
misérable [mizerabl]	miserable; poor

■■■■■ Evaluating ■■■■■

la **comparaison** [kɔ̃parɛzɔ̃]	comparison
la **conclusion** [kɔ̃klyzjɔ̃]	conclusion
considérer [kɔ̃sidere]	consider
convenir [kɔ̃vnir]	suit; be convenient
Cette heure vous convient?	Does that time suit you?
dépendre de [depɑ̃drdə]	depend on
Ça dépend.	That depends.
estimer [ɛstime]	estimate; esteem; deem
juger [ʒyʒe]	judge
Jugez-en vous-même.	Judge that yourself.
relatif, -ive [rəlatif, iv]	relative
ressembler [rəsɑ̃ble]	resemble
tragique [traʒik]	tragic

■■■■■ Varying Evaluations ■■■■■

assez [ase]	enough, rather
François est assez grand.	Francois is rather tall.
cher, chère [ʃɛr]	expensive; dear
clair, e [klɛr]	light; clear
C'est clair qu'il a raison.	It's clear that he's right.
connu, e [kɔny]	known; well-known
courant, e [kurɑ̃, t]	current; usual, ordinary

définitif, -ive [definitif, iv] definitive

général, e, -aux [ʒeneral, o] general

nécessaire [nesesɛr] necessary

normal, e, -aux [nɔrmal, o] normal

original, e, -aux [ɔriʒinal, o] original, odd, quaint

possible [pɔsibl] possible

rare [rar] rare

sérieux, -euse [serjø, z] serious

simple [sɛ̃pl] simple

sûr, e [syr] sure
Tu es sûr que c'est le bon train? Are you sure that it's the right train?

mystérieux, -euse [misterjø, z] mysterious

la **nécessité** [nesesite] necessity

sentimental, e, -aux sentimental
[sɑ̃timɑ̃tal, o]

Positive Evaluations

accepter [aksɛpte] accept
Paul a esprit large, il accepte tout. Paul is very tolerant; he accepts everything.

agréable [agreabl] agreeable

approuver [apruve] approve, approve of
J'approuve ta décision. I approve of your decision.

l'**avantage** *m* [avɑ̃taʒ] advantage

avoir raison [avwarrɛzɔ̃] be right

bien [bjɛ̃] well

certain, e [sɛrtɛ̃, ɛn] certain, sure; true
C'est une affaire sûre et certaine. It's a sure thing.
C'est certain que tu n'as pas le temps? Is it true that you don't have time?

la **chance** [ʃɑ̃s] luck, good luck; chance

commode [kɔmɔd]	comfortable
correct, e [kɔrɛkt]	correct
élémentaire [elemãtɛr]	elementary
essentiel, le [esãsjɛl]	essential
évident, e [evidã, t]	evident, obvious
C'est évident qu'il a fait une gaffe.	It's obvious that he has made a blunder.
exact, e [ɛgzakt]	exact, correct, accurate
C'est exact qu'il a dit ça.	It's true that he said that.
l'**importance** f [ɛ̃pɔrtãs]	importance
important, e [ɛ̃pɔrtã, t]	important
incroyable [ɛ̃krwajabl]	incredible
indispensable [ɛ̃dispãsabl]	indispensable
Il est indispensable que tu viennes.	You absolutely have to come.
intéressant, e [ɛ̃terɛsã, t]	interesting
juste [ʒyst]	just; proper; right, true
logique [lɔʒik]	logical
louer [lwe]	praise
meilleur, e [mɛjœr]	better; best
C'est mon meilleur ami.	That's my best friend.
mieux [mjø]	better
Jean travaille mieux que Philippe.	Jean works better than Philippe.
C'est mieux.	That's better.
naturel, le [natyrɛl]	natural
obligatoire [ɔbligatwar]	obligatory, compulsory
porter bonheur [pɔrtebɔnœr]	bring good luck
positif, -ive [pozitif, iv]	positive
pratique [pratik]	practical
préférable [preferabl]	preferable
principal, e, -aux [prɛ̃sipal, o]	principal
probable [prɔbabl]	probable

raisonnable [rɛzɔnabl]	reasonable
sympa(thique) [sɛ̃pa tik]	likable, congenial
utile [ytil]	useful
valable [valabl]	valid, good
la **vérité** [verite]	truth
vrai, e [vrɛ]	true, real, genuine
C'est vrai qu'il a dit ça?	Is it true that he said that?

Incroyable! C'est délicieux, c'est meilleur que n'importe quoi que j'aie mangé dans n'importe quel restaurant!

Incredible! It's delicious, it's better than anything I have eaten in any restaurant!

Negative Evaluations

avoir tort [avwartɔr]	be wrong
banal, e [banal]	banal; commonplace, trite
C'est une question banale.	It's a trite question.
condamner [kɔ̃dane]	condemn
confus, e [kɔ̃fy, z]	confused, muddled, vague
critique [kritik]	critical
le **défaut** [defo]	defect; lack; flaw
difficile [difisil]	difficult; hard to please
dur, e [dyr]	hard
l'**échec** *m* [eʃɛk]	failure, blow, loss
C'est un échec complet.	It's a total failure.
ennuyeux, -euse [ãnɥijø, z]	boring
l'**erreur** *f* [ɛrœr]	error
exagérer [ɛgzaʒere]	exaggerate; overdo
5000 FF pour une robe, tu exagères.	5000 francs for a dress; you're overdoing it.
fatigant, e [fatigã, t]	fatiguing, tiring
faux, fausse [fo, fos]	false
la **folie** [fɔli]	madness, folly
C'est de la folie de dépenser tant pour une robe.	It's madness to spend so much for a dress.
fou, fol, folle [fu, fɔl]	mad; foolish, silly
gênant, e [ʒɛnã, t]	troublesome, embarrassing
grave [grav]	heavy, grave, serious
impossible [ɛ̃pɔsibl]	impossible
indiscret, -ète [ɛ̃diskrɛ, t]	indiscreet, tactless
injuste [ɛ̃ʒyst]	unjust, unfair
l'**injustice** *f* [ɛ̃ʒystis]	injustice
inutile [inytil]	useless
mauvais, e [mɔvɛ̃, z]	bad
J'ai une mauvaise habitude, je fume.	I have a bad habit: I smoke.

pire [pir]   worse; worst
Henri va de pire en pire.   Henri is doing increasingly poorly.
C'est encore pire.   That's even worse.

porter malheur [pɔrtemalœr]   bring bad luck

le **préjugé** [preʒyʒe]   prejudice

le **problème** [prɔblɛm]   problem

secondaire [səgɔ̃dɛr]   secondary; subordinate

vague [vag]   vague, unclear

---

l'**inconvénient** *m* [ɛ̃kɔ̃venjɑ̃]   disadvantage; inconvenience

inévitable [inevitabl]   inevitable

insuffisant, e [ɛ̃syfizɑ̃, t]   insufficient

médiocre [medjɔkr]   mediocre

▬▬▬ Expressing Astonishment ▬▬▬

bizarre [bizar]   strange, bizarre, whimsical

curieux, -euse [kyrjø, z]   curious, strange

drôle [drol]   funny, strange
C'est une drôle d'histoire.   That's a funny story.

étonnant, e [etɔnɑ̃, t]   astonishing

étonner [etɔne]   astonish, amaze

étonner (s') [setɔne]   be astonished, wonder

étrange [etrɑ̃ʒ]   strange, odd, extraordinary

frappant, e [frapɑ̃, t]   striking, surprising
J'en ai ici la preuve frappante.   I have here the convincing proof.
C'est une idée frappante.   It is a surprising idea.

ne pas en revenir   not get over it
[nəpazɑ̃rəvnir]
Tu ne fumes plus? Je n'en reviens pas.   You've quit smoking? I can't get
                                             over it.

inexplicable [inɛksplikabl]   inexplicable

invraisemblable [ɛ̃vrɛsɑ̃blabl]   improbable, unlikely

51

9 | Fixed Expressions

Greeting and Farewell

A bientôt. [abiɛ̃to]	So long!
A plus tard. [aplytar]	See you later.
A tout à l'heure. [atutalœr]	See you later.
Allô! [alo]	Hello!
Au revoir. [orvwar]	Goodbye.
Bonjour! [bɔ̃ʒur]	Good morning!, Good day!
Bonsoir! [bɔ̃swar]	Good evening!
Comment allez-vous? [kɔmãtalevu]	How are you?
Comment ça va? [kɔmãsava]	How are you?
Eh! [e]	Ah!, Well!, Hey!
Enchanté, e. [ãʃãte]	Pleased to meet you!
Il y a du monde? [iljadymɔ̃d]	Is anyone there?
Madame [madam]	Mrs. . . .
Mademoiselle [madmwazɛl]	Miss. . . .
Monsieur [məsjø]	Mr. . . .
Salut! [saly]	Hi!

Wishes

A tes/vos souhaits! [ate/vosuɛ]	God bless you! (after sneezing)
Bon anniversaire! [bɔnaniversɛr]	Happy birthday!
Bon appétit! [bɔ̃napeti]	I wish you a good appetite!
Bonne année! [bɔnane]	Happy New Year!
Bonne chance! [bɔnʃãs]	Good luck!
Bonne fête! [bɔnfɛt]	Many happy returns!
Félicitations! [felisitasjɔ̃]	Congratulations!
Joyeux Noël [ʒwajønɔɛl]	Merry Christmas

52

Merci! [mɛrsi]   Thank you!, Thanks!
Salutations [salytɑsjɔ̃]   Greetings; Yours truly
Santé! [sɑ̃te]   Cheers!
Vive . . . ! [viv]   Long live . . . !

(Tous mes) regrets.   My (heartfelt) sympathy.
[tumerəgrɛ]

━━━━━━ **Exhortations** ━━━━━━

Attention! [atɑ̃sjɔ̃]   Look out!
Au secours! [oskur]   Help!
Chut! [ʃyt]   Hush!
Fiche le camp! [fiʃləkɑ̃]   Beat it!, Get lost!
Fous-moi la paix! [fumwalapɛ] Leave me alone!
La ferme! [lafɛrm]   Shut up!, Shut your trap!
La paix! [lapɛ]   Leave me alone!
Ne te gêne pas. [nətʒɛnpa]   Don't mind me; Don't let me
                                 disturb you.
Silence! [silɑ̃s]   Quiet!
Ta gueule! [tagœl]   Shut up!

━━━━━━ **Regret and Consolation** ━━━━━━

C'est dommage. [sɛdɔmaʒ]   It's a pity.
Ça ne fait rien. [sanfɛrjɛ̃] It doesn't matter.
Ce n'est pas grave. [snɛpagrav] It's not serious.
Ce n'est rien. [sənɛrjɛ̃]   It doesn't matter; You're welcome.
Dommage. [dɔmaʒ]   Pity; Too bad.
Je n'y peux rien. [ʒnipørjɛ̃] I can't help it.
Je regrette. [ʒrəgrɛt]   I am sorry.
Je suis désolé, e. [ʒsɥidezole] I am very sorry.
Je vous en prie. [ʒvuzɑ̃pri] You're welcome!, I beg your
                                 pardon!

malheureusement [malœrøzmã]	unfortunately
Ne vous en faites pas. [nvuzãfɛtpɑ]	Don't worry.
Pardon. [pardɔ̃]	Pardon me!, Excuse me!
Tant pis. [tãpi]	Never mind!, So much the worse!
Tu m'en veux? [tymãvø]	Are you angry with me?

■ Annoyance and Pain ■

Aïe! [aj]	Oh!, Oh dear!
Arrête! [arɛt]	Stop!
C'est du vol! [sɛdyvɔl]	It's highway robbery!
C'est gênant. [sɛʒenã]	It's troublesome.
Ça alors! [saalɔr]	That does it!, That's the limit!
Ça gratte. [sagrat]	That scratches.
Ça pique. [sapik]	That stings.
Ça suffit. [sasyfi]	That's enough.
le **con** [kɔ̃] Pauvre con!	stupid fool You moron!
la **connerie** [kɔnri]	stupidity, stupid action
espèce de [ɛspɛsdə] Espèce d'idiot!	damn Damn fool!
Et après? [eaprɛ]	And then?; What next?; So what?
Faute de mieux [fotdəmjø]	For want of something better
Franchement [frãʃmã]	Really!, Frankly!
l'**imbécile** *m* [ɛ̃besil]	imbecile, idiot
J'en ai assez. [ʒãnɛase]	I've had enough.
J'en ai marre. [ʒãnɛmar]	I've had enough!
La vache! [lavaʃ]	Damn it!
Merde! [mɛrd]	Damn it!, Shit!
Mon Dieu! [mɔ̃djø]	My God!
Ne fais pas l'idiot! [nfɛpalidjo]	Don't act like an idiot!

Oh putain! [opytɛ̃]	Damn it all!
Oh! [o]	Oh!
Penses-tu! [pɑ̃sty]	That's what you think!
Salaud! [salo]	Skunk!, Scoundrel!
Salopard! [salɔpar]	Swine!, Bastard!
Tu es vache. [t y ɛvaʃ]	You're mean; You're beastly.
Tu m'embêtes. [tymɑ̃bɛt]	You drive me up the wall.
Tu m'énerves. [tymenɛrv]	You get on my nerves.
Zut! [zyt]	Damnation!, Bother!

Ça me révolte. [samrevɔlt]	That disgusts me.
Sacré menteur! [sakremɑ̃tœr]	Damn liar!

■■■■■ Praise and Agreement ■■■■■

Ah! [ɑ]	Oh!
Bien! [bjɛ̃]	Good!
bien entendu [bjɛ̃nɑ̃tɑ̃dy]	naturally, of course
bien sûr [bjɛ̃syr]	of course
Bravo! [bravo]	Bravo!
C'est le cas. [sɛlka]	That is so.
Ça revient au même. [sarəvjɛ̃omɛm]	It amounts to the same thing.
Ça y est. [sajɛ]	Now the fat's in the fire.
D'accord! [dakɔr]	Agreed!, Granted!
entendu [ɑ̃tɑ̃dy]	settled; agreed; all right
exactement [ɛgzaktəmɑ̃]	exactly
justement [ʒystəmɑ̃] Tu n'es pas bête.—Justement. Justement, te voilà.	precisely, exactly; just You're not stupid.—Right! You're just on time.
naturellement [natyrɛlmɑ̃]	naturally
oui [wi]	yes
parfaitement [parfɛtmɑ̃]	perfectly

55

Si tu veux. [sityvø]	If you wish.
super *inv* [sypɛr]	super
volontiers [vɔlɔ̃tje]	gladly, willingly
vraiment [vrɛmā]	truly; indeed, really

Rejection and Skepticism

à aucun prix [aokɛ̃pri]	by no means; not at any price
Ah bon? [abɔ̃]	Oh, indeed?
Ça m'est égal. [samɛtegal]	It's all the same to me.
Ça manque. [samāk]	That's (what's) missing.
Ça n'empêche pas. [sanāpɛʃpa]	All the same; For all that.
Ce n'est pas malin. [snɛpamalɛ̃]	It's easy.
non [nɔ̃]	no
pas du tout [padytu]	not at all
pas grand-chose [pagrāʃoz]	not much, nothing special
Quelle horreur! [kɛlɔrœr]	How horrible!
rien à faire [rjɛ̃nafɛr]	nothing can be done
sans blague [sāblag]	no kidding, seriously
Voyons! [vwajɔ̃]	See here!, Come now!

Ça ne vaut rien. [sanvorjɛ̃]	It's good for nothing.

Terms of Endearment

chéri, e [ʃeri]	darling
ma bien-aimée [mabjɛ̃neme]	beloved, darling . . .
ma biquette [mabikɛt]	darling, honey
mon mignon, ma mignonne [mɔ̃miɲɔ̃, mamiɲɔn]	sweetie, sugar
mon amour [mɔnamur]	my darling
mon bien-aimé [mɔ̃bjɛ̃nemə]	beloved, darling . .

mon chou [mɔ̃ʃu]	sweetheart
mon trésor [mɔ̃trezɔr]	darling, dear, my treasure
mon vieux, ma vieille [mɔ̃vjø, mavjɛj]	my friend, old friend

━━━━━ Appraisal ━━━━━

à part ça [aparsa]	apart from that
au contraire [okɔ̃trɛr]	on the contrary
au fait [ofɛt]	to the point; after all
C'est bon signe. [sɛbɔ̃siɲ]	It's a good sign.
C'est différent. [sɛdiferã]	That's different.
C'est obligé. [sɛtɔbliʒe]	It has to be.
Ça dépend. [sadepã]	That depends.
Ça m'a frappé, e. [samafrape]	I noticed that.
Ça se peut. [saspø]	That's possible.
Ça tombe bien. [satɔ̃bbjɛ̃]	That comes at the right time.
Ça vaut le coup. [savolku]	It's worth trying.
chouette [ʃwɛt]	swell, great
comme ci, comme ça [kɔmsikɔmsa]	so so, indifferently
comme il faut [kɔmilfo]	proper; properly; the right kind of
comme tout [kɔmtu] Il est bête comme tout.	exceedingly, extremely He's as dumb as they come.
d'ailleurs [dajœr]	besides, moreover
Dieu merci! [djømɛrsi]	Thank God!
en effet [ãnefɛ]	in reality, indeed, in fact
en principe [ãprɛ̃sip]	as a rule, theoretically
évidemment [evidamã]	evidently
extra [ɛkstra]	extra
il est interdit de [ilɛtɛ̃tɛrdidə]	it is forbidden to
il n'y a qu'à [ilnjaka] Il n'y a qu'a lire le journal.	you only have to You only have to read the newspaper.

Il n'y a pas de mal. [ilnjapadmal]	It's not serious.
Je n'en peux plus. [ʒnãpøply]	I can't keep on.
malgré tout [malgretu]	in spite of everything
merveilleux, -euse [mɛrvejø, z]	marvelous, fantastic
par exemple [parɛksãpl]	for example
pas mal [pɑmal]	not bad
pour ainsi dire [purɛ̃sidir]	so to speak, as it were
Quel monde! [kɛlmɔ̃d]	What a crowd there is!
tant mieux [tãmjø]	so much the better

Ça varie. [savari]	That varies.
Ça vaut la peine. [savolapɛn]	It is worth while.
étant donné que [etãdɔnekə]	whereas, since
soi-disant [swadizã]	so-called, self-styled

▬▬▬ Expletives and Transition Words ▬▬▬

à mon avis [amɔ̃navi]	in my opinion
à propos [apropo]	by the way, incidentally
dis/dites (donc) [di/dit dɔ̃k]	tell me, say
disons [dizɔ̃]	let's say . . .
Eh bien! [ebjɛ̃]	Well!
Hein? [ɛ̃]	Isn't it?; Eh?, What?
quoi [kwa]	which; what
s'il te plaît [siltəplɛ]	please
s'il vous plaît [silvuplɛ]	please
tiens! tiens! [tjɛ̃tjɛ̃]	Well, hello!
tiens/tenez [tjɛ̃/təne]	look here; you don't say
tu sais [tysɛ]	you know
voilà [vwala]	there, there is, there are
vous savez [vusave]	you know

================ **Confirmation** ================

ainsi [ɛsi]   so, thus
C'est ainsi.   That's so.

bien [bjɛ̃]   good
C'est bien.   That's good.

certainement [sɛrtɛnmã]   certainly

d'ordinaire [dɔrdinɛr]   ordinarily

de cette manière [dəsɛtmanjɛr]   in this way

également [egalmã]   equally; also, likewise, too

en effet [ãnefɛ]   in reality, indeed, in fact

en fait [ãfɛt]   as a matter of fact

en tout cas [ãtuka]   at all events, however

entièrement [ãtjɛrmã]   entirely

évidemment [evidamã]   evidently, obviously

exactement [ɛgzaktəmã]   exactly

généralement [ʒeneralmã]   in general, generally

habituellement [abituɛlmã]   habitually, usually

précisément [presizemã]   precisely

sans aucun doute [sãzokɛ̃dut]   without any doubt

sans faute [sãfot]   without fail

sûrement [syrmã]   surely, certainly

tout à fait [tutafɛ]   entirely

vraiment [vrɛmã]   truly, really

à coup sûr [akusyr]   certainly

ça correspond à [sakɔrɛspõa]   that corresponds to

en somme [ãsɔm]   in short, when all is said and done

nettement [nɛtmã]   clearly, distinctly

pur et simple [pyresɛ̃mpl]   pure and simple, unconditional
C'est de la folie pure et simple.   It's utter madness.

Intensity

à feu doux [afødu]	over a low flame
à fond [afɔ̃]	thoroughly
à tout prix [atupri]	at all costs
au fond [ofɔ̃]	basically
autant [otã]	as much, as many
Je travaille autant.	I work just as much.
Je travaille autant que toi.	I work just as much as you.
bref *adv* [brɛf]	brief, short
complètement [kɔ̃plɛtmã]	completely
d'autant plus [dotãply]	the more, so much the more
D'autant plus qu'il a raison.	And besides he's right.
Dommage qu'elle ne vienne pas,	Too bad she's not coming, all the
d'autant plus que je comptais sur elle.	more so since I was counting on her.
d'un (seul) coup [dɛ̃ sœl ku]	(all) at once
de plus en plus [dəplyzãplus]	more and more
de trop [dətro]	too much; in the way
Je me sens de trop.	I feel that I'm in the way.
doucement [dusmã]	gently; slowly
en moyenne [ãmwajɛn]	on the average
énormément [enɔrmemã]	enormously
ensemble [ãsãbl]	together, at the same time
être à bout [ɛtrabu]	be at the end
Je suis à bout de souffle.	I'm bushed.
il suffit de [ilsyfitdə]	it suffices to
Il suffit d'apprendre.	It suffices to learn.
il suffit que [ilsyfikə]	it suffices that
Il suffit que tu me préviennes et j'arrive.	You only have to notify me, and I'll come.
largement [larʒəmã]	fully; plenty; by far
Ça suffit largement.	That's enough by a long shot.
mal [mal]	wrong, badly
mieux [mjø]	better
C'est mieux.	It's better.

parfaitement [parfɛtmā]	perfectly
pas mal [pɑmal]	not bad
Elle n'est pas mal.	She's not bad-looking.
Il n'est pas mal.	He's not bad-looking.
sans peine [sāpɛn]	without difficulty
sans succès [sāsyksɛ]	without success
tellement [tɛlmā]	so much, so
C'est tellement bon.	That's so good.
terriblement [tɛribləmā]	terribly
trop [tro]	too much, too many
C'en est trop.	Now that's enough.

à la rigueur [alarigœr]	as a last resort
Ça va à la rigueur.	It'll do as a last resort.
à quel point [akɛlpwɛ̄]	to what degree
à toute allure [atutalyr]	at full speed
à voix basse [avwabɑs]	in a low voice, softly
à voix haute [avwa'ot]	in a loud voice, loudly
brusquement [bryskəmā]	brusquely, abruptly
de mieux en mieux [dəmjøzāmjø]	better and better
de moins en moins [dəmwɛ̄zāmwɛ̄]	less and less, fewer and fewer
On se voit de moins en moins.	We see each other less and less.
de peu [dəpø]	by a very little
Je l'ai raté de peu.	I barely missed him.
décidément [desidemā]	decidedly
en entier [ānātje]	in full, wholly
Avale la pilule en entier.	Swallow the tablet whole.
en masse [āmas]	in a body, in the mass
en vitesse [āvitɛs]	swiftly
sans effort [sāzefɔr]	without effort

Subjective Perception

avec peine [avɛkpɛn]	with difficulty
comme [kɔm]	like, how
de mon côté [dəmɔ̄kote]	for my part
Moi, de mon côté, je m'en vais.	I, for my part, am going.
en fin de compte [ãfɛdkɔ̄t]	when all is said and done
en réalité [ãrealite]	in reality
en vain [ãvɛ̃]	in vain
enfin [ãfɛ̃]	finally, at last
être de bonne humeur [ɛtrdəbɔnymœr]	be in a good humor
exprès [ɛksprɛ]	expressly, on purpose
Tu l'as fait exprès.	You did it on purpose.
finalement [finalmã]	finally, at last
heureusement [œrøzmã]	luckily, fortunately
Heureusement qu'il n'est pas venu.	Fortunately he didn't come.
horriblement [ɔriblǝmã]	horribly
il me semble que [ilməsãblǝkǝ]	it seems to me that
Il me semble que tout va bien.	It seems to me that everything is all right.
il semble que [ilsãblǝkǝ]	it seems that
Il semble que tu n'aies pas compris.	It seems that you didn't understand.
il vaut mieux que [ilvomjøkǝ]	it's better that
Il vaudrait mieux que tu viennes.	It would be better if you came.
malheureusement [malœrøzmã]	unfortunately
normalement [nɔrmalmã]	normally
par hasard [parazar]	by chance
personnellement [pɛrsɔnɛlmã]	personally
sans doute [sãdut]	without doubt
sans le vouloir [sãlvulwar]	without wishing it
sans raison [sãrɛzɔ̄]	groundless(ly)

spécialement [spesjalmɑ̃]	especially, particularly
volontiers [vɔlɔ̃tje]	gladly, willingly

au hasard [oˈazar]	at random
avec intérêt [avɛkɛ̃terɛ]	with interest, attentively
J'ai suivi votre discours avec intérêt.	I followed your talk with interest.
avec succès [avɛksyksɛ]	with success, successfully
la **circonstance** [sirkɔ̃stɑ̃s]	circumstance
le **coup de chance** [kudʃɑ̃s]	stroke of luck
de bon cœur [dəbɔ̃kœr]	willingly, heartily
de rêve [dərɛv]	dream, of one's dreams
Une femme de rêve.	A dream woman.
en colère [ɑ̃kɔlɛr]	angry
en personne [ɑ̃pɛrsɔn]	in person, personally
en secret [ɑ̃skrɛ]	in secret, secretly
forcément [fɔrsemɑ̃]	inevitably, necessarily
J'ai forcément raison.	I'm inevitably right!
Pas forcément.	Not necessarily.
par malheur [parmalœr]	unfortunately
sans façons [sɑ̃fasɔ̃]	informal
sur mesure [syrməzyr]	to measure, to order

Qualification

après tout [aprɛtu]	after all
Après tout ce que j'ai fait pour toi.	After all I've done for you.
au moins [omwɛ̃]	at least
autrement [otrəmɑ̃]	otherwise
autrement dit [otrəmɑ̃di]	in other words
d'un autre côté [dɛ̃notrkote]	on the other hand
d'un côté [dɛ̃kote]	on the one hand
D'un côté . . . de l'autre côté.	On the one hand . . . on the other hand.
de toute façon [dətutfasɔ̃]	at any rate, in any event
Je viens de toute façon.	I'm coming in any event.

de toute manière [dətutmanjɛr]	in any case
du moins [dymwɛ̃]	at least
en dernier [ãdɛrnje]	last
Tu viens toujours en dernier.	You always come last.
plutôt [plyto]	rather; instead
Il fait plutôt froid ici.	It's rather cold here.
pratiquement [pratikmã]	practically
simplement [sɛ̃pləmã]	simply
tout de même [tudmɛm]	however, all the same
Qu'il soit un pauvre type, je veux bien, mais il nous a volés tout de même.	He may well be a poor fellow, but he robbed us all the same.
uniquement [ynikmã]	solely

le cas échéant [ləkazeʃeã]	if necessary, should the occasion arise
plus ou moins [plyzumwɛ̃]	more or less
provisoirement [prɔvizwarmã]	temporarily, provisionally
sans plus [sãplys]	simply, without more ado
Le maire a répondu aux questions, sans plus.	The mayor answered the questions, without more ado.
sous réserve [surezɛrv]	subject to
tout compte fait [tukɔ̃tfɛ]	all in all

Humans and Their Needs

Shops

le **boucher** [buʃe]	butcher
Je vais chez le boucher.	I'm going to the butcher's.
la **boucherie** [buʃri]	butcher shop
Je vais à la boucherie.	I'm going to the butcher shop.
le **boulanger** [bulɑ̃ʒe]	baker
la **boutique** [butik]	small shop
le **bureau de tabac** [byrodtaba]	tobacco shop
l'**épicerie** *f* [episri]	grocery store
la **librairie** [librɛri]	bookstore
le **magasin** [magazɛ̃]	store, shop
le **marché** [marʃe]	market
la **pâtisserie** [pɑtisri]	pastry shop
le **supermarché** [sypɛrmarʃe]	supermarket

le **bar** [bar]	bar
le **bistro(t)** [bistro]	pub
la **boulangerie** [bulɑ̃ʒri]	bakery
le **café** [kafe]	cafe
la **charcuterie** [ʃarkytri]	pork butcher shop; delicatessen
l'**épicier** *m* [episje]	grocer
la **maison de la presse** [mɛzɔ̃dlaprɛs]	newsstand
la **papeterie** [papetri]	stationery store
la **parfumerie** [parfymri]	perfumery, cosmetics store
le **traiteur** [trɛtœr]	caterer, delicatessen

Shopping

l'**achat** *m* [aʃa]	purchase
acheter [aʃte]	buy, purchase
l'**argent** *m* [arʒɑ̃]	money
augmenter [ɔgmɑ̃te]	increase; augment
Les prix ont encore augmenté.	Prices have increased again.
avoir besoin de [avwarbəzwɛ̃də]	need
avoir de la monnaie [avwardlamonɛ]	have small change
la **caisse** [kɛs]	cash register
cher, chère [ʃɛr]	expensive
Cette année les pommes sont très chères.	This year apples are very expensive.
le **client,** la **cliente** [klijɑ̃, t]	customer, client
combien [kɔ̃bjɛ̃]	how much, how many
Combien de tranches?	How many slices?
les **courses** *fpl* [kurs]	shopping
coûter [kute]	cost
Ça coûte combien?	How much does it cost?
coûter cher [kuteʃɛr]	cost a great deal
Cette année les pommes coûtent très cher.	This year apples cost a great deal.
dépenser [depɑ̃se]	spend
désirer [dezire]	wish
Vous désirez?	May I help you?
faire la queue [fɛrlakø]	get in line, stand in line
le **franc** [frɑ̃]	franc
le **grand magasin** [grɑ̃magazɛ̃]	department store
gratuit, e [gratɥi, t]	free, gratis
le **litre** [litr]	liter
Un litre de lait s.v.p.	A liter of milk, please.
la **livre** [livr]	pound
Une livre de beurre salé s.v.p.	A pound of salted butter, please.

la **marchandise** [marʃãdiz]	merchandise
la **monnaie** [mɔnɛ]	small change
le **morceau, x** [mɔrso]	piece
Un bon morceau de porc.	A nice piece of pork.
payer [peje]	pay
payer cher [pejeʃɛr]	pay a high price
payer comptant [pejekõtã]	pay in cash
la **pièce de monnaie** [pjɛsdəmɔnɛ]	coin
le **portefeuille** [pɔrtəfœj]	wallet, billfold
le **porte-monnaie** [pɔrtmɔnɛ]	coin purse
le **prix** [pri]	price
la **réduction** [redyksjõ]	reduction in price
rendre la monnaie [rãdrəlamɔnɛ]	make change
la **tranche** [trãʃ]	slice
le **vendeur,** la **vendeuse** [vãdœr, øz]	salesman; saleslady
vendre [vãdr]	sell
la **vitrine** [vitrin]	show window, showcase

l'**alimentation** *f* [alimãtɑsjõ]	nourishment
bon marché *inv* [bõmarʃe]	cheap; cheaply
Les fraises sont bon marché en ce moment.	Strawberries are cheap right now.
la **clientèle** [klijãtɛl]	customers; clientele
coûteux, -euse [kutø, z]	costly, expensive

Cooking

à feu doux [afødu]	on a low flame
ajouter [aʒute]	add
Ajoutez trois jaunes d'œuf au sucre.	Add three egg yolks to the sugar.

la **boîte** [bwat]   can

bouillir [bujir]   boil
Faites bouillir le lait.   Bring the milk to a boil.

la **casserole** [kasrɔl]   saucepan

la **conserve** [kɔ̃sɛrv]   canned food, preserves

couper [kupe]   cut

cuire [kɥir]   cook
J'ai fait cuire un steak.   I cooked a steak.

la **cuisine** [kɥizin]   cooking; kitchen; cuisine
La cuisine française.   French cuisine.
La nouvelle cuisine.   Nouvelle cuisine.

essayer [eseje]   try, try out

faire la cuisine [fɛrlakɥizin]   cook
C'est papa qui fait la cuisine   Papa does the cooking at
chez nous.   our house.

le **four** [fur]   oven

goûter [gute]   taste, try

la **goutte** [gut]   drop

griller [grije]   grill, broil; toast

l'**huile** *f* [ɥil]   oil

mélanger [melɑ̃ʒe]   mix

la **nourriture** [nurityr]   nourishment, food

l'**œuf** *m* [œf, ø]   egg

la **pâte** [pɑt]   paste; dough; pasta

la **poêle** [pwal]   frying pan

préparer [prepare]   prepare

la **recette** [rəsɛt]   recipe

le **réfrigérateur** [refriʒeratœr]   refrigerator

refroidir [rəfrwadir]   cool

le **vinaigre** [vinɛgr]   vinegar

l'**ail** *m* [aj]	garlic
la **farine** [farin]	flour
les **herbes** *fpl* [ɛrb]	herbs
la **levure** [ləvyr]	yeast
l'**oignon** *m* [ɔɲɔ̄]	onion
l'**os** *m* [ɔs, o]	bone
l'**ouvre-boîte** *m* [uvrbwat]	can-opener
la **pâte brisée** [pɑtbrize]	short pastry
la **pâte feuilletée** [pɑtfœjte]	puff pastry
le **persil** [pɛrsi]	parsley
la **pincée** [pɛ̄se]	pinch
remuer [rəmɥe]	stir

Setting the Table

l'**assiette** *f* [asjɛt]	plate
le **couteau, x** [kuto]	knife
la **cuiller** [kɥijɛr]	spoon
débarrasser [debarase]	clear (the table)
la **fourchette** [furʃɛt]	fork
le **pain** [pɛ̄]	bread
le **panier** [panje]	basket
le **poivre** [pwavr]	pepper
le **sel** [sɛl]	salt
la **serviette** [sɛrvjɛt]	napkin
la **table** [tabl]	table
la **tasse** [tas]	cup
la **vaisselle** [vɛsɛl]	dishes
le **verre** [vɛr]	glass

le **bol** [bɔl]	bowl, basin; cup
J'ai bu deux bols de café ce matin.	I drank two cups of coffee this morning.
la **cafetière** [kaftjɛr]	coffee machine; coffee pot
la **carafe** [karaf]	carafe, decanter
le **couvert** [kuvɛr]	cover (plate, spoon, knife, fork)
mettre la table [mɛtrəlatabl]	set the table
mettre le couvert [mɛtrləkuvɛr]	set the table
le **plateau, x** [plato]	tray
le **saladier** [saladje]	salad bowl
la **soupière** [supjɛr]	soup tureen
la **théière** [tejɛr]	teapot

In a Restaurant

l'**addition** *f* [adisjɔ̃]	check, bill
L'addition s.v.p.	The check, please.
l'**ambiance** *f* [ãbjãs]	atmosphere; surroundings
l'**appétit** *m* [apeti]	appetite, hunger
L'appétit vient en mangeant.	The more one has, the more one wants.
avoir envie de [avwarãvidə]	want
J'ai envie d'un éclair.	I want an eclair.
avoir faim [avwarfɛ̃]	be hungry
J'ai faim.	I'm hungry.
J'ai une faim de loup.	I'm hungry as a wolf.
avoir soif [avwarswaf]	be thirsty
boire [bwar]	drink
Je bois à ta santé.	I drink to your health.
la **boisson** [bwasɔ̃]	beverage, drink
le **bouchon** [buʃɔ̃]	cork
la **bouteille** [butɛj]	bottle
On a pris une bonne bouteille.	We drank a very good bottle of wine.
le **chef** [ʃɛf]	chef
commander [kɔmãde]	order; command

71

la **consommation** [kɔ̃sɔmasjɔ̃] Le tarif des consommations est affiché.	food, drinks, refreshments, expense The price list is posted.
digérer [diʒere]	digest
être au régime [ɛtroreʒim]	be on a diet
la **faim** [fɛ̃]	hunger
le **garçon** [garsɔ̃] Garçon!	waiter Waiter!
le **goût** [gu]	taste
ivre [ivr]	drunk
la **liste** [list]	list
manger [mɑ̃ʒe]	eat
le **menu** [mǝny] Qu'est-ce qu'il y a au menu?	menu, bill of fare What's on the menu?
nourrir [nurir]	nourish, feed
offrir [ɔfrir]	offer
le **patron,** la **patronne** [patrɔ̃, ɔn]	proprietor
le **plat** [pla] plat du jour	course, dish special dish of the day
le **pourboire** [purbwar]	tip
prendre [prɑ̃dr] Je prends un café.	take I'll take a cup of coffee.
la **qualité** [kalite]	quality
le **régime** [reʒim]	diet
réserver [rezɛrve] Faites réserver à l'avance.	reserve Reserve in advance.
le **restaurant** [rɛstɔrɑ̃]	restaurant
le **reste** [rɛst]	rest, remainder
le **service** [sɛrvis] service compris	service service included
servir [sɛrvir]	serve
la **soif** [swaf]	thirst
soûl, e [su, l]	drunk
la **spécialité** [spesjalite]	specialty
le **tarif** [tarif]	price list

le **consommateur** [kɔ̃sɔmatœr]	eater, drinker, guest, consumer
le **glaçon** [glasɔ̃]	ice cube
le **libre-service** [librəsɛrvis]	self-service
la **réclamation** [reklamasjɔ̃]	claim; complaint
recommander [rəkɔmɑ̃de]	recommend
le **salon de thé** [salɔ̃dəte]	tearoom

The Menu

Breakfast

la **baguette** [bagɛt]	baguette, long thin loaf of bread
le **beurre** [bœr]	butter
le **café** [kafe]	coffee
le **chocolat** [ʃɔkɔla]	chocolate
le **citron** [sitrɔ̃]	lemon
la **confiture** [kɔ̃fityr]	marmelade, jam
le **croissant** [krwasɑ̃]	croissant, crescent roll
le **lait** [lɛ]	milk
le **petit déjeuner** [ptidezœne]	breakfast
J'ai pris mon petit déjeuner à 7 heures ce matin.	I had breakfast at 7 this morning.
le **sandwich** [sɑ̃dwitʃ]	sandwich
la **tartine** [tartin]	slice of bread and butter
le **thé** [te]	tea

Other Meals

le **déjeuner** [dezœne]	lunch
déjeuner [dezœne]	eat lunch
le **dîner** [dine]	dinner
dîner [dine]	eat dinner, dine
le **repas** [rəpɑ]	meal, repast

Appetizers

au choix [oʃwa]	at one's discretion
le **hors-d'œuvre** ['ɔrdœvr]	hors d'oeuvre, appetizer
le **jambon** [ʒɑ̃bɔ̃]	ham
l'**omelette** *f* [ɔmlɛt]	omelet
le **pâté** [pate]	pate
le **saucisson** [sosisɔ̃]	large dry sausage, salami
la **soupe** [sup]	soup

l'**artichaut** *m* [artiʃo]	artichoke
la **crudité** [krydite]	raw fruit or vegetable
l'**entrée** *f* [ɑ̃tre]	appetizer, starter
le **potage** [pɔtaʒ]	soup

Fish

le **poisson** [pwasɔ̃]	fish

la **lotte** [lɔt]	monkfish
la **sole** [sɔl]	sole
la **truite** [tryit]	trout

Meat

le **bifteck** [biftɛk]	steak
le **bœuf** [bœf, bø]	beef
le **canard** [kanar]	duck
le **cheval, -aux** [ʃval, o]	horsemeat
le **foie** [fwa]	liver
la **langue** [lɑ̃g]	tongue
le **lapin** [lapɛ̃]	rabbit
le **mouton** [mutɔ̃]	mutton
le **porc** [pɔr]	pork
le **poulet** [pulɛ]	chicken

le **rôti** [roti]	roast
la **sauce** [sos]	sauce; gravy
le **veau, x** [vo]	veal
la **viande** [vjãd]	meat

la **côtelette** [kotlɛt]	cutlet, chop
l'**escalope** *f* [ɛskalɔp]	scallop (veal, pork)

Vegetables

la **carotte** [karɔt]	carrot
le **champignon** [ʃãpiɲõ]	mushroom
les **frites** *fpl* [frit]	French fries
les **haricots verts** *mpl* ['arikovɛr]	green beans
le **légume** [legym]	vegetable
les **nouilles** *fpl* [nuj]	noodles
les **petits pois** *mpl* [ptipwa]	peas
la **pomme de terre** [pɔmdətɛr]	potato
le **riz** [ri]	rice

l'**aubergine** *f* [obɛrʒin]	eggplant
le **chou-fleur** [ʃuflœr]	cauliflower
l'**endive** *f* [ãdiv]	endive

Salad

la **salade** [salad]	salad
la **tomate** [tɔmat]	tomato

le **concombre** [kõkõbr]	cucumber
la **frisée** [frize]	curly endive, escarole, chicory
la **laitue** [lety]	lettuce

Cheese

le **fromage** [frɔmaʒ]	cheese
le **plateau de fromage** [platodfrɔmaʒ]	cheese platter

Fruit

la **banane** [banan]	banana
la **cerise** [səriz]	cherry
la **fraise** [frɛz]	strawberry
les **fruits** *mpl* [frɥi]	fruits
l'**orange** *f* [ɔrɑ̃ʒ]	orange
la **poire** [pwar]	pear
la **pomme** [pɔm]	apple
le **raisin** [rɛzɛ̃]	grape

l'**ananas** *m* [anana]	pineapple
la **framboise** [frɑ̃bwaz]	raspberry
le **melon** [məlɔ̃]	melon
la **pêche** [pɛʃ]	peach

Dessert

le **bonbon** [bɔ̃bɔ̃]	bonbon, piece of candy
la **crème** [krɛm]	cream; custard
le **dessert** [desɛr]	dessert
le **gâteau, x** [gɑto]	cake
la **glace** [glas]	ice; ice cream
la **mousse au chocolat** [musoʃɔkɔla]	chocolate mousse
la **tarte** [tart]	tart
la **tarte aux abricots** [tartozabriko]	apricot tart
le **yaourt** [jaurt]	yogurt

la **coupe** [kup]	cup, goblet
la **crème Chantilly** [krɛmʃɑ̃tiji]	whipped cream
la **crème caramel** [krɛmkaramɛl]	caramel custard
la **crêpe** [krɛp]	crepe, thin pancake
le **flan** [flɑ̃]	vanilla custard with caramel
le **gâteau sec** [gɑtosɛk]	cookie
la **gaufre** [gofr]	wafer

Beverages

l'**alcool** *m* [alkɔl]	alcohol
la **bière** [bjɛr]	beer
l'**eau, x** *f* [o]	water
le **jus** [ʒy]	juice
la **limonade** [limɔnad]	soft drink; lemon soda
l'**orangeade** *f* [ɔrɑ̃ʒad]	orange soda
le **vin** [vɛ̃]	wine
le **vin ordinaire** [vɛ̃ɔrdinɛr]	table wine

l'**apéritif** *m* [aperitif]	aperitif
le **blanc** [blɑ̃]	white wine
le **champagne** [ʃɑ̃paɲ]	champagne
le **cidre** [sidr]	cider
le **digestif** [diʒɛstif]	digestive
l'**eau minérale** *f* [omineral]	mineral water
le **rosé** [roze]	rose wine
le **rouge** [ruʒ]	red wine
le **sirop** [siro]	syrup

▬▬▬ Characteristics of Dishes ▬▬▬

amer, amère [amɛr]	bitter
avoir du goût [avwardygu]	have taste
bon, bonne [bɔ̃, bɔn]	good
brûlant, e [brylɑ̃, t]	very hot
chaud, e [ʃo, d]	warm, hot
cru, e [kry]	raw
cuit, e [kɥi, t]	done; cooked
doux, douce [du, dus]	sweet
dur, e [dyr]	hard
épais, se [epɛ, s]	thick
frais, fraîche [frɛ, frɛʃ]	fresh
froid, e [frwa, d]	cold
gras, se [grɑ, s]	fat; greasy
maigre [mɛgr]	lean
mou, molle [mu, mɔl] Les frites sont molles.	soft The French fries are too soft.
mûr, e [myr]	ripe
pur, e [pyr]	pure
sec, sèche [sɛk, sɛʃ]	dry
spécial, e, -aux [spesjal, o]	special
tendre [tɑ̃dr] Mon steak est très tendre.	tender My steak is very tender.
tiède [tjɛd]	lukewarm

à point [apwɛ̃]	to a turn, medium
bien cuit, e [bjɛ̃kɥi, t]	well done
saignant, e [sɛɲɑ̃, t]	rare
salé, e [sale]	salted
sucré, e [sykre]	sweet, sugared
varié, e [varje]	varied, assorted
vert, e [vɛr, t]	unripe, green
Je suis malade. j'ai mangé des prunes vertes.	I'm sick, I ate some green plums.
vide [vid]	empty

Smoking

allumer [alyme]	light
le **briquet** [brikɛ]	lighter
le **cendrier** [sɑ̃drije]	ashtray
la **cigarette** [sigarɛt]	cigarette
éteindre [etɛ̃dr]	put out, extinguish
fumer [fyme]	smoke
la **pipe** [pip]	pipe
le **tabac** [taba]	tobacco

l'**allumette** f [alymɛt]	match
la **cendre** [sɑ̃dr]	ash
le **cigare** [sigar]	cigar

━━━━━━━━━━━━━━ **Shopping** ━━━━━━━━━━━━━━

à l'endroit [alãdrwa] right side out

à l'envers [alãvɛr] wrong side out, inside out, backwards

Tu as mis ton pull à l'envers. You've put on your sweater inside out.

à la mode [alamɔd] in style, fashionable
Le rose est à la mode cet été. Pink is in style this summer.

l'**achat** *m* [aʃa] purchase

acheter [aʃte] buy, purchase

avoir besoin de [avwarbəzwɛ̃də] need
J'ai besoin d'une nouvelle robe. I need a new dress.

avoir du goût [avwardygu] have taste

avoir envie de [avwarãvidə] want
J'ai envie d'acheter un pantalon. I want to buy a pair of pants.

la **boutique** [butik] boutique, small shop

Ça coûte une fortune. That costs a fortune.
[sakutynfɔrtyn]

le **client**, la **cliente** [klijã, t] customer; client

essayer [eseje] try on
Vous voulez essayer? Would you like to try it on?

l'**étiquette** *f* [etikɛt] label

le **grand magasin** [grãmagazɛ̃] department store
J'achète toujours mes vêtements dans les grands magasins. I always buy my clothes in the department stores.

la **marchandise** [marʃãdiz] merchandise

la **mode** [mɔd] style, fashion

le **modèle** [mɔdɛl] model

la **paire** [pɛr] pair
J'ai acheté trois paires de chaussures. I've bought three pairs of shoes.

payer [peje] pay
Je les ai payées pas trop cher. I got them at a good price.

le **prix** [pri] price

la **qualité** [kalite] quality

la **réduction** [redyksjɔ̃] reduction in price

rendre la monnaie [rãdrəlamɔnɛ]	make change
la **taille** [taj]	size
Vous faites quelle taille?	What is your size?
le **vendeur,** la **vendeuse** [vãdœr, øz]	salesman; saleslady
vendre [vãdr]	sell
la **vitrine** [vitrin]	shop window, showcase

aller avec [aleavɛk]	go with, suit
Cette couleur va avec mes cheveux.	This color goes with my hair.
coûteux, -euse [kutø, z]	costly, expensive
faire un prix [fɛrɛ̃pri]	give a discount
Le vendeur m'a fait un prix.	The salesman gave me a discount.
la **pointure** [pwɛ̃tyr]	shoe size
les **soldes** *mpl* [sɔld]	clearance sales
J'ai acheté ce pull en soldes.	I bought this pullover on sale.

■ Garments ■

la **botte** [bɔt]	boot
changer [ʃãʒe]	change
J'ai déjà changé de chemise.	I've already changed my shirt.
changer (se) [səʃãʒe]	change clothes
Je vais me changer.	I'm going to change clothes.
le **chapeau, x** [ʃapo]	hat
la **chaussure** [ʃosyr]	shoe
la **chemise** [ʃmiz]	shirt
le **costume** [kɔstym]	suit
Etienne a mis son costume neuf.	Etienne has his new suit on.
couvrir (se) [səkuvrir]	dress warmly
Couvre-toi, il fait froid.	Dress warmly, it's cold!
la **cravate** [kravat]	necktie

déshabiller (se) [sədezabije]	get undressed
enlever [ɑ̃lve]	take off
Si tu as chaud, enlève ta veste.	If you're hot, take off your jacket.
le **gant** [gɑ̃]	glove
habiller (s') [sabije]	get dressed
l'**imper(méable)** *m* [ɛ̃pɛr meabl]	raincoat
la **jupe** [ʒyp]	skirt
le **maillot** [majo]	bathing suit; bathing trunks
le **manteau, x** [mɑ̃to]	coat
mettre [mɛtr]	put on
Oh, tu as mis ta nouvelle robe.	Oh, you've put on your new dress.
le **pantalon** [pɑ̃talɔ̃]	trousers, pair of pants
porter [pɔrte]	wear
Le vert se porte beaucoup cette année.	Green is being worn a lot this year.
le **pull** [pyl]	pullover, sweater
le **pyjama** [piʒama]	pajamas
la **robe** [rɔb]	dress
le **slip** [slip]	panties, briefs
le **vêtement** [vɛtmɑ̃]	clothing

l'**anorak** *m* [anorak]	anorak, parka
le **bas** [bɑ]	stocking
le **basket** [baskɛt]	high-top athletic shoe
le **bikini** [bikini]	bikini
la **blouse** [bluz]	smock
le **blouson** [bluzɔ̃]	jacket
le **blue-jean** [bludʒin]	bluejeans
le **bonnet** [bɔnɛ]	cap
le **boot** [but]	ankle boot
le **cardigan** [kardigɑ̃]	cardigan sweater
le **casque** [kask]	helmet

le **chemisier** [ʃəmizje]	blouse
le **ciré** [sire]	raincoat; waterproof garment
Pour aller en mer, mets ton ciré jaune.	To go out on the ocean, put on your yellow slicker.
le **collant** [kɔlā]	pantyhose
la **combinaison** [kɔ̃binɛzɔ̃]	coveralls; slip, undergarment
le **corsage** [kɔrsaʒ]	blouse
la **culotte** [kylɔt]	panties
l'**espadrille** *f* [ɛspadrij]	canvas shoe with cord soles
le **gilet** [ʒilɛ]	vest
le **peignoir** [pɛɲwar]	bathrobe, dressing gown
la **sandale** [sādal]	sandal
le **short** [ʃɔrt]	shorts
les **sous-vêtements** *mpl* [suvɛtmā]	underwear
le **soutien-gorge** [sutjɛ̃gɔrʒ]	bra
le **tailleur** [tɑjœr]	suit
le **tee-shirt** [tiʃœrt]	T-shirt
le **training** [trɛnŋ]	jogging suit, track suit
la **veste** [vɛst]	jacket
Mon mari a déchiré la veste de son costume.	My husband has torn the jacket of his suit.

■■■■■■■ Characteristics and Materials ■■■■■■■

chaud, e [ʃo, d]	warm
Il est chaud, mon pull.	My sweater is warm.
la **chaussette** [ʃosɛt]	stocking, sock
chic *unv* [ʃik]	chic, stylish
Françoise ne porte que des vêtements chic.	Françoise wears only stylish clothing.
confortable [kɔ̃fɔrtabl]	comfortable
le **coton** [kɔtɔ̃]	cotton
court, e [kur, t]	short

le **cuir** [kɥir]
Je ne porte que des chaussures
en cuir.

leather
I wear only leather shoes.

élégant, e [elegã, t]

elegant

en or [ãnɔr]

(made of) gold

épais, se [epɛ, s]
Mon manteau est très épais.

thick, warm
My coat is very thick.

fin, fine [fɛ, fin]
Ma mère porte une chaîne fine en or.

fine
My mother wears a fine gold
necklace.

la **fourrure** [furyr]

fur

gai, e [gɛ]
Ce tissu a des couleurs gaies.

cheerful, lively, gay
This fabric has cheerful colors.

la **laine** [lɛn]

wool

large [larʒ]

large, big

léger, -ère [leʒe, ɛr]

light

long, longue [lɔ̃, g]

long

moderne [mɔdɛrn]

modern

neuf, neuve [nœf, nœv]
Les chaussures neuves font mal
aux pieds.

new
New shoes hurt one's feet.

nouveau, -vel, -velle, x
[nuvo, nuvɛl]
Je n'aime pas la nouvelle mode.

new

I don't like the new fashion.

le **nylon** [nilɔ̃]

nylon

propre [prɔpr]

clean

pure laine [pyrlɛn]

pure wool

rayé, e [reje]

striped

sale [sal]

dirty

spécial, e, -aux [spesjal, o]
Le cuir de mon blouson a subi un
traitement spécial.

special
The leather of my jacket under-
went a special treatment.

le **tissu** [tisy]

fabric; cloth; tissue

triste [trist]

sad

uni, e [yni]

solid-colored

usé, e [yze]
Ton pull est usé aux coudes.

worn-out, threadbare
Your sweater is worn-out on the elbows.

véritable [veritabl]

genuine

à carreaux [akaro]
La nouvelle mode propose des jupes à carreaux.

checked
The new fashion recommends checked skirts.

à pois [apwa]
Ridicules, ces collants à pois.

polka-dotted
Ridiculous, these polka-dotted pantyhose.

à talon haut [atalɔ'o]

high-heeled

démodé, e [demɔde]

old-fashioned, outmoded

la **dentelle** [dɑ̃tɛl]
Comment tu trouves ce col en dentelle?

lace; lacework
What do you think of this lace collar?

doublé, e [duble]
Ce pantalon est doublé.

lined
These trousers are lined.

en argent [ɑ̃narʒɑ̃]

(made of) silver

l'**étoffe** *f* [etɔf]

stuff; material, fabric

habillé, e [abije]
Cette robe fait très habillé.

elegant, becoming
This dress is very becoming.

imprimé, e [ɛprime]

printed

précieux, -euse [presjø, z]

valuable, precious

la **soie** [swa]

silk

souple [supl]

supple; pliant

le **tricot** [triko]

knitting; knitted garment

================= **Articles and Accessories** =================

le **bijou, x** [biʒu]

jewel

le **bouton** [butɔ̃]

button

la **ceinture** [sɛ̃tyr]

belt

la **chaîne** [ʃɛn]
Mon frère porte une chaîne en or.

necklace
My brother wears a gold necklace.

le **col** [kɔl]	collar
la **manche** [mɑ̃ʃ]	sleeve
la **montre** [mɔ̃tr]	clock, watch
le **mouchoir** [muʃwar]	handkerchief
le **nœud** [nø]	knot; bowtie
Tu mets ton nœud papillon?	Are you wearing your bowtie?
le **parapluie** [paraplɥi]	umbrella
la **pièce** [pjɛs]	piece of clothing, garment
le **pli** [pli]	fold; pleat
la **poche** [pɔʃ]	pocket
le **sac** [sak]	handbag

la **bague** [bag]	ring
le **bracelet** [braslɛ]	bracelet
le **col en V** [kɔlɑ̃ve]	V-neck
le **col roulé** [kɔlrule]	turtleneck
Je ne supporte pas les pulls à col roulé.	I can't stand turtleneck sweaters.
le **collier** [kɔlje]	necklace; collar
Il est splendide, ton collier de perles.	Your pearl necklace is splendid.
le **diamant** [djamɑ̃]	diamond
l'**élastique** *m* [elastik]	rubber band
Mon élastique a lâché.	My rubber band broke.
la **fermeture éclair** [fɛrmtyreklɛr]	zipper
le **foulard** [fular]	scarf
la **perle** [pɛrl]	pearl
la **pierre précieuse** [pjɛrpresjøz]	precious stone

Tasks

abîmer [abime]	spoil; damage
l'**aiguille** *f* [egɥij]	needle
les **ciseaux** *mpl* [sizo]	scissors

coudre [kudr]	sew
déchirer [deʃire]	tear
faire nettoyer [fɛrnetwaje]	have cleaned
le **fil** [fil]	thread
laver [lave]	wash
préparer [prepare]	prepare
repasser [rəpɑse]	iron
serrer [sere]	squeeze, be tight
Il serre, ton pantalon.	Your pants are too tight.
la **tache** [taʃ]	spot
le **trou** [tru]	hole

broder [brɔde]	embroider
J'ai brodé mes mouchoirs moi-même.	I embroidered my handkerchiefs myself.
la **broderie** [brɔdri]	embroidery
Tu fais de la broderie?	What, you do embroidery?
le **canevas** [kanva]	embroidery netting
élargir [elarʒir]	let out, make larger
faire du crochet [fɛrdykrɔʃɛ]	crochet
faire qqc au crochet [fɛrkɛlkəʃozokrɔʃɛ]	crochet s.th.
la **machine à coudre** [maʃinakudr]	sewing machine
raccourcir [rakursir]	make shorter, shorten
rallonger [ralɔ̃ʒe]	make longer, lengthen
repriser [rəprize]	darn
rétrécir [retresir]	take in
la **teinturerie** [tɛ̃tyrri]	dry cleaning
tricoter [trikɔte]	knit

Home

---

l'**appartement** *m* [apartəmã]	apartment
l'**ascenseur** *m* [asãsœr]	elevator
le **balcon** [balkɔ̃]	balcony
la **cave** [kav]	cellar, basement
la **chambre** [ʃãbr] Va dans ta chambre.	(bed)room Go to your room.
la **chambre d'enfants** [ʃãbrdãfã]	children's room, nursery
le, la **concierge** [kɔ̃sjɛrʒ] M. Muller n'est pas là, adressez- vous au concierge.	building superintendent, concierge Mr. Müller is not here; please speak to the superintendent.
la **cuisine** [kɥizin]	kitchen
donner sur [dɔnesyr] Le salon donne sur le jardin.	overlook, open onto The living room opens onto the garden.
l'**entrée** *f* [ãtre]	entrance, entry
l'**escalier** *m* [ɛskalje]	stairs, staircase
l'**espace** *m* [ɛspas] Vous n'avez pas mal d'espace.	room; space You have a good amount of space.
l'**étage** *m* [etaʒ] J'habite au troisième (étage).	floor, story I live on the third floor.
le **garage** [garaʒ] Tu as mis la voiture au garage?	garage Did you put the car in the garage?
l'**immeuble** *m* [imœbl]	building, apartment building
le **jardin** [ʒardɛ̃]	garden
le **luxe** [lyks] Appartement de luxe	luxury luxury apartment
la **maison** [mɛzɔ̃]	house
la **pièce** [pjɛs] C'est un trois pièces.	room It's a three-room apartment.
la **piscine** [pisin]	swimming pool
le **rez-de-chaussée** [redʃose]	ground floor

la **salle** [sal]	room; hall
la **salle à manger** [salamãʒe]	dining room
la **salle de bain** [saldəbɛ̃]	bathroom
la **salle de séjour** [saldəseʒur]	living room
le **salon** [salɔ̃]	living room, parlor
le **sol** [sɔl]	floor
le **sous-sol** [susɔl]	basement
la **terrasse** [tɛras]	terrace
les **toilettes** *fpl* [twalɛt]	toilet
Les toilettes s.v.p.	Where is the toilet, please?
le **toit** [twa]	roof
la **tour** [tur]	tower
La tour Montparnasse est le plus grand bâtiment de Paris.	The Montparnasse Tower is the tallest building in Paris.
les **W.-C.** *mpl* [vese]	toilet

l'**antenne** *f* [ãtɛn]	antenna
le **building** [bildŋ]	building
les **cabinets** *mpl* [kabinɛ]	toilet
la **chambre d'amis** [ʃãmbrdami]	guestroom
le **couloir** [kulwar]	corridor; hallway
de grand standing [dəgrãstãdŋ]	luxury
le **débarras** [debara]	catchall
le **foyer** [fwaje]	foyer, lobby
le **grenier** [grənje]	attic, loft
luxueux, -euse [lyksɥø, z]	luxurious
la **maison individuelle** [mɛzɔ̃ɛ̃dividɥəl]	single-family house
le **palier** [palje]	landing (of stairs)
le **pavillon** [pavijɔ̃]	one-story house
la **résidence** [rezidãs]	residence
J'ai une résidence secondaire dans l'Eure.	I have a second residence in Eure Department.
la **villa** [vila]	villa; small one-story home

Features of the Home

la **baignoire** [bɛɲwar]	bathtub
central, e, -aux [sãtral, o]	central
Nous avons le chauffage central.	We have central heating.
le **chauffage** [ʃofaʒ]	heating
la **cheminée** [ʃəmine]	chimney; fireplace
Tu allumes la cheminée?	Will you light the fireplace?
Ma cheminée tire mal.	My chimney draws badly.
le **coin** [kwɛ̃]	corner
la **douche** [duʃ]	shower
l'**électricité** f [elɛktrisite]	electricity
la **fenêtre** [fənɛtr]	window
le **gaz** [gaz]	gas
le **lavabo** [lavabo]	washbasin
la **lumière** [lymjɛr]	light
la **marche** [marʃ]	step (of staircase)
le **mur** [myr]	wall
Pousse l'armoire contre le mur.	Push the wardrobe against the wall.
le **placard** [plakar]	cupboard (in a wall)
le **plafond** [plafɔ̃]	ceiling
la **porte** [pɔrt]	door
la **prise (de courant)** [priz dəkurã]	(electrical) outlet
la **vitre** [vitr]	windowpane

le **carrelage** [karlaʒ]	tiling
le **courant** [kurɑ̃]	current
l'**éclairage** m [eklɛraʒ]	lighting
la **moquette** [mɔkɛt]	pile carpet
le **papier peint** [papjepɛ̃]	wallpaper
la **persienne** [pɛrsjɛn]	Persian blind, slatted shutter
le **plancher** [plɑ̃ʃe]	floor
le **radiateur** [radjatœr]	radiator
le **volet** [vɔlɛ]	shutter

Inhabitants

déménager [demenaʒe]	move out, change one's residence
la **femme de ménage** [famdəmenaʒ]	cleaning woman
habiter [abite]	live, reside; inhabit
J'habite dans un H.L.M.	I live in public housing.
J'habite en banlieue.	I live in the suburbs.
J'habite un immeuble neuf.	I live in a new building.
J'habite un appartement en banlieue.	I live in an apartment in the suburbs.
installer (s') [sɛ̃stale]	settle down, set up shop
le, la **locataire** [lɔkatɛr]	tenant, renter
de location [dəlɔkɑsjɔ̃]	rental
J'ai pris un appartement de location.	I've taken a rental apartment.
le **logement** [lɔʒmɑ̃]	lodging, lodgings
loger [lɔʒe]	lodge, live; put up
Tu peux loger chez moi.	You can put up at my place.
Je peux te loger.	I can put you up.
louer [lwe]	rent
le **loyer** [lwaje]	rent
le, la **propriétaire** [prɔprijetɛr]	owner; landlord/lady

la **bonne** [bɔn]	maid
les **charges** *fpl* [ʃarʒ]	additional expenses
emménager [ãmenaʒe]	move in
le, la **sous-locataire** [sulɔkatɛr]	subtenant
le **voisin de palier** [vwazɛ̃dpalje]	neighbor across the landing

Furnishings

le **bouton** [butɔ̃]	button, light switch
le **bureau, x** [byro]	desk
le **cadre** [kadr]	frame
la **chaîne** [ʃɛn]	stereo system
la **chaise** [ʃɛz]	chair
le **confort** [kɔ̃fɔr]	comfort
confortable [kɔ̃fɔrtabl]	comfortable
le **coussin** [kusɛ̃]	pillow
le **cuir** [kɥir]	leather
le **fauteuil** [fotœj]	armchair, easy chair
la **glace** [glas]	mirror
la **lampe** [lãp]	lamp
le **lit** [li]	bed
le **meuble** [mœbl]	piece of furniture
la **plante verte** [plãtvɛrt]	indoor plant, house plant
le **poste (de radio)** [pɔst dəradjo]	radio
le **rideau, x** [rido]	curtain
la **table** [tabl]	table
le **tableau, x** [tablo]	picture
le **tapis** [tapi]	carpet; rug
la **télé(vision)** [teleəvizjɔ̃ɲ]	television, TV
Nous avons la télé.	We have a TV set.

le **téléphone** [telefɔn]	telephone
Nous avons le téléphone.	We have a telephone.
le **tiroir** [tirwar]	drawer
le **tourne-disque** [turnədisk]	turntable
le **vase** [vaz]	vase

l'**armoire** *f* [armwar]	wardrobe; cabinet
le **baladeur** [baladœr]	Walkman
le **canapé** [kanape]	sofa
le **double rideau** [dublərido]	(over)drape, curtain
l'**étagère** *f* [etaʒɛr]	rack, shelf
l'**évier** *m* [evje]	sink
le **magnétophone** [maɲetɔfɔn]	tape recorder
le **magnétoscope** [maɲetɔskɔp]	video tape recorder
le **minitel** [minitɛl]	home minicomputer
le **miroir** [mirwar]	mirror
l'**oreiller** *m* [ɔreje]	pillow
la **platine** [platin]	record player
le **sofa** [sɔfa]	sofa
le **store** [stɔr]	blind, window shade
le **transistor** [trãsistɔr]	transistor radio

Household Objects

l'**appareil** *m* [aparɛj]	appliance, machine, apparatus
le **briquet** [brikɛ]	cigarette lighter
la **brosse** [brɔs]	brush
le **cendrier** [sãdrije]	ashtray
le **chiffon** [ʃifɔ̃]	rag, cloth
J'ai vite passé le chiffon.	I dusted it quickly.
les **ciseaux** *mpl* [sizo]	scissors, shears
la **clé** [kle]	key

le **clou** [klu]	nail
la **couverture** [kuvɛrtyr]	cover; blanket, bedspread
le **drap** [dra]	sheet
l'**échelle** *f* [eʃɛl]	ladder
électrique [elɛktrik]	electric(al)
être sous garantie [ɛtrəsugarãti]	be under warranty
le **fer à repasser** [fɛrarəpase]	iron
fonctionner [fɔ̃ksjɔne]	function
le **four** [fur] Faites dorer au four.	oven Brown it in the oven.
le **frigo** [frigo] Qu'est-ce que tu as pris dans le frigo? Tu mets tout au frigo?	refrigerator, fridge What did you take out of the refrigerator? Do you put everything in the refrigerator?
garantir [garãtir]	guarantee
le **linge** [lɛ̃ʒ] Avec trois enfants, on a tout le temps du linge à laver.	linen With three children, there's always laundry to do.
la **machine** [maʃin]	machine
neuf, neuve [nœf, nœv] Ma machine à laver est toute neuve.	new My washing machine is brand new.
nouveau, -vel, -velle, x [nuvo, nuvɛl] J'ai un nouveau toaster.	new I have a new toaster.
la **pile** [pil]	battery
la **poubelle** [pubɛl]	garbage can
le **réfrigérateur** [refriʒeratœr]	refrigerator
le **réveil** [revɛj]	alarm clock
le **robinet** [rɔbinɛ] Qui a ouvert le robinet?	faucet, tap Who turned on the faucet?
la **vaisselle** [vɛsɛl]	dishes

l'**appareil ménager** *m* [aparɛjmenaʒe]	household appliance
l'**aspirateur** *m* [aspiratœr]	vacuum cleaner
le **batteur** [batœr]	(electric) mixer
la **cafetière** [kaftjɛr]	coffee machine; coffee pot
le **chauffe-eau** [ʃofo]	water heater
le **congélateur** [kɔ̃ʒelatœr]	freezer
la **cuisinière** [kɥizinjɛr]	kitchen stove
l'**équipement** *m* [ekipmɑ̃]	equipment
le **gadget** [gadʒɛt]	gadget
la **garantie** [garɑ̃ti]	guarantee
La cuisinière est encore sous garantie.	The stove is still under warranty.
le **lave-vaisselle** [lavvɛsɛl]	dishwasher
la **machine à écrire** [maʃinaekrir]	typewriter
la **machine à laver** [maʃinalave]	washing machine
le **robot** [rɔbo]	kitchen appliance; mixer
le **sèche-cheveux** [sɛʃʃəvø]	hairdryer
le **sèche-linge** [sɛʃlɛ̃ʒ]	clothes dryer
vide [vid]	empty
le **vide-ordures** [vidɔrdyr]	garbage disposal

Household Chores

accrocher [akrɔʃe]	hang up
allumer [alyme]	light, turn on
Allume le four s.t.p.	Please turn on the oven.
balayer [baleje]	sweep, sweep out
J'ai balayé la cave.	I swept the cellar.
chauffer [ʃofe]	heat
Nous, on chauffe au mazout.	We heat with oil.
C'est bien chauffé chez vous.	Our house is well heated.
le **courant d'air** [kurɑ̃dɛr]	air current, draft

les **courses** *fpl* [kurs]
Va me faire les courses.

shopping
Go do my shopping for me.

débarrasser [debarase]
Qui débarrasse?

clear
Who's clearing the table?

le **désordre** [dezɔrdr]

disorder

donner un coup de balai
[dɔneɛ̃kudbalɛ]

make a clean sweep

éclairer [eklere]
Cette pièce est mal éclairée.

light
This room is poorly lit.

enlever [ɑ̃lve]
Enlève cette horrible nappe.

remove, take away
Take away this horrible tablecloth.

essuyer [esɥije]

wipe; wipe dry

éteindre [etɛ̃dr]
Eteins la lumière.

put out, extinguish
Put out the light.

faire du feu [fɛrdyfø]

light a fire

faire le ménage [fɛrlmenaʒ]

clean, do the housework

fermer [fɛrme]
Ferme la lumière.
Ferme la télé.

close; turn off
Turn off the light.
Turn off the TV.

frapper à la porte [frapealapɔrt]

knock at (on) the door

humide [ymid]

humid

l'**incendie** *m* [ɛ̃sɑ̃di]

fire

laver [lave]

wash

la **lessive** [lesiv]
Je suis occupée, je fais la lessive.

cleaning agent; washing
I'm busy, I'm doing the washing.

le **ménage** [menaʒ]

household

nettoyer [nɛtwaje]

clean; wash up or out

ouvrir [uvrir]

open; turn on

la **poussière** [pusjɛr]
Tu fais la poussière?

dust
Are you doing the dusting?

propre [prɔpr]
Quelle maison propre.

clean
What a clean house.

ranger [rɑ̃ʒe]

put in order

réparer [repare]

repair

repasser [rəpɑse]

iron

sale [sal]	dirty
sécher [seʃe]	dry
sonner [sɔne]	ring
On sonne.	The doorbell is ringing.
utiliser [ytilize]	use

aérer [aere]	air; ventilate
le **court-circuit** [kursirkɥi]	short circuit
donner un coup de main [dɔneɛ̃kudmɛ̃]	lend a hand
Tu me donnes un coup de main?	Will you lend me a hand?
faire la cuisine [fɛrlakɥizin]	cook, do the cooking
Je n'aime pas faire la cuisine.	I don't like to cook.
faire la vaisselle [fɛrlavɛsɛl]	do the dishes
la **fuite d'eau** [fɥitdo]	water leak
mettre la table [mɛtrəlatabl]	set the table
le **plomb** [plɔ̃]	fuse
Le plomb a sauté.	The fuse blew out.

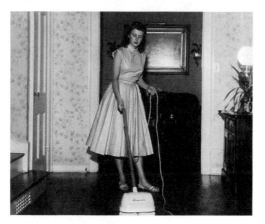

Marie se sert de sa cireuse neuve.
Marie is using her new floor polishing machine.

================ **The Human Body** ================

la **bouche** [buʃ]	mouth
le **bras** [bra]	arm
le **cœur** [kœr]	heart
le **corps** [kɔr]	body
le **cou** [ku]	neck
le **coude** [kud]	elbow
la **dent** [dã]	tooth
le **doigt** [dwa]	finger
le **doigt de pied** [dwadpje]	toe
le **dos** [do]	back
l'**épaule** *f* [epol]	shoulder
l'**estomac** *m* [ɛstɔma]	stomach
la **figure** [figyr]	face
le **foie** [fwa]	liver
le **front** [frɔ̃]	forehead
le **genou, x** [ʒnu]	knee
la **gorge** [gɔrʒ]	throat; bust
la **jambe** [ʒãb]	leg
la **joue** [ʒu]	cheek
la **langue** [lãg]	tongue
la **lèvre** [lɛvr]	lip
la **main** [mɛ̃]	hand
le **menton** [mãtɔ̃]	chin
le **nerf** [nɛr]	nerve
le **nez** [ne]	nose
nu, e [ny]	nude, naked
l'**œil, yeux** *m* [œj, jø]	eye
l'**oreille** *f* [ɔrɛj]	ear
la **peau, x** [po]	skin

le **pied** [pje]	foot
le **poing** [pwɛ̃]	fist
la **poitrine** [pwatrin]	chest; breast; bosom
le **poumon** [pumɔ̃]	lung
la **respiration** [rɛspirasjɔ̃]	respiration, breathing
respirer [rɛspire]	breathe
le **sang** [sɑ̃]	blood
le **système** [sistɛm]	system
la **tête** [tɛt]	head
le **ventre** [vɑ̃tr]	belly; stomach
la **voix** [vwa]	voice
la **vue** [vy]	(eye)sight

l'**appendice** m [apɛ̃dis]	appendix
l'**artère** f [artɛr]	artery
le **cerveau, x** [sɛrvo]	brain
la **cheville** [ʃəvij]	knuckle
la **colonne vertébrale** [kɔlɔnvɛrtebral]	spinal column
le **crâne** [krɑn]	skull
la **cuisse** [kɥis]	thigh
le **derrière** [dɛrjɛr]	rear, backside
les **fesses** fpl [fɛs]	buttocks
la **hanche** ['ɑ̃ʃ]	hip
l'**intestin** m [ɛtɛstɛ̃]	intestine
le **muscle** [myskl]	muscle
le **nombril** [nɔ̃bril]	navel
la **nuque** [nyk]	nape
les **organes sexuels** mpl [ɔrgansɛksɥɛl]	sexual organs
l'**os** m [ɔs, o]	bone
le **poignet** [pwaɲɛ]	wrist
le **pouce** [pus]	thumb

le **rein** [rɛ̃]	kidney
le **sein** [sɛ̃]	breast; bosom
sexuel, le [sɛksyɛl]	sexual
le **sourcil** [sursi]	eyebrow
le **système nerveux** [sistɛmnɛrvø]	nervous system
le **talon** [talɔ̃]	heel
le **tendon** [tãdɔ̃]	tendon
la **veine** [vɛn]	vein

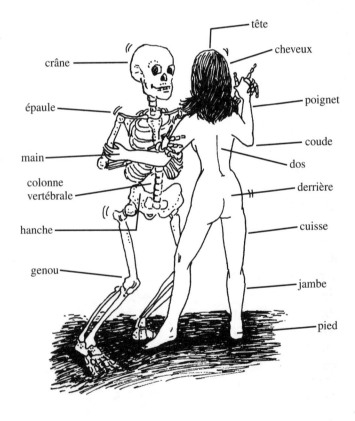

Illnesses

l'**accident** *m* [aksidā]	accident
attraper froid [atrapefrwa]	catch cold
attraper une maladie [atrapeynmaladi]	catch a disease
aveugle [avœgl]	blind
avoir le mal de mer [avwarləmaldəmɛr]	be seasick
avoir mal [avwarmal]	have a pain
avoir mal au cœur [avwarmalokœr]	feel sick
J'ai mal au cœur.	I feel sick.
avoir mal au foie [avwarmalofwa]	be bilious, have gastric distress caused by liver or gallbladder
J'ai mal au foie, j'ai mangé trop de chocolat.	I'm bilious; I ate too much chocolate.
blessé, e [blese]	injured, wounded
blessé, e grave [blesegrav]	seriously wounded
brûler (se) [səbryle]	be burned, get burned
la **chute** [ʃyt]	fall
le **coup de soleil** [kudsɔlɛj]	sunburn
J'ai pris un coup de soleil.	I got a sunburn.
couper (se) [səkupe]	cut oneself
la **crise** [kriz]	crisis, attack, fit
la **crise de foie** [krizdəfwa]	gallbladder attack, bilious colic
le **danger** [dāʒe]	danger
enceinte [āsɛ̃t]	pregnant
Marie est enceinte de quatre mois.	Marie is four months pregnant.
faire une dépression nerveuse [fɛryndepresjɔ̃nɛrvøz]	have a nervous breakdown
la **fièvre** [fjɛvr]	fever
la **folie** [fɔli]	madness, lunacy

grave [grav]	serious, grave
la **grippe** [grip]	influenza, flu
le **mal, maux** [mal, mo]	pain, hurt
malade [malad]	sick, ill
la **maladie** [maladi]	disease, sickness
malin, maligne [malɛ̃, iɲ]	malignant
Le cancer est une tumeur maligne.	Cancer is a malignant tumor.
muet, te [mɥɛ, t]	mute
prendre froid [prãdrəfrwa]	catch cold
le **rhume** [rym]	head cold
saigner [seɲe]	bleed
se faire mal [səfɛrmal]	hurt oneself
souffrir [sufrir]	suffer
Paul souffre de migraines.	Paul suffers from migraines.
tomber malade [tɔ̃bemalad]	fall ill
urgent, e [yrʒã, t]	urgent

l'**abcès** *m* [apsɛ]	abscess
aggraver (s') [sagrave]	become more serious
l'**angine** *f* [ãʒin]	tonsillitis
l'**appendicite** *f* [apɛ̃disit]	appendicitis
asphyxier (s') [sasfiksje]	be asphyxiated
Il a failli s'asphyxier au gaz.	He almost was asphyxiated by gas.
la **blessure** [blesyr]	wound, injury
la **bronchite** [brɔ̃ʃit]	bronchitis
le **cancer** [kãsɛr]	cancer
le **choc** [ʃɔk]	shock
la **coqueluche** [kɔklyʃ]	whooping cough
la **coupure** [kupyr]	cut
les **courbatures** *fpl* [kurbatyr]	stiffness in the back and limbs
la **crise cardiaque** [krizkardjak]	heart attack
le **diabète** [djabɛt]	diabetes

la **diarrhée** [djare]	diarrhea
la **douleur** [dulœr]	pain
empoisonner (s') [sãpwazɔne]	be poisoned
évanouir (s') [sevanwir]	faint; lose consciousness
la **fracture** [fraktyr]	fracture, break
l'**insolation** *f* [ɛsɔlasjɔ̃]	sunstroke
l'**intoxication** *f* [ɛ̃tɔksikasjɔ̃]	poisoning
la **morsure** [mɔrsyr]	bite
les **oreillons** *mpl* [ɔrɛjɔ̃]	mumps
l'**otite** *f* [ɔtit]	middle ear infection
la **plaie** [plɛ]	wound
le **poison** [pwazɔ̃]	poison
la **rage** [raʒ]	rabies
le **rhumatisme** [rymatism]	rheumatism
la **rougeole** [ruʒɔl]	measles
la **rubéole** [rybeɔl]	German measles
se casser le bras [səkaselbra]	break one's arm
le **SIDA** [sida]	AIDS
sourd, e [sur, d]	deaf
sourd-muet, sourde-muette [surmɥə, surdmɥɛt]	deaf-mute
la **tension** [tãsjɔ̃]	blood pressure; high blood pressure
Il faut prendre sa tension régulièrement.	You should take your blood pressure often.
J'ai de la tension.	I have high blood pressure.
le **tétanos** [tetanɔs]	tetanus
la **varicelle** [varisɛl]	chicken pox

Effects of Illness

avoir chaud [avwarʃo]	be hot
avoir des jambes molles [avwardeʒɑ̃bmɔl]	be weak-kneed
avoir froid [avwarfrwa] J'ai froid.	be cold I'm cold.
avoir mauvaise mine [avwarmɔvɛzmin]	look bad or unwell
avoir sommeil [avwarsɔmɛj] J'ai sommeil.	be sleepy I'm sleepy.
brûlant, e [brylɑ̃, t]	very hot
l'**état** *m* [eta] Son état est très grave.	state, condition His condition is very serious.
éternuer [etɛrnɥe]	sneeze
faible [fɛbl]	weak
faire mal [fɛrmal] Où ça fait mal?	hurt Where does it hurt?
la **fatigue** [fatig]	fatigue, tiredness
fatiguer [fatige]	weary, get tired
fragile [fraʒil]	fragile
grossir [grosir] J'ai grossi de trois kilos.	gain weight I've gained 3 kilos.
maigre [mɛgr]	thin, lean
maigrir [megrir] J'ai maigri de deux kilos.	lose weight I've lost 2 kilos.
pâle [pɑl]	pale
se sentir bien/mal [səsɑ̃tirbjɛ̃/mal]	feel well/unwell

tomber de fatigue [tɔ̃bedfatig] collapse from exhaustion

tomber de sommeil [tɔ̃bedsɔmɛj] be overcome with sleep

tousser [tuse] cough

transpirer [trãspire] sweat

trembler [trãble] tremble, shake

---

avoir le vertige [avwarləvɛrtiʒ] be dizzy
J'ai le vertige. I'm dizzy.

Ça me démange. [samdemãʒ] I itch all over.

la **démangeaison** [demãʒɛzõ] itch

épuisé, e [epɥize] tired out, exhausted

étouffer [etufe] suffocate, smother, choke
On étouffe dans cette pièce. It's stifling in this room.

être trempé, e [ɛtrətrãpe] be soaked or drenched

handicapé, e ['ãdikape] handicapped

la **toux** [tu] cough

Treatment of Illness

l'**aide** f [ɛd] aid, help

aider [ede] help, aid
Vous êtes là pour aider les malades. You're here to help the sick.

améliorer [ameljɔre] improve

avoir bonne mine [avwarbɔnmin] look well

bien [bjẽ] well; fine

le **cachet** [kaʃɛ] tablet

le **chirurgien**, la **chirurgienne** [ʃiryrʒjẽ, ɛn] surgeon

le **client**, la **cliente** [klijã, t] patient

la **clinique** [klinik] clinic; private hospital

le **comprimé** [kõprime] tablet, lozenge

le **docteur** [dɔktœr]   doctor

efficace [efikas]   effective

être au régime [ɛtroreʒim]   be on a diet

être en forme [ɛtrãfɔrm]   be fit, be in shape

examiner [ɛgzamine]   examine

l'**exercice** *m* [ɛgzɛrsis]   exercise

guérir [gerir]   heal

l'**hôpital, -aux** *m* [ɔpital, o]   hospital

l'**infirmier, -ère** [ɛ̃firmje, ɛr]   nurse

l'**instrument** *m* [ɛ̃strymã]   instrument

les **lunettes** *fpl* [lynɛt]   (eye)glasses
Je porte des lunettes.   I wear glasses.

le **médecin** [mɛdsɛ̃]   physician, doctor

la **médecine** [mɛdsin]   medicine

le **médicament** [medikamã]   medication

l'**opération** *f* [ɔperasjɔ̃]   operation

opérer [ɔpere]   operate

la **pharmacie** [farmasi]   pharmacy

la **pilule** [pilyl]   pill; birth control pill

porter (se) [səpɔrte]   feel

prendre [prãdr]   take

la **prise de sang** [prizdəsã]   blood specimen

la **radio** [radjo]   X ray

le **régime** [reʒim]   diet

le **repos** [rəpo]   rest

reposer (se) [sərəpoze]   rest

sain, e [sɛ̃, sɛn]   healthy

la **santé** [sãte]   health

sauver [sove]   save

soigner [swaɲe]   nurse, take care of
Je me fais soigner les dents   I have my teeth cleaned
régulièrement.   regularly.

le **soin** [swɛ̃]
care; treatment

Les soins sont peu efficaces.
The treatment is not very effective.

Les soins du visage.
Care of the face.

solide [sɔlid]
solid; sound

René a une santé solide.
René's health is sound.

suivre un régime [sɥivrɛ̃reʒim]
follow a diet

le **traitement** [trɛtmɑ̃]
treatment

traiter [trete]
treat

J'ai été traité à la cortisone.
I was treated with cortisone.

J'ai été traité pour mon asthme.
I've been treated for my asthma.

la **vie** [vi]
life

vivant, e [vivɑ̃, t]
alive, living

vivre [vivr]
live

Vous avez une bonne assurance? Excellent! Vous irez à l'hôpital, vous prendrez beaucoup de médicaments, vous subirez des examens médicaux, et puis je vais opérer. Mais d'abord, permettez-moi de voir quel mal il y a.

You have good health insurance? Excellent! You will go to the hospital, take a lot of medicines and examinations, and then I will operate on you. But first, let me see what's wrong.

l'**ambulance** *f* [ābylās]	ambulance
le **bandage** [bādaʒ]	bandage
le **diagnostic** [djagnɔstik]	diagnosis
les **gouttes** *fpl* [gut]	drops
le **mercurochrome** [mɛrkyrɔkrɔm]	mercurochrome
l'**ordonnance** *f* [ɔrdɔnās]	prescription
Faites-moi une ordonnance.	Write me a prescription.
le **pansement** [pāsmā]	dressing
le **pharmacien,**	pharmacist
la **pharmacienne** [farmasjɛ̃, ɛn]	
la **piqûre** [pikyr]	injection, shot
le **plâtre** [plɑtr]	plaster cast
J'ai le bras dans le plâtre.	I have my arm in a cast.
la **pommade** [pɔmad]	salve
Appliquer la pommade sur la peau.	Apply the ointment to the skin.
la **précaution** [prekosjɔ̃]	precaution
protéger (se) [səprɔteʒe]	protect oneself
récupérer [rekypere]	recuperate
J'ai besoin de récupérer.	I have to recuperate.
le **remède** [rəmɛd]	remedy
remettre (se) [sərəmɛtr]	recover
Tu t'es remis de ta grippe?	Have you recovered from your flu?
reprendre des forces [rəprādrədefɔrs]	regain strength
la **Sécurité sociale** [sekyritesɔsjal]	social security, National Health Service
le **sparadrap** [sparadra]	adhesive tape
vacciner [vaksine]	vaccinate

Personal Grooming

le **bain** [bɛ̃]	bath
la **barbe** [barb]	beard
le **bouton** [butɔ̃]	pimple
la **brosse** [brɔs]	brush
chaud, e [ʃo, d]	warm, hot
le **cheveu, x** [ʃəvø]	hair
les **ciseaux** *mpl* [sizo]	scissors, shears
coiffer (se) [səkwafe]	do one's hair
le **coiffeur,** la **coiffeuse** [kwafœr, øz]	hairdresser
Je vais chez le coiffeur.	I'm going to the hairdresser.
la **crème** [krɛm]	cream
le **dentifrice** [dãtifris]	toothpaste
la **douche** [duʃ]	shower
Prends une douche.	Take a shower.
l'**éponge** *f* [epɔ̃ʒ]	sponge
froid, e [frwa, d]	cold, cool
frotter [frɔte]	rub
laver [lave]	wash
laver (se) [səlave]	wash oneself
Tu t'es lavé les dents?	Have you brushed your teeth?
la **ligne** [liɲ]	figure
Je fais attention à ma ligne.	I watch my figure.
les **lunettes de soleil** *fpl* [lynɛtdəsɔlɛj]	sunglasses
maquiller (se) [səmakije]	make up, put on make-up
mouillé, e [muje]	wet
l'**ongle** *m* [ɔ̃gl]	nail
le **parfum** [parfɛ̃]	perfume; scent
le **peigne** [pɛɲ]	comb
peigner (se) [səpeɲe]	comb one's hair

peser [pəse]	weigh
propre [prɔpr]	clean
raser (se) [sərɑze]	shave (oneself)
le **rouge à lèvres** [ruʒalɛvr]	lipstick
J'ai mis du rouge à lèvres.	I've put on lipstick.
sale [sal]	dirty
le **savon** [savɔ̃]	soap
sécher [seʃe]	dry
la **serviette** [sɛrvjɛt]	towel
la **toilette** [twalɛt]	dress, outfit

le **cil** [sil]	eyelash
le **coton** [kɔtɔ̃]	absorbent cotton
l'**eau de toilette** *f* [odətwalɛt]	toilet water
faire couler [fɛrkulə]	let run
Fais-moi couler un bain.	Run me a bath.
la **lame de rasoir** [lamdərazwar]	razor blade
la **laque** [lak]	hair spray
la **lime à ongles** [limaɔ̃gl]	nail file
moucher (se) [səmuʃe]	blow one's nose
la **moustache** [mustaʃ]	mustache
la **paupière** [pɔpjɛr]	eyelid
le **poil** [pwal]	hair (other than that of the head)
la **poudre** [pudr]	powder
le **produit de beauté** [prɔdyidbote]	beauty product
le **rasoir** [rɑzwar]	razor
se faire la barbe [səfɛrlabarb]	shave
le **sèche-cheveux** [sɛʃʃəvø]	hairdryer
le **teint** [tɛ̃]	complexion; hue; dye
le **vernis à ongles** [vɛrniaɔ̃gl]	nail polish

General Terms

actif, -ive [aktif, iv]	active
l'**activité** *f* [aktivite]	activity
avoir besoin de [avwarbəzwɛ̃də]	need
J'ai besoin de courir un peu.	I need to run some.
avoir envie de [avwarãvidə]	want
J'ai envie de faire un footing.	I want to do some walking (for training).
la **distraction** [distraksjɔ̃]	distraction; recreation
distraire (se) [sədistrɛr]	amuse oneself
faire la queue [fɛrlakø]	get in line, wait in line
le **jeu, x** [ʒø]	game
jouer [ʒwe]	play
Tu joues au volley avec nous?	Will you play volleyball with us?
les **loisirs** [lwazir]	leisure, spare time
L'industrie des loisirs.	The leisure industry.
le **monde** [mɔ̃d]	people; world
Le monde du sport.	The world of sports.
l'**occupation** *f* [ɔkypasjɔ̃]	occupation, pursuit
Mon occupation préférée.	My favorite pursuit.
participer [partisipe]	participate
J'ai participé à une course populaire.	I participated in an open cross-country race.
la **partie** [parti]	game
passer son temps à [pasesɔ̃tãa]	spend one's time in
Je passe mon temps à tricoter.	I spend my time in knitting.
le **plaisir** [plezir]	pleasure
l'**amateur** *m* [amatœr]	amateur
coûteux, -euse [kutø, z]	costly, expensive
détendre (se) [sədetãdr]	unbend
le **divertissement** [divɛrtismã]	recreation, amusement, entertainment
le **pro** [prɔ]	pro(fessional)

Hobbies

l'**appareil photo** *m* [aparɛjfɔtɔ]	camera
arracher [araʃe]	pull up
Qui m'aide à arracher les mauvaises herbes?	Who'll help me pull weeds?
bricoler [briɔle]	do odd jobs; putter around
le **bricoleur**, la **bricoleuse** [brikɔlœr, øʒ]	jack-of-all-trades, putterer
Jean Pierre est un bricoleur fanatique.	Jean Pierre is a fanatical putterer.
la **caméra** [kamera]	movie camera
la **carte** [kart]	map; ticket
la **cassette** [kasɛt]	cassette
Tu me prends une cassette vidéo?	Will you bring me a video-cassette?
le **catalogue** [katalɔg]	catalog
la **colle** [kɔl]	glue
la **collection** [kɔlɛksjɔ̃]	collection
coller [kɔle]	glue
développer [devlɔpe]	develop
les **éches** *mpl* [eʃɛk]	chess
On fait une partie d'échecs?	Shall we play a game of chess?
enregistrer [ɑ̃rəʒistre]	record
j'ai enregistré le concert.	I recorded the concert.
l'**épreuve** *f* [eprœv]	proof, print
le **film** [film]	film
la **fleur** [flœr]	flower
la **guitare** [gitar]	guitar
l'**herbe** *f* [ɛrb]	herb, grass
le **jardin** [ʒardɛ̃]	garden
le **jouet** [ʒwɛ]	toy
la **musique** [myzik]	music
la **peinture** [pɛ̃tyr]	painting

la **photo** [fɔto]	photo
la **plante** [plãt]	plant
planter [plãte]	plant
le **rythme** [ritm]	rhythm
le **timbre** [tɛ̃mbr]	stamp

arroser [aroze]	water, sprinkle
J'ai arrosé le gazon.	I sprinkled the lawn.
cultiver [kyltive]	cultivate
le **folklore** [fɔlklɔr]	folklore
le **gazon** [gazɔ̃]	lawn
inscrire (s') [sɛ̃skrir]	register, sign up
Je vais m'inscrire à un cours de danse.	I'm going to sign up for a dance course.
la **mauvaise herbe** [mɔvɛzɛrb]	weed
le **music-hall** [myzikol]	music hall
la **pellicule** [pɛlikyl]	film
Je prends toujours des pellicules de 400 ASA.	I always use 400 ASA film.
la **sensibilité** [sãsibilite]	sensitivity
tondre [tɔ̃dr]	mow

Sports Terms

battre [batr]	beat
Paris a battu Marseille 3 à 1.	Paris beat Marseille 3 to 1.
Personne ne battra le record du monde de saut en longueur.	No one will break the world record in the broad jump.
le **but** [byt]	goal; point (scored)
Quel joli but!	What a nice point!
le **champion,** la **championne** [ʃãpjɔ̃, ɔn]	champion, winner
Alain Prost a été deux fois champion du monde.	Alain Prost was world champion twice.
le **club** [klœb]	club
entraîner (s') [sãtrene]	train

113

l'**équipe** *f* [ekip]   team
L'équipe nationale.   The national team.

l'**étape** *f* [etap]   stage; lap
Qui a gagné la troisième étape du   Who won the third lap of the
Tour de France?   Tour de France?

être en forme [ɛtrãfɔrm]   be fit, be in shape
Je suis en pleine forme.   I'm in top shape.

la **force** [fɔrs]   force, strength

gagner [gaɲe]   win

gonfler [gɔ̃fle]   swell, inflate
Quel type gonflé!   What a conceited fellow!

la **ligne** [liɲ]   fishing line
Je n'aime pas la pêche à la ligne.   I don't like angling.

le **maillot** [majo]   swimming suit

l'**outil** *m* [uti]   tool, implement

perdre [pɛrdr]   lose

le **record** [rəkɔr]   record

le **règlement** [rɛgləmã]   rule, regulation

remporter [rãpɔrte]   win; carry off
Alain Prost a remporté la victoire.   Alain Prost won the victory.

le **résultat** [rezylta]   result

siffler [sifle]   whistle; hiss, boo
Le public a sifflé les joueurs.   The spectators booed the players.
L'arbitre a sifflé la mi-temps.   The referee blew the whistle at
                                                    half-time.

le **sport** [spɔr]   sport

le **stade** [stad]   stadium

le **terrain de sport** [tɛrɛ̃dspɔr]   playing field

transpirer [trãspire]   sweat

la **victoire** [viktwar]   victory

l'**adversaire** *mf* [advɛrsɛr] — opponent, adversary

l'**arbitre** *m* [arbitr] — umpire, referee

l'**athlète** *mf* [atlɛt] — athlete

la **belle** [bɛl] — deciding match
Henri Leconte a perdu la belle contre Boris Becker. — Henri Leconte lost the deciding match to Boris Becker.

le **championnat** [ʃãpjɔna] — championship
Le championnat d'Europe. — The European championship.
Le championnat du monde. — The world championship.

la **compétition** [kɔ̃petisjɔ̃] — competition

la **coupe** [kup] — cup
La coupe du monde. — The World (Soccer) Cup.

la **défaite** [defɛt] — defeat

le **défi** [defi] — challenge
Le défi de Kasparov contre Karpov. — Kasparov's challenge to Karpov.

les **Jeux Olympiques** *mpl* [ʒøzɔlɛ̃pik] — Olympic Games

lutter [lyte] — fight, wrestle

la **médaille** [medaj] — medal
Qui a gagné la médaille d'or? — Who won the gold medal?

la **mi-temps** [mitã] — half-time

le **participant,** la **participante** [partisipã, t] — participant

pratiquer [pratike] — practice, engage in
Vous pratiquez quel sport? — Which sport do you engage in?

le **professionnel,** la **professionnelle** [prɔfɛsjɔnɛl] — pro, professional athlete

la **revanche** [rəvãʃ] — revenge; return match or bout

rival, e, -aux [rival, o] — rival

tirer au sort [tireosɔr] — draw lots; toss

le **vainqueur** [vɛ̃kœr] — victor

Athletic Activities

la **balle** [bal]	ball
le **ballon** [balɔ̄]	(soccer) ball
le **bateau, x** [bato]	boat
J'ai acheté un petit bateau à voiles.	I bought a small sailboat.
la **chasse** [ʃas]	hunting, hunt
La chasse aux canards est ouverte.	The duck hunting season is open.
chasser [ʃase]	hunt
la **course** [kurs]	race
la **descente** [desãt]	downhill
faire de la gymnastique [fɛrdlaʒimnastik]	do gymnastics
faire du ski [fɛrdyski]	ski
faire du sport [fɛrdyspɔr]	play games, engage in sports
le **foot(ball)** [fut bol]	soccer
le **gardien de but** [gardjɛ̄dbyt]	goalkeeper
grimper [grɛ̄pe]	climb
la **gym(nastique)** [ʒim nastik]	gymnastics
lancer [lãse]	throw
le **match** [matʃ]	match, contest, game
nager [naʒe]	swim
la **neige** [nɛʒ]	snow
l'**obstacle** *m* [ɔpstakl]	obstacle
Une course d'obstacles.	An obstacle course.
pêcher [peʃe]	fish, angle
plonger [plɔ̄ʒe]	dive
le **rugby** [rygbi]	rugby
sauter [sote]	jump
le **ski** [ski]	ski
le **vélo** [velo]	bicycle, bike

aller à la pêche [alealapɛʃ]	go fishing
l'**alpiniste** *mf* [alpinist]	mountain climber
l'**arc** *m* [ark]	bow
l'**athlétisme** *m* [atletism]	athletics
l'**aviron** *m* [avirɔ̃]	oar; rowing
la **bicyclette** [bisiklɛt]	bicycle
la **boxe** [bɔks]	boxing
le **chasseur,** la **chasseuse** [ʃasœr, øz]	hunter
le **cyclisme** [siklism]	cycling
le, la **cycliste** [siklist]	cyclist
l'**escrime** *f* [ɛskrim]	fencing
faire de l'alpinisme [fɛrdəlalpinism]	do mountain climbing
faire de la voile [fɛrdəlavwal]	sail
faire du cheval [fɛrdyʃval]	ride
le **filet** [filɛ]	net
le **golf** [gɔlf]	golf
la **marche à pied** [marʃapje]	march (on foot)
la **natation** [natɑsjɔ̃]	swimming
le **patinage** [patinaʒ]	ice-skating
les **patins à roulettes** *mpl* [patɛ̃arulɛt]	roller skates
le **pêcheur,** la **pêcheuse** [pɛʃœr, øz]	angler, fisherman
le **ping-pong** [piʒpɔʒ]	ping-pong, table tennis
la **planche à roulettes** [plɑ̃ʃarulɛt]	skateboard
la **planche à voile** [plɑ̃ʃavwal]	surfboard
le **skieur,** la **skieuse** [skjœr, øz]	skier
les **sports d'hiver** *mpl* [spɔrdivɛr]	winter sports
les **sports nautiques** *mpl* [spɔrnotik]	water sports
la **voile** [vwal]	sailing
le **volley** [vɔlɛ]	volleyball

■■■■ Travel Preparations ■■■■

l'**agence de voyages** *f* [aʒɑ̃sdəvwajaʒ]	travel agency
le **catalogue** [katalɔg]	catalog
le **client,** la **cliente** [klijɑ̃, t]	client, customer
l'**employé, e** [ɑ̃plwaje]	employee
faire sa valise [fɛrsavaliz]	pack one's bag
le, la **guide** [gid] Tu peux me prêter ton guide Michelin?	guide Can you lend me your Michelin guide?
l'**indication** *f* [ɛdikasjɔ̃]	indication; sign
l'**itinéraire bis** *m* [itinerɛrbis] L'itinéraire bis est indiqué par des flèches vertes.	bypass, detour, alternate route Alternate routes are marked with green arrows.
la **liste** [list]	list
de location [dəlɔkasjɔ] On prendra une voiture de location?	rental Shall we take a rental car?
louer [lwe] On loue les patins sur place?	rent Do we rent the skates on the spot?
le **projet** [prɔʒɛ]	project; plan
le **renseignement** [rɑ̃sɛɲəmɑ̃]	information
réserver [rezɛrve]	reserve, book
le **séjour** [seʒur]	stay
le **syndicat d'initiative** [sɛ̃dikadinisjativ]	tourist information bureau
le, la **touriste** [turist]	tourist
les **vacances** *fpl* [vakɑ̃s] Nous avons passé de bonnes vacances.	vacation We had a good vacation.
la **valise** [valiz]	suitcase, bag
le **voyage** [vwajaʒ] Je suis parti en voyage.	trip I went on a trip.
le **voyage organisé** [vwajaʒɔrganize]	group tour

voyager [vwajaʒe]	travel
la **vue d'ensemble** [vydɑ̃sɑ̃bl]	overall view

les **arrhes** *fpl* [ar]	down-payment, deposit
la **carte routière** [kartrutjɛr]	road map
informer (s') [sɛ̃fɔrme]	inquire
Tu t'es informé des conditions de location?	Have you inquired about the conditions of rental?
l'**itinéraire** *m* [itinerɛr]	itinerary, route
recommander [rəkɔmɑ̃de]	recommend
la **réservation** [rezɛrvasjɔ̃]	reservation, booking
le **vacancier,** la **vacancière** [vakɑ̃sje, ɛr]	vacationer

Traveling

accompagner [akɔ̃paɲe]	accompany
l'**aéroport** *m* [aerɔpɔr]	airport
l'**aller et retour** *m* [aleɛrtur]	round-trip ticket
Tu prends deux aller et retour.	You get two round-trip tickets.
l'**arrivée** *f* [arive]	arrival
arriver [arive]	arrive
Nous sommes arrivés.	We have arrived.
l'**avion** *m* [avjɔ̃]	airplane
avoir le mal de mer [avwarləmaldəmɛr]	be seasick
les **bagages** *mpl* [bagaʒ]	baggage, luggage
le **bateau, x** [bato]	boat
le **bord** [bɔr]	board; side (of a ship); shore
Nous avons une petite maison au bord de la mer.	We have a little house at the seashore.
Bienvenus à bord.	Welcome on board.
le **car** [kar]	sightseeing bus
le **carnet** [karnɛ]	book of tickets
la **classe** [klɑs]	class

la **consigne** [kõsiɲ]	baggage room, checkroom
J'ai mis la valise à la consigne.	I put my suitcase in the checkroom.
le **contrôle** [kõtrol]	inspection booth, ticket-check
la **couchette** [kuʃɛt]	couchette, second-class sleeper
coûter cher [kuteʃɛr]	be expensive
déclarer [deklare]	declare
Avez-vous quelque chose à déclarer?	Do you have anything to declare?
le **départ** [depar]	departure
direct, e [dirɛkt]	direct, through
C'est un train direct?	Is it a through train?
la **douane** [dwan]	customs
en règle [ãrɛglə]	in order
Vos papiers ne sont pas en règle.	Your papers are not in order.
faire la queue [fɛrlakø]	get in line, wait in line
la **formalité** [fɔrmalite]	formality
fouiller [fuje]	search, inspect
On nous a fouillés.	We were searched.
la **frontière** [frõtjɛr]	border
la **gare** [gar]	train station
l'**horaire** *m* [ɔrɛr]	schedule
partir [partir]	leave, depart
Jean-Marc est parti pour l'Afrique.	Jean-Marc has left for Africa.
le **passager**, la **passagère** [pasaʒe, ɛr]	passenger
le **passeport** [paspɔr]	passport
payer cher [pejeʃɛr]	pay a high price
la **pièce d'identité** [pjɛsdidãtite]	identification papers
le **port** [pɔr]	port
premier, -ère [prəmje, ɛr]	first
Je ne voyage jamais en première classe.	I never travel first class.
prendre [prãdr]	take
le **quai** [ke]	(R.R.) platform; wharf, quay
De quel quai part le bateau?	From which wharf does the boat sail?
rapide [rapid]	rapid

rater [rate]	miss
le **retard** [rətar]	delay
Le train est en retard.	The train is late.
second, e [səgɔ̃, d]	second
le **supplément** [syplemɑ̃]	supplement
le **train** [trɛ̃]	train
la **voiture** [vwatyr]	car; railroad car
voler [vɔle]	fly
le **wagon-lit** [wagɔ̃li]	sleeping car
le **wagon-restaurant** [wagɔ̃rɛstɔrɑ̃]	dining car

le **compartiment** [kɔ̃partimɑ̃]	compartment
composter [kɔ̃pɔste]	cancel or invalidate (ticket)
N'oubliez pas de composter votre billet.	Don't forget to have your ticket canceled.
l'**escalier roulant** *m* [ɛskaljerulɑ̃]	escalator
faire du stop [fɛrdystɔp]	hitch-hike
le **ferry** [fɛri]	ferry
la **passerelle** [pɑsrɛl]	gangway
le **péage** [peaʒ]	toll
Péage à 800 m.	Toll booth, 800 meters.
le **tapis roulant** [tapirulɑ̃]	conveyor belt; moving sidewalk
le **T.G.V.** [teʒeve]	high-speed train
la **T.V.A.** [tevea]	VAT, value-added tax

On the Trip

ancien, ne [ɑ̃sjɛ̃, ɛn]	ancient; former
Le Louvre est un ancien château.	The Louvre is a former palace.
Marseille est une ville très ancienne.	Marseille is a very ancient city.
l'**appareil photo** *m* [aparɛjfɔto]	camera
l'**aventure** *f* [avɑ̃tyr]	adventure
baigner (se) [səbeɲe]	bathe; swim
On va se baigner?	Are we going swimming?

le **bain de soleil** [bɛ̃dsɔlɛj]	sun bath
le **bateau-mouche** [batomuʃ]	excursion boat
bronzé, e [brõze]	tanned
célèbre [selɛbr]	famous, celebrated
le **coup de soleil** [kudsɔlɛj]	sunburn
J'ai attrapé un coup de soleil.	I got sunburned.
la **découverte** [dekuvɛrt]	discovery
A la découverte du Népal!	Discover Nepal!
découvrir [dekuvrir]	discover
en plein soleil [ãplɛ̃sɔlɛj]	right in the sun
l'**étranger** *m* [etrãʒe]	foreign countries
Je passe mes vacances à l'étranger.	I spend my vacations abroad.
étranger, -ère [etrãʒe, ɛr]	foreign; foreigner
l'**excursion** *f* [ɛkskyrsjõ]	excursion
faire du feu [fɛrdyfø]	light a fire
international, e, -aux [ɛ̃tɛrnasjɔnal, o]	international
les **lunettes de soleil** *fpl* [lynɛtdəsɔlɛj]	sunglasses
la **mer** [mɛr]	ocean, sea
le **Midi** [midi]	south of France
la **neige** [nɛʒ]	snow
le **pays** [pei]	country
la **plage** [plaʒ]	beach
la **région** [reʒjõ]	region, area
le **repos** [rəpo]	rest, repose
reposer (se) [sərəpoze]	rest
J'ai dû me reposer du voyage.	I had to rest from the trip.
les **ruines** *fpl* [rɥin]	ruins
le **sable** [sabl]	sand
Attention aux sables mouvants dans la baie.	Caution: Quicksand in the bay!

la **spécialité** [spesjalite]	specialty
Une spécialité du pays.	A local specialty.
la **statue** [staty]	statue
typique [tipik]	typical
visiter [vizite]	visit

aller danser [aledãse]	go dancing
au grand air [ogrãtɛr]	in the fresh air
la **baignade** [bɛɲad]	bathing, swimming
la **boîte de nuit** [bwatdənɥi]	night club
bronzer [brõze]	tan
la **croisière** [krwazjɛr]	cruise
en plein air [ãplɛnɛr]	in the open air, outdoors
le **folklore** [fɔlklɔr]	folklore
la **grande randonnée (GR)** [grãdrãdɔne ʒeɛr]	long walk, long hike
la **Manche** [mãʃ]	English Channel
la **marée basse** [marebɑs]	low tide, ebb
les **marées** *fpl* [mare]	tides
L'horaire des marées.	The tide table.
la **Méditerranée** [mediterane]	Mediterranean
la **mer du Nord** [mɛrdynɔr]	North Sea
pittoresque [pitɔrɛsk]	picturesque
la **pleine mer** [plɛnmɛr]	high tide, flow
la **randonnée** [rãdɔne]	walk, hike, ramble
le **site** [sit]	scenic site, beauty spot

▬▬▬ Accommodations ▬▬▬

l'**ascenseur** *m* [asãsœr]	elevator
Il y a un ascenseur à l'hôtel?	Is there an elevator in the hotel?
l'**auberge de jeunesse** *f* [obɛrʒdəʒœnɛs]	youth hostel

123

le **balcon** [balkɔ̃]	balcony
bruyant, e [brɥijã, t]	loud, noisy
C'est bruyant chez vous!	It's noisy in your room!
calme [kalm]	calm, quiet
le **camping** [kãpiŋ]	camping
Cette année, on a fait du camping.	This year we went camping.
la **catégorie** [kategɔri]	category
central, e, -aux [sãtral, o]	central
la **chambre** [ʃãbr]	room
C'est une chambre à deux lits?	Is it a room with two beds?
la **clé** [kle]	key
le **club** [klœb]	club
complet, -ète [kɔ̃plɛ, t]	full
le **confort** [kɔ̃fɔr]	comfort
donner sur [dɔnesyr]	open onto, overlook
Ma chambre donne sur la mer.	My room overlooks the ocean.
la **douche** [duʃ]	shower
l'**étoile** *f* [etwal]	star
le **grand lit** [grãli]	double bed
le **hall** ['ol]	lobby
l'**hôtel** *m* [ɔtɛl]	hotel
l'**interprète** *mf* [ɛ̃tɛrprɛt]	interpreter
le **lavabo** [lavabo]	washbasin
le **lit** [li]	bed
le **luxe** [lyks]	luxury
la **pension** [pãsjɔ̃]	pension; private hotel, boarding-house
Réservez une chambre en demi-pension.	Reserve a room with half-pension.
Réservez une chambre en pension complète.	Reserve a room with full pension.
J'habite dans une petite pension de famille.	I'm staying in a small family-run residential hotel.
le **personnel** [pɛrsɔnɛl]	personnel
le **petit déjeuner** [ptideʒøne]	breakfast
la **règle** [rɛgl]	rule, regulation
C'est la règle du jeu.	Those are the rules of the game.

le **restaurant** [rɛstɔrā]	restaurant
le **service** [sɛrvis]	service
le **terrain** [tɛrɛ̃]	terrain, ground
la **terrasse** [tɛras]	terrace
les **W.-C.** *mpl* [vese]	toilets

la **caravane** [karavan]	camping trailer, house trailer
la **clientèle** [klijātɛl]	clientele, customers
la **colo(nie de vacances)** [kɔlɔ nidvakās]	summer camp
faire du camping [fɛrdykāpiŋ ɲ]	camping
luxueux, -euse [lyksɥø, z]	luxury, luxurious
le **prix forfaitaire** [prifɔrfɛtɛr]	lump-sum price
la **réception** [resɛpsjɔ̃]	reception
la **réclamation** [reklamasjɔ̃]	complaint
la **tente** [tāt] J'ai couché sous la tente.	tent I slept in the tent.

Nous nous sommes assis sur nos sacs de couchage et avons bu du vin.
We sat on our sleeping bags and drank wine.

━━━━━━━━ **School System** ━━━━━━━━

la **bibliothèque** [biblijɔtɛk]	library
la **classe** [klɑs]	class; classroom
Je vais en classe.	I'm going to class.
le **collège** [kɔlɛʒ]	high school; preparatory school
Tous les Français vont quatre ans au collège.	All the French go to high school for four years.
l'**échange** m [eʃɑ̃ʒ]	exchange
l'**école** f [ekɔl]	school
l'**élève** mf [elɛv]	pupil, student
l'**enseignement** m [ɑ̃sɛɲəmɑ̃]	teaching, education
L'enseignement public est laïque et gratuit en France.	Public education is secular and free in France.
l'**instituteur, -trice** [ɛ̃stitytœr, tris]	schoolteacher
l'**instruction** f [ɛ̃stryksjɔ̃]	instruction
le **lycée** [lise]	high school, lyceum
privé, e [prive]	private
le **prof(esseur)** [prɔf ɛsœr]	teacher; professor
le **programme** [prɔgram]	curriculum; program, syllabus
Qu'est-ce que vous avez au programme cette année?	What's in your curriculum this year?
la **réforme** [refɔrm]	reform
la **salle** [sal]	room; hall; auditorium
scolaire [skɔlɛr]	school
secondaire [səgɔ̃dɛr]	secondary
surveiller [syrveje]	supervise, monitor
le **système** [sistɛm]	system

l'**analphabète** mf [analfabɛt]	illiterate
bilingue [bilɛ̃g]	bilingual
Nous aimerions être bilingues.	We would like to be bilingual.
le **bilinguisme** [bilɛ̃gyism]	bilingualism

l'**enseignement primaire** *m* [ɑ̃sɛɲəmɑ̃primɛr]	elementary education
l'**enseignement secondaire** *m* [ɑ̃sɛɲəmɑ̃səgɔ̃dɛr]	secondary education
enseigner [ɑ̃sɛɲe]	teach
la **formation professionnelle** [fɔrmɑsjɔ̃prɔfɛsjɔnɛl]	professional training
francophone [frɑ̃kɔfɔn]	Francophone, French-speaking
la **francophonie** [frɑ̃kɔfɔni]	French-speaking world
l'**indigène** *mf* [ɛdʒɛn]	native
la **maternelle** [matɛrnɛl]	kindergarten
mixte [mikst]	coeducational, mixed
l'**option** *f* [ɔpsjɔ̃]	option; branch of study
le **primaire** [primɛr]	elementary school
le **proviseur** [prɔvizœr]	headmaster
redoubler [rəduble]	repeat (a class or grade)
la **scolarité** [skɔlarite] La scolarité obligatoire est de dix ans.	school attendance School attendance is compulsory for 10 years.
le **surveillant**, la **surveillante** [syrvɛjɑ̃, t]	superintendent, overseer

========== **Subjects of Instruction** ==========

le **calcul** [kalkyl]	arithmetic, calculation; calculus
la **chimie** [ʃimi]	chemistry
le **cours** [kur] Les cours durent une heure entière.	course The courses each last an entire hour.
le **dessin** [desɛ̃]	drawing
l'**éducation physique** *f* [edykɑsjɔ̃fizik]	physical education
l'**étude** *f* [etyd]	study
la **géographie** [ʒeɔgrafi]	geography

la **gym(nastique)** [ʒim nastik]	gym(nastics)
l'**histoire** *f* [istwar]	history
la **langue** [lãg]	language
les **mathématiques** *fpl* [matematik]	mathematics
les **maths** *fpl* [mat]	math
la **matière** [matjɛr]	subject, subject matter
la **musique** [myzik]	music
la **physique** [fizik]	physics
les **sciences naturelles** *fpl* [sjãsnatyrɛl]	natural sciences

l'**instruction civique** *f* [ɛstryksjõsivik]	civics
la **langue étrangère** [lãgetrãʒɛr]	foreign language
la **langue maternelle** [lãgmatɛrnɛl]	mother tongue
la **philo(sophie)** [filɔ zɔfi]	philosophy
le **travail manuel** [travajmanɥɛl]	manual labor

	8 à 9	9 à 10	10 à 11	11 à 12	2 à 3	3 à 4
Lundi	Français	Anglais	Géographie	Mathématiques	Allemand	Gymnastique
Mardi	Mathématiques		Etude	Anglais	Chimie	
Mercredi	Physique	Etude	Mathématiques	Français		
Jeudi	Allemand	Français		Anglais	Plein air	
Vendredi	Physique	Etude	Histoire	Allemand	Anglais	Français
Samedi	Mathématiques	Histoire	Instruction civique			

■■■■■■■ **Teaching Objectives** ■■■■■■■

le **but** [byt]   objective, goal

le **candidat,** la **candidate**   candidate; applicant
[kãdida, t]

le **certificat** [sɛrtifika]   certificate; diploma
J'ai eu mon certificat d'études.   I've obtained my diploma.

le **concours** [kɔ̃kur]   competitive examination
Tu as passé ton concours?   Did you pass your competitive
                                                         exam?

correct, e [kɔrɛkt]   correct, right

la **culture** [kyltyr]   culture
Il n'a aucune culture générale.   He lacks an all-round education.

le **diplôme** [diplom]   diploma

écrit, e [ekri, t]   written

l'**écriture** f [ekrityr]   writing

l'**éducation** f [edykɑsjɔ̃]   education

être reçu, e [ɘɛtrərəsy]   pass an exam
J'ai été reçu au bac.   I passed the school-leaving exam.

l'**examen** m [ɛgzamɛ̃]   exam(ination), test
J'ai passé mon examen de maths.   I passed my math exam.

moyen, ne [mwajɛ̃, ɛn]   average, middle

oral, e, -aux [ɔral, o]   oral

l'**orthographe** f [ɔrtɔgraf]   spelling, orthography

le **prix** [pri]   prize

le **progrès** [prɔgrɛ]   progress

le **résultat** [rezylta]   result
J'ai eu des bons résultats.   I got good grades.

savoir [savwar]   know; be able
Sabine sait bien le français.   Sabine knows French well.

la **solution** [sɔlysjɔ̃]   solution

l'**usage** m [yzaʒ]   custom, usage; use

le **vocabulaire** [vɔkabylɛr]   vocabulary

129

distribuer [distribчe]	distribute
la **distribution** [distribysjɔ̃]	distribution
le **lexique** [lɛksik]	lexicon; abridged dictionary
la **linguistique** [lɛ̃gчistik]	linguistics
le **niveau, x** [nivo]	level
la **phonétique** [fɔnetik]	phonetics
la **syntaxe** [sɛ̃taks]	syntax

Les lettres de l'alphabet

A [a]	**J** [ʒi]	**S** [ɛs]
B [be]	**K** [ka]	**T** [te]
C [se]	**L** [ɛl]	**U** [y]
D [de]	**M** [ɛm]	**V** [ve]
E [ə]	**N** [ɛn]	**W** [dublǝve]
F [ɛf]	**O** [o]	**X** [iks]
G [ʒe]	**P** [pe]	**Y** [igrɛk]
H [aʃ]	**Q** [ky]	**Z** [zɛd]
I [i]	**R** [ɛr]	

In the Classroom

absent, e [apsã, t]	absent
Qui est absent?	Who is absent?
apprendre [aprãdr]	learn, study
avoir de la volonté [avwardlavɔlɔ̃te]	have will(power)
bref, brève [brɛf, brɛv]	brief, short

calculer [kalkyle]	calculate, reckon
le **chiffre** [ʃifr]	figure, number
compliqué, e [kɔ̃plike]	complicated
la **composition** [kɔ̃pozisjɔ̃]	paper, test, essay; composition
comprendre [kɔ̃prɑ̃dr]	understand
compter [kɔ̃te]	count
copier [kɔpje]	copy
corriger [kɔriʒe]	correct
décrire [dekrir]	describe
définir [definir]	define; determine
dessiner [desine]	draw
développer [devlɔpe]	develop
les **devoirs** *mpl* [dəvwar]	homework
la **dictée** [dikte]	dictation
la **difficulté** [difikylte]	difficulty
la **discussion** [diskysjɔ̃]	discussion
discuter [diskyte]	discuss
diviser [divize]	divide
écrire [ekrir]	write
employer [ɑ̃plwaje]	use, employ
l'**épreuve** *f* [eprœv]	proof

étudier [etydje]
study, learn, read
J'ai étudié la grammaire basque.
I have studied Basque grammar.
Nous étudions l'histoire des Francs.
We're learning the history of the Franks.

l'**exercice** *m* [ɛgzɛrsis]	exercise
l'**explication** *f* [ɛksplikɑsjɔ̃]	interpretation; explanation
expliquer [ɑɛksplike]	explain, expound, construe

l'**expression** *f* [ɛksprɛsjɔ̃]
expression
C'est une expression toute faite.
It is a fixed expression.

familier, -ère [familje, ɛr]
familiar
"Piger" est un mot familier.
"Piger" is a colloquial word.

la **faute** [fot]
C'est une faute grave.

mistake, error
It's a serious error.

ignorer [iɲɔre]

be ignorant of, not know

l'**image** *f* [imaʒ]

image; picture

incompréhensible
[ɛ̃kɔ̃preɑ̃sibl]

incomprehensible

le **langage** [lɑ̃gaʒ]
Le langage des jeunes

language; speech, diction
The language of young people

la **leçon** [ləsɔ̃]

lesson; reading

la **lettre** [lɛtr]

letter

lire [lir]

read

la **note** [nɔt]
Tu as pris des notes?

note; mark, grade
Did you take notes?

noter [nɔte]

note; mark; note down

nouveau, -vel, -velle, x
[nuvo, nuvɛl]

new

l'**occupation** *f* [ɔkypɑsjɔ̃]

occupation

par cœur [parkœr]

by heart

par écrit [parekri]

in writing

paresseux, -euse [parɛsø, z]

lazy

parler [parle]
Tu parles anglais?
Parle plus fort.

speak
Do you speak English?
Speak louder.

préparer [prepare]
Vous préparez l'examen des
Grandes Ecoles?

prepare
Are you preparing for the entrance
exam of the Grandes Ecoles?

la **preuve** [prœv]

proof

le **problème** [prɔblɛm]
J'ai résolu mon problème de maths.

problem
I solved my math problem.

prouver [pruve]
Qu'est-ce que ça prouve?

prove
What does that prove?

la **question** [kɛstjɔ̃]
Qui a posé la question?

question
Who asked the question?

rater [rate]
J'ai raté mon interro.

miss; fail
I failed my examination.

résumer [rezyme]

sum up, give a summary

la **serviette** [sɛrvjɛt]	briefcase, portfolio
signifier [siɲifje]	signify, mean
la **table des matières** [tablədəmatjɛr]	table of contents
le **texte** [tɛkst]	text
traduire [tradɥir]	translate
transformer [trãsfɔrme]	transform

analyser [analize]	analyze
l'**arc** *m* [ark]	arc
le **brouillon** [brujõ]	rough draft, rough copy
citer [site]	quote, cite
cocher [kɔʃe]	notch; check off
Cochez la case.	Make a check in the box.
le **contenu** [kõtny]	contents
le **corrigé** [kɔriʒe]	correction
la **définition** [definisjõ]	definition
démontrer [demõtre]	show, demonstrate
la **description** [dɛskripsjõ]	description
le **dossier** [dosje]	notes, papers filed together
dresser [drese]	set up; lay out; make out
l'**esquisse** *f* [ɛskis]	sketch, outline, rough draft
l'**introduction** *f* [ɛ̃trɔdyksjõ]	introduction
la **lecture** [lɛktyr]	reading; perusal
le **paragraphe** [paragraf]	paragraph
prendre des notes [prãdrədenɔt]	make notes, take notes
la **prononciation** [prɔnõsjɑsjõ]	pronunciation
souligner [suliɲe]	underline
la **traduction** [tradyksjõ]	translation

Teaching Aids

le **bouquin** [bukɛ̃]	book
le **cahier** [kaje]	notebook
la **calculette** [kalkylɛt]	pocket calculator
le **crayon** [krɛjɔ̃]	pencil
le **dictionnaire** [diksjɔnɛr]	dictionary
l'**encre** *f* [ãkrə]	ink
l'**éponge** *f* [epɔ̃ʒ]	sponge
la **feuille** [fœj]	leaf; sheet
la **feuille de papier** [fœjdəpapje]	sheet of paper
la **liste** [list]	list
le **livre** [livr]	book
le **stylo** [stilo]	fountain pen
le **stylo (à) bille** [stilo a bij]	ballpoint pen
le **tableau, x** [tablo]	blackboard

le **classeur** [klasœr]	file; ring binder
le **compas** [kɔ̃pa]	pair of compasses
la **craie** [krɛ]	chalk
la **gomme** [gɔm]	rubber eraser
le **manuel** [manɥɛl]	manual, handbook, textbook
Le manuel scolaire.	The schoolbook.
le **scotch** [skɔtʃ]	Scotch® tape
le **taille-crayons** [tɑjkrɛjɔ̃]	pencil sharpener

Grammar

l'**accent** *m* [aksã]	accent
l'**adjectif** *m* [adʒɛktif]	adjective
l'**adverbe** *m* [advɛrb]	adverb

l'**article** *m* [artikl]	article
la **cause** [koz]	cause
la **condition** [kɔ̃disjɔ̃]	condition
le **discours** [diskur]	discourse, speech
l'**exception** *f* [ɛksɛpsjɔ̃]	exception
l'**exemple** *m* [ɛgzãpl]	example
féminin, e [feminɛ̃, in]	feminine
le **genre** [ʒãr]	gender
la **grammaire** [gramɛr]	grammar
masculin, e [maskylɛ̃, in]	masculine
le **mot** [mo]	word
négatif, -ive [negatif, iv]	negative
le **nom** [nɔ̃]	noun
la **phrase** [fraz]	sentence
le **pluriel** [plyrjɛl]	plural
le **point** [pwɛ̃]	period
positif, -ive [pozitif, iv]	positive
le **présent** [prezã]	present
relatif, -ive [rəlatif, iv]	relative
le **singulier** [sɛ̃gylje]	singular
le **sujet** [syʒɛ]	subject
le **temps** [tã]	tense
le **verbe** [vɛrb]	verb

le **complément d'objet direct** [kɔ̃plemãdɛdirɛkt]	direct object
le **complément d'objet indirect** [kɔ̃plemãdɔbʒɛ̃dirɛkt]	indirect object
le **conditionnel** [kɔ̃disjɔnɛl]	conditional
la **conjonction** [kɔ̃ʒɔ̃ksjɔ̃]	conjunction
défini, e [defini]	definite
le **déterminant** [detɛrminã]	determinative word
le **futur composé** [fytyrkɔ̃pose]	compound future

le **futur simple** [fytyrsɛ̃pl]	simple future
l'**imparfait** *m* [ɛparfɛ]	imperfect
l'**impératif** *m* [ɛperatif]	imperative, command form
indéfini, e [ɛ̃defini]	indefinite
l'**indicatif** *m* [ɛdikatif]	indicative
l'**infinitif** *m* [ɛfinitif]	infinitive
la **manière** [manjɛr]	manner
marquer [marke]	indicate; denote
le **passé composé** [pasekɔ̃poze]	compound past
le **passé simple** [pasesɛ̃pl]	simple past
le **plus-que-parfait** [plyskəparfɛ]	pluperfect
la **préposition** [prepozisjɔ̃]	preposition
le **pronom** [prɔnɔ̃]	pronoun
la **règle** [rɛgl]	rule
le **subjonctif** [sybʒɔ̃ktif]	subjunctive
la **subordonnée** [sybɔrdɔne]	subordinate clause
la **syllabe** [silab]	syllable
la **virgule** [virgyl]	comma
la **voix active** [vwaaktiv]	active voice
la **voix passive** [vwapasiv]	passive voice

University

le **droit** [drwa]	law
René est étudiant en droit.	René is a law student.
l'**étudiant, e** [etydjɑ̃, t]	student
l'**expérience** *f* [ɛksperjɑ̃s]	experience; experiment
l'**invention** *f* [ɛvɑ̃sjɔ̃]	invention
la **médecine** [mɛdsin]	medicine
la **psychologie** [psikɔlɔʒi]	psychology
le **savant**, la **savante** [savɑ̃, t]	scholar, scientist
la **science** [sjɑ̃s]	science

les **sciences humaines** *fpl* [sjãsymɛn]	liberal arts, humanities
les **sciences naturelles** *fpl* [sjãsnatyrɛl]	natural sciences
scientifique [sjãtifik]	scientific
l'**université** *f* [ynivɛrsite]	university

l'**assistant, e** [asistã, t]	assistant
l'**autorité** *f* [ɔtɔrite]	authority
le **cours magistral** [kurmaʒistral]	lecture course
la **discipline** [disiplin]	subject; discipline
les **études** *fpl* [etyd] J'ai fait mes études à Rennes.	studies I studied in Rennes.
la **fac(ulté)** [fak ylte]	faculty; school, college
la **faculté des lettres** [fakyltedelɛtr]	Faculty of Arts (or Humanities)
inscrire (s') [sɛ̃skrir]	register
la **recherche** [rəʃɛrʃ]	research
le **resto-U** [rɛstɔy]	university cafeteria
les **sciences économiques** *fpl* [sjãsekɔnɔmik]	economics, economic science
les **sciences politiques** *fpl* [sjãspɔlitik]	political science

Les étudiants en médecine à l'université doivent étudier pendant sept ans au moins.
Medical students at the university must study for at least seven years.

General Terms

à la mode [alamɔd]
Le pop art n'est plus à la mode.

in fashion, in style
Pop art is no longer in fashion.

amusant, e [amyzã, t]

amusing

applaudir [aplodir]
L'artiste a été applaudi longuement.

applaud
The artist was applauded for a long time.

l'**art** *m* [ar]
L'art pour l'art.

art
Art for art's sake.

au premier plan [oprəmjeplãʃ]

in the foreground

beau, bel, belle, x [bo, bɛl]

beautiful

le **billet** [bijɛ]

ticket

bref, brève [brɛf, brɛv]

brief, short

célèbre [selɛbr]

famous, celebrated

classique [klasik]

classical

complet, -ète [kɔ̃plɛ, t]
Les œuvres complètes de Diderot.

complete
The complete works of Diderot.

créer [kree]
Picasso a créé Guernica.

create
Picasso created Guernica.

critiquer [kritike]

criticize, censure; review

découvrir [dekuvrir]

discover

distraire (se) [sədistrɛr]

amuse oneself

l'**esprit** *m* [ɛspri]
L'esprit critique.
Voltaire est un auteur plein d'esprit.

wit; spirit; intellect
The subtle mind.
Voltaire is a witty writer.

faire la queue [fɛrlakø]

get in line, stand in line

incompréhensible [ɛ̃kɔ̃preãsibl]

incomprehensible

laid, e [lɛ, d]

ugly

la **liberté** [libɛrte]
La liberté de l'art.

liberty, freedom
Artistic liberty.

la **matinée** [matine]

matinee

moderne [mɔdɛrn]

modern

nouveau, -vel, -velle, x [nuvo, nuvɛl]	new
l'**œuvre** _f_ [œvr]	work
l'**original, -aux** _m_ [ɔriʒinal, o] L'original de la Joconde est au Louvre.	original The original of the Mona Lisa is in the Louvre.
participer [partisipe] Nous avons participé à un concert pop.	participate We participated in a pop concert.
populaire [pɔpylɛr] J'aime les chansons populaires.	popular I like folk songs.
premier, -ère [prəmje, ɛr]	first
le **prix** [pri] Il y a 1500 prix littéraires en France.	prize There are 1500 literary prizes in France.
le **public** [pyblik]	public
rare [rar]	rare
réaliste [realist] Courbet est un peintre réaliste.	realistic Courbet is a realistic painter.
réel, le [reɛl]	real
siffler [sifle] La chanteuse s'est fait siffler.	whistle; hiss, boo The singer was booed.
la **sortie** [sɔrti]	exit
sortir [sɔrtir]	leave, go out
le **style** [stil]	style
le **sujet** [syʒɛ]	subject
le **titre** [titr]	title
typique [tipik]	typical
la **valeur** [valœr]	value

l'**artiste** _mf_ [artist]	artist
artistique [artistik]	artistic
baroque [barɔk]	baroque
la **beauté** [bote]	beauty
la **créativité** [kreativite]	creativity

139

doué, e [dwe]	gifted
Paul est doué pour la musique.	Paul is musically gifted.
Les Italiens sont doués en musique.	The Italians have a gift for music.
la **fascination** [fasinɑsjɔ̃]	fascination
fasciner [fasine]	fascinate
le **festival, s** [fɛstival]	festival
gothique [gɔtik]	Gothic
historique [istɔrik]	historic(al)
Woodstock a été un événement historique.	Woodstock was a historic event.
inconnu, e [ə̃ɛ̃kɔny]	unknown
médiéval, e, -aux [medjeval, o]	medieval
L'art médiéval.	Medieval art.
la **nouveauté** [nuvote]	novelty
le **prestige** [prɛstiʒ]	prestige
la **réalisation** [realizɑsjɔ̃]	realization; production
La réalisation d'un film.	The production of a film.
roman, e [rɔmɑ̃, an]	Romanesque
le **talent** [talɑ̃]	talent, gift

Literature

l'**auteur** *m* [otœr]	author, writer
avoir de l'esprit [avwardəlɛspri]	be witty
le **bouquin** [bukɛ̃]	book
l'**écrivain** *m* [ekrivɛ̃]	writer
l'**histoire** *f* [istwar]	history; tale, story
la **lettre** [lɛtr]	letter
Un roman par lettres.	An epistolary novel.
la **littérature** [literatyr]	literature
le **livre** [livr]	book
la **nouvelle** [nuvɛl]	novella, short story
la **page** [paʒ]	page

le **passage** [pɑsaʒ]	passage
la **poésie** [pɔezi]	poetry, verse; poem
le **roman** [rɔmã]	novel
le **volume** [vɔlym]	volume
Les œuvres complètes de Goethe comprennent 138 volumes.	The complete works of Goethe comprise 138 volumes.

la **bande dessinée** [bãddesine]	comic strip, comics
La b.d. est la littérature populaire moderne.	Comic strips are modern popular literature.
le **dialecte** [djalɛkt]	dialect
intellectuel, le [ɛ̃telɛktɥɛl]	intellectual
la **maison d'édition** [mɛzɔ̃dedisjɔ̃]	publishing house
les **mémoires** *fpl* [memwar]	memoirs
le **poème** [pɔɛm]	poem
le **poète** [pɔɛt]	poet
la **préface** [prefas]	preface
le **récit** [resi]	narrative, story, account
le **recueil** [rəkœj]	collection
Les Fleurs du Mal sont un recueil de poèmes.	*Flowers of Evil* is a collection of poems.
le **roman policier** [rɔmãpɔlisje]	detective novel
le **romancier**, la **romancière** [rɔmãsje, ɛr]	novelist
le **tome** [tɔm]	volume
le **vers** [vɛr]	verse
L'alexandrin est un vers de douze syllabes.	An Alexandrine is a verse of 12 syllables.

Music

l'**air** *m* [ɛr]	tune, melody
J'aime bien l'air de cette chanson.	I like the tune of this song.
la **chanson** [ʃãsɔ̃]	song
chanter [əʃãte]	sing
Adamo chante l'amour.	Adamo sings about love.

le **chanteur,** la **chanteuse** [ʃɑ̃tœr, øz]	singer
la **clarinette** [clarinɛt]	clarinet
le **concert** [kɔ̃sɛr]	concert
J'ai assisté à un concert symphonique.	I attended a symphony concert.
le **disque** [disk]	record
la **flûte** [flyt]	flute
la **guitare** [gitar]	guitar
Tu joues de la guitare?	Do you play the guitar?
l'**instrument** *m* [ɛ̃strymɑ̃]	instrument
l'**interprète** *mf* [ɛ̃tɛrprɛt]	interpreter
le **jazz** [dʒaz]	jazz
la **marche** [marʃ]	march
La marche funèbre.	The funeral dead march.
le **mouvement** [muvmɑ̃]	movement
La symphonie a quatre mouvements.	The symphony has four movements.
le **musicien,** la **musicienne** [myzisjɛ̃, ɛn]	musician
la **musique** [myzik]	music
la **note** [nɔt]	note
l'**opéra** *m* [ɔpera]	opera
l'**orchestre** *m* [ɔrkɛstr]	orchestra; band
L'orchestre du village a ouvert le bal.	The village band opened the ball.
L'orchestre philharmonique de Vienne a donné un concert.	The Viennese Philharmonic gave a concert.
l'**orgue** *m* [ɔrg]	organ
le **piano** [pjano]	piano
la **pièce** [pjɛs]	piece
le **rythme** [ritm]	rhythm
la **séance** [seɑ̃s]	performance
le **son** [sɔ̃]	sound
L'armée avance aux sons des tambours.	The army advances to the sound of the drums.
la **trompette** [trɔ̃pɛt]	trumpet
le **violon** [vjɔlɔ̃]	violin

l'**alto** *m* [alto]	viola
la **batterie** [batri]	percussion instruments
le **concerto** [kɔ̃sɛrto] Un concerto pour violon.	concerto A violin concerto.
la **contre-basse** [kɔ̃trəbas]	double-bass, contrabass
la **corde** [kɔrd]	string; chord
la **gamme** [gam]	scale
la **harpe** ['arp]	harp
le **hautbois** ['obwa]	oboe
l'**instrument à cordes** *m* [ɛ̃strymãakɔrd]	string(ed) instrument
l'**instrument à percussion** *m* [ɛ̃strymãapɛrkysjɔ̃]	percussion instrument
l'**instrument à vent** *m* [ɛ̃strymãavã]	wind instrument
le **lied, lieder** [lid, lidœr] Les lieder de Schubert.	lied, lieder Schubert's lieder.
le **quatuor** [kwatyɔr]	quartet
le **violoncelle** [vjɔlɔ̃sɛl]	cello
majeur [maʒœr] La symphonie en mi bémol majeur de Mozart.	major Mozart's Symphony in E Flat Major.
mineur [minœr] La messe en si mineur de Bach.	minor Bach's Mass in B Minor.
do, ut [do, yt]	C, do
ré [re]	D, re
mi [mi]	E, mi
fa [fa]	F, fa
sol [sɔl]	G, sol
la [la]	A, la
si [si]	B, ti (si)
dièse [djɛz]	sharp
bémol [bemɔl]	flat

Visual Arts

le **cadre** [kadr]	frame
le **dessin** [desɛ̃]	drawing
l'**exposition** *f* [ɛkspozisjɔ̃]	exhibition, show
le **gardien,** la **gardienne** [gardjɛ̃, ɛn]	guard
le **musée** [myze]	museum
peindre [pɛ̃dr]	paint
le **peintre** [pɛ̃tr]	painter
la **peinture** [pɛ̃tyr]	painting, picture
la **sculpture** [skyltyr]	sculpture
la **statue** [staty]	statue
le **tableau, x** [tablo] Le tableau le plus connu c'est la Joconde.	picture, painting, tableau The best-known painting is the Mona Lisa.
la **toile** [twal] Les voleurs ont découpé la toile.	canvas; painting, picture, piece The thieves cut out the canvas.

abstrait, e [apstrɛ, t]	abstract
l'**arc** *m* [ark]	arc
la **galerie** [galri]	gallery
le **sculpteur** [skyltœr]	sculptor

Theater and Film

l'**acteur, -trice** [aktœr, tris]	actor, actress
la **caméra** [kamera]	movie camera
le **cinéma** [sinema] Tu vas souvent au cinéma?	movie theater, movies Do you go to the movies often?
la **comédie** [kɔmedi]	comedy
comique [kɔmik]	funny, comic(al)

le **costume** [kɔstym] — costume

dramatique [dramatik] — dramatic

l'**entracte** *m* [ãtrakt] — interval, intermission
On vend des glaces pendant l'entracte. — Ice cream is sold during the intermission.

l'**entrée** *f* [ãtre] — entrance; admission; debut

faire du théâtre [fɛrdyteatr] — perform a play

le **film** [film] — film

la **mise en scène** [mizãsɛn] — production, staging; direction

le **personnage** [pɛrsɔnaʒ] — character, part
Le personnage de Maigret est joué par Jean Richard. — The part of Maigret is played by Jean Richard.

la **pièce de théâtre** [pjɛsdəteatr] — play, piece

le **rang** [rã] — tier (of boxes)

la **représentation** [rəprezãtasjɔ̃] — performance, production; show
La représentation est un succès total. — The production is a complete success.

représenter [rəprezãte] — perform, act

la **revue** [rəvy] — revue, show

le **rôle** [rol] — role

la **salle** [sal] — hall, (theater) house

la **scène** [sɛn] — stage; scenery, scene
L'acteur est entré en scène. — The actor came on stage.

le **spectacle** [spɛktakl] — play, performance; spectacle
L'industrie du spectacle. — The entertainment industry; show business.

Quel spectacle, toi sur un vélo. — What a spectacle: you on a bike.

le **spectateur,** la **spectatrice** [spɛktatœr, tris] — spectator

le **théâtre** [teatr] — theater

tourner un film [turneɛ̃film] — shoot a film

la **vedette** [vədɛt] — star
J.P. Belmondo est la vedette du cinéma français. — J. P. Belmondo is the star of French film.

l'**acte** *m* [akt]	act
le **cirque** [sirk]	circus
le **décor** [dekɔr]	decoration; scenery
le **dénouement** [denumã]	denouement, unraveling
Ce film a un dénouement inattendu.	This film has an unexpected denouement.
le **dessin animé** [desɛ̃anime]	animated film
Cendrillon, un grand dessin animé de Walt Disney.	Cinderella, a great animated film by Walt Disney.
la **distribution** [distribysjɔ̃]	cast, casting
le **drame** [dram]	drama
l'**éclairage** *m* [eklɛraʒ]	lighting
le **film de cape et d'épée** [filmdəkapedepe]	cloak-and-dagger film
Les trois mousquetaires est un film de cape et d'épée.	The Three Musketeers is a cloak-and-dagger film.
le **film de conte de fées** [filmdəkõtdəfe]	fairy-tale film
le **film de science fiction** [filmdəsjãsfiksjɔ̃]	science fiction film
le **film policier** [filmpɔlisje]	detective film
le **metteur en scène** [mɛtœrãsɛn]	director
Claude Chabrol est un metteur en scène très connu.	Claude Chabrol is a very famous director.
le **monologue** [mɔnɔlɔg]	monologue
le **prologue** [prɔlɔg]	prologue
le **scénario** [senarjo]	film scenario, film script
le, la **scénariste** [senarist]	script writer, scenario writer
la **tragédie** [traʒedi]	tragedy
le **western** [wɛstɛrn]	Western

Philosophy

le **bon sens** [bɔ̃sɑ̃s]	good sense, common sense
la **catégorie** [kategɔri]	category
causer [koze]	cause
concret, -ète [kɔ̃krɛ, t]	concrete
la **contradiction** [kɔ̃tradiksjɔ̃]	contradiction
définitif, -ive [definitif, iv]	definitive
l'**effet** *m* [efɛ]	effect
Les causes et les effets.	Causes and effects.
élémentaire [elemɑ̃tɛr]	elementary
l'**esprit** *m* [ɛspri]	intellect, mind, spirit
L'esprit critique.	The subtle mind.
l'**idée** *f* [ide]	idea
l'**individu** *m* [ɛ̃dividy]	individual
le **mal** [mal]	evil
Le bien et le mal.	Good and evil.
la **méthode** [metɔd]	method
La méthode cartésienne.	The Cartesian method.
le **modèle** [mɔdɛl]	model
moderne [mɔdɛrn]	modern
la **mort** [mɔr]	death
l'**œuvre** *f* [œvr]	work
L'œuvre complète.	The complete works.
l'**origine** *f* [ɔriʒin]	origin
De l'origine des espèces.	On the origin of species.
l'**ouvrage** *m* [uvraʒ]	work
la **pensée** [pɑ̃se]	thought, notion
penser [pɑ̃se]	think
Je pense donc je suis.	I think, therefore I am.
la **raison** [rɛzɔ̃]	reason; sense
raisonnable [rɛzɔnabl]	reasonable
le, la **réaliste** [realist]	realist

réel, le [reɛl]	real
le **sens** [sɑ̃s]	sense; judgement
la **théorie** [teɔri]	theory
la **vérité** [verite]	truth
la **volonté** [vɔlɔ̃te]	will
vrai, e [vrɛ, ɲ]	true

l'**acte** *m* [akt]	act, action
la **conception** [kɔ̃sɛpsjɔ̃]	conception; notion
concevoir [kɔ̃səvwar]	imagine, understand
la **dimension** [dimɑ̃sjɔ̃]	dimension
douter [dute]	doubt
Le nihiliste doute de tout.	The nihilist doubts everything.
l'**existence** *f* [ɛgzistɑ̃s]	existence
le **hasard** ['azar]	chance
l'**ignorance** *f* [iɲɔrɑ̃s]	ignorance; error
les **mœurs** *fpl* [mœrs]	morals; manners, customs
moral, e, -aux [mɔral, o]	moral
la **morale** [mɔral]	moral
spirituel, le [spiritɥɛl]	spiritual
le **symbole** [sɛ̃bɔl]	symbol
le **terme** [tɛrm]	term, concept
vain, e [vɛ̃, ɛn]	vain, fruitless; empty
Tout est vain.	Everything is futile.
Un vain espoir.	A vain hope.

Religion

catholique [katɔlik]	Catholic
chrétien, ne [kretjɛ̃, ɛn]	Christian
le **ciel** [sjɛl]	heaven
le **clergé** [klɛrʒe]	clergy
Dieu [djø]	God
Je crois en Dieu.	I believe in God.

l'**Eglise** *f* [egliz] — the Church
L'Eglise catholique. — The Catholic Church.

Jésus-Christ [əʒezykri] — Jesus Christ

le **mariage** [marjaʒ] — wedding
Le mariage à l'église. — The church wedding.
Le mariage civil. — The civil wedding.

Noël *m* [nɔɛl] — Christmas
Joyeux Noël — Merry Christmas

Pâques *fpl* [pɑk] — Easter

la **Pentecôte** [pɑ̃tkot] — Pentecost

prier [prije] — pray
Priez Dieu. — Pray to God.
Priez pour les âmes en peine. — Pray for the souls in torment.

protestant, e [prɔtɛstɑ̃, t] — Protestant

religieux, -euse [rəliʒjø, z] — religious

la **religion** [rəliʒjɔ̃] — religion

l'**ange** *m* [ɑ̃ʒ] — angel
L'ange gardien. — The guardian angel.

le **baptême** [batɛm] — baptism

la **Bible** [bibl] — Bible

confesser (se) [səkɔ̃fese] — confess

le **culte** [kylt] — worship

le **curé** [kyre] — parish priest

le **diable** [djɑbl] — devil
Je ne crois ni à Dieu ni au diable. — I believe neither in God nor in the devil.

l'**enfer** *m* [ɑ̃fɛr] — hell

la **foi** [fwa] — faith
La profession de foi. — The profession of faith.

la **messe** [mɛs] — mass

le **miracle** [mirakl] — miracle

le **pape** [pap] — pope

le **paradis** [paradi] — paradise

le **pasteur** [pastœr] — pastor

le **péché** [peʃe]	sin
Le péché originel.	The original sin.
le **prêtre** [prɛtr]	priest
sacré, e [sakre]	sacred
saint, e [sɛ̃, t]	holy; saintly; sainted
La Sainte Vierge.	The Blessed Virgin.
Le Saint Esprit.	The Holy Spirit.
solennel, le [sɔlanɛl]	solemn
la **Toussaint** [tusɛ̃]	All Saints' Day

History

battre [batr]	beat; defeat
Les Romains ont battu les Gaulois.	The Romans defeated the Gauls.
la **bourgeoisie** [burʒwazi]	middle class, bourgeoisie
le **château, x** [ʃato]	palace; castle
la **colonie** [kɔlɔni]	colony
la **conquête** [kɔ̃kɛt]	conquest
La conquête du Nouveau Monde.	The conquest of the New World.
la **constitution** [kɔ̃stitysjɔ̃]	constitution
la **découverte** [dekuvɛrt]	discovery
l'**empire** m [ɑ̃pir]	empire
L'empire romain.	The Roman Empire.
L'Empire.	The Empire (Napoleon's).
la **Gaule** [gol]	Gaul
le **Gaulois**, la **Gauloise** [golwa, z]	Gaul
la **guerre** [gɛr]	war
la **guillotine** [gijɔtin]	guillotine
la **légion** [leʒjɔ̃]	legion
La Légion.	The Foreign Legion.
la **liberté** [libɛrte]	liberty, freedom
Les libertés individuelles.	The individual liberties.
la **Marseillaise** [marsɛjɛz]	French national anthem

la **monarchie** [mɔnarʃi] La monarchie absolue.	monarchy The absolute monarchy.
la **noblesse** [nɔblɛs]	nobility
occuper [ɔkype]	occupy
la **prise de la Bastille** [prizdəlabastij]	storming of the Bastille
la **reine** [rɛn]	queen
la **révolution** [revɔlysjɔ̃]	revolution
la **Révolution** [revɔlysjɔ̃]	French Revolution of 1789
le **roi** [rwa]	king
romain, e [rɔmɛ̃, ɛn]	Roman
la **tradition** [tradisjɔ̃]	tradition

absolu, e [apsɔly]	absolute
l'**absolutisme** *m* [apsɔlytism]	absolutism
Charlemagne [əʃarləmaɲ]	Charlemagne
le **citoyen,** la **citoyenne** [sitwajɛ̃, ɛn]	citizen
colonial, e, -aux [kɔlɔnjal, o]	colonial
le **combat** [kɔ̃ba]	combat, fight, battle
combattre [kɔ̃batr]	fight, combat, wage war against
le **Débarquement** [debarkəmã]	Allied landing on June 6, 1944
dominer [dɔmine]	rule; dominate
les **droits de l'homme** *mpl* [drwadlɔm]	human rights
l'**égalité** *f* [egalite] Liberté, Egalité, Fraternité	equality Liberty, Equality, Fraternity
l'**empereur** *m* [ãprœr] L'empereur Napoléon III.	emperor Emperor Napoleon III.
envahir [ãvair] Guillaume le Conquérant a envahi l'Angleterre.	invade, overrun William the Conqueror invaded England.
l'**esclave** *mf* [ɛsklav]	slave
les **Etats généraux** *mpl* [etaʒenero]	Estates General

l'**exécution** *f* [ɛgzekysjɔ̃]	execution
fonder [fɔ̃de]	found
la **fraternité** [fratɛrnite]	brotherhood, fraternity
la **gloire** [glwar]	glory, fame
l'**invasion** *f* [ɛ̃vɑzjɔ̃]	invasion
libérer [libere]	liberate, free
la **lutte** [lyt] La lutte de la classe ouvrière.	struggle, contest, strife The struggle of the working class.
misérable [mizerabl]	miserable, poor
la **misère** [mizɛr] Le peuple a vécu dans la misère.	misery, poverty The people lived in poverty.
le **plébiscite** [plebisit] Louis-Napoléon a éte élu par plébiscite.	plebiscite Louis-Napoleon was elected by means of a plebiscite.
la **population** [pɔpylasjɔ̃]	population
la **Première guerre mondiale** [prəmjɛrgɛrmɔ̃djal]	First World War
le **privilège** [privilɛʒ]	privilege
le **règne** [rɛɲ]	reign, rule
régner [reɲe] Louis XIV a régné de 1643 à 1715.	reign, rule Louis XIV reigned from 1643 to 1715.
la **Résistance** [rezistɑ̃s]	French Resistance in World War II
royal, e, -aux [rwajal, o]	royal
le **royaume** [rwajom]	kingdom
la **séparation des pouvoirs** [separasjɔ̃depuvwar]	separation of powers
le **Siècle des lumières** [sjɛklədəlymjɛr] Les philosophes ont marqué le Siècle des lumières.	Age of Enlightenment The philosophers molded the Age of Enlightenment.
le **tiers état** [tjɛrzeta]	third estate, the bourgeoisie
la **torture** [tɔrtyr]	torture
traditionnel, le [tradisjɔnɛl]	traditional
victorieux, -euse [viktɔrjø, z]	victorious

Humans in Society

Family

l'**aîné, e** [ene]	elder, eldest, oldest; senior
le **bébé** [bebe]	baby
cadet, te [kadɛ, t]	younger, youngest, junior
C'est moi la cadette.	I'm the youngest.
le **cousin**, la **cousine** [kuzɛ̃, in]	cousin
enceinte [ɑ̃sɛ̃t]	pregnant
Je suis enceinte de trois mois.	I'm three months pregnant.
l'**enfant** *mf* [ɑ̃fɑ̃]	child
l'**enfant unique** *mf* [ɑ̃fɑ̃ynik]	only child
faire partie de [fɛrpartidə]	belong to
Le chien fait partie de la famille.	The dog belongs to the family.
la **famille** [famij]	family
la **femme** [fam]	woman; wife
fiancé, e [fjɑ̃se]	engaged
la **fille** [fij]	daughter
le **fils** [fis]	son
le **frère** [frɛr]	brother
le **garçon** [garsɔ̃]	boy
le, la **gosse** [gɔs]	kid, youngster
la **grand-mère** [grɑ̃mɛr]	grandmother
le **grand-père** [grɑ̃pɛr]	grandfather
les **grands-parents** *mpl* [grɑ̃parɑ̃]	grandparents
l'**homme** *m* [ɔm]	man
L'homme était le chef de la famille.	The man was the head of the family.
la **maman** [mamɑ̃]	mama
le **mari** [mari]	husband
Mon mari est malade.	My husband is ill.
le **membre** [mɑ̃br]	member
la **mère** [mɛr]	mother

le **neveu, x** [nvø]	nephew
la **nièce** [njɛs]	niece
l'**oncle** *m* [ɔ̃kl]	uncle
le **papa** [papa]	papa
les **parents** *mpl* [parã]	parents
le **père** [pɛr]	father
la **petite-fille** [ptitfij]	granddaughter
le **petit-fils** [ptifis]	grandson
les **petits-enfants** *mpl* [ptizãfã]	grandchildren
la **sœur** [sœr]	sister
la **tante** [tãt]	aunt

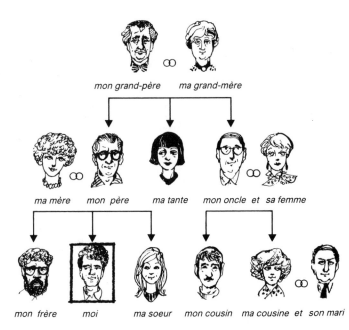

mon grand-père   ma grand-mère

ma mère   mon père   ma tante   mon oncle et sa femme

mon frère   moi   ma soeur   mon cousin   ma cousine et son mari

l'**ancêtre** *m* [ãsɛtr]	ancestor
le **beau-fils** [bofis]	son-in-law; stepson
le **beau-père** [bopɛr]	father-in-law; stepfather
les **beaux-parents** *mpl* [boparã]	parents-in-law
la **belle-fille** [bɛlfij]	daughter-in-law; stepdaughter
la **belle-mère** [bɛlmɛr]	mother-in-law; stepmother
la **famille nombreuse** [famijnõbrøz]	large family
Ils ont trois enfants, c'est une famille nombreuse.	They have three children; it's a large family.
la **génération** [ʒenerasjõ]	generation
Les gens de ma génération ont été élevés autrement.	My generation was raised differently.
la **mamie** [mami]	granny
la **marraine** [marɛn]	godmother
la **mémé** [meme]	granny
mineur, e [minœr]	minor
Le film est interdit aux mineurs.	The film is off limits to minors.
le **papi** [papi]	grandpa
le **parrain** [parɛ̃]	godfather
le **pépé** [pepe]	grandpa

Family Life

abandonner [abãdɔne]	abandon; give up
Janine a dû abandonner son bébé.	Janine had to give up her baby.
l'**amour** *m* [amur]	love
l'**anniversaire** *m* [anivɛrsɛr]	birthday
Bon anniversaire.	Happy Birthday!
attendre (s') [satãdr]	expect, be prepared for
Je m'attends à tout.	I'm prepared for anything.
Je ne m'y suis pas attendu.	I didn't expect that.
le **cadeau, x** [kado]	gift
le **cimetière** [simtjɛr]	cemetery

commun, e [kɔmɛ̃, yn]
Nous, on fait tout en commun.

common, joint
We do everything jointly.

Dieu *m* [djø]

God

le **divorce** [divɔrs]

divorce

l'**éducation** *f* [edykasjɔ̃]

education

élever [elve]

raise, bring up; educate

l'**émotion** *f* [emosjɔ̃]
Mémé pleure d'émotion.

emotion; stir, commotion
Granny is crying with emotion.

ému, e [emy]

moved, touched, affected

l'**enterrement** *m* [ɑ̃tɛrmɑ̃]

burial, interment, funeral

l'**excursion** *f* [ɛkskyrsjɔ̃]

excursion, outing

la **fête** [fɛt]
Bonne fête, Paulette.

holiday; saint's day; party
Many happy returns, Paulette.

l'**intérêt** *m* [ɛ̃terɛ]

interest

le **mariage** [marjaʒ]

wedding; marriage

marier (se) [səmarje]
Odile s'est mariée avec son cousin.

marry
Odile married her cousin.

le **ménage** [menaʒ]
Scène de ménage.

household; married couple
Marital quarrel.

la **mort** [mɔr]

death

mort, e [mɔr, t]

dead

mourir [murir]

die

la **naissance** [nɛsɑ̃s]

birth

obéir [ɔbeir]

obey

religieux, -euse [rəliʒjø, z]

religious

la **religion** [rəliʒjɔ̃]

religion

la **retraite** [rətrɛt]

retirement; pension

séparer [separe]

separate

uni, e [yni]
Stéphane et Berthe forment un
couple uni.

united, harmonious
Stephane and Berthe are a
harmonious couple.

le **baptême** [batɛm]	baptism
baptiser [batize]	baptize
la **cérémonie** [seremɔni]	ceremony
la **communion solennelle** [kɔmynjɔ̃sɔlanɛl]	confirmation; solemn communion
conjugal, e, -aux [kɔ̃ʒygal, o]	conjugal
le **couple** [kupl]	couple, pair
divorcer [divɔrse] Si tu continues, je divorce.	get a divorce If you keep it up, I'm getting a divorce.
épouser [epuze]	marry
fiancer (se) [səfjãse]	become engaged
l'**héritage** m [eritaʒ]	heritage, inheritance
hériter [erite] J'ai hérité de la maison. Il a tout hérité de son père.	inherit I inherited the house. He's the very image of his father.
marier [marje] J'ai marié ma fille cadette.	marry; marry off I've married off my youngest daughter.
parent, e [parã, t]	related
la **première communion** [prəmjɛrkɔmynjɔ̃]	first communion
rompre [rɔ̃pr] J'ai rompu mes fiançailles avec Guy.	break I've broken my engagement to Guy.
la **séparation** [separasjɔ̃]	separation
séparer (se) [səsepare]	separate

Relations with Others

aimer [eme] J'aime les bébés.	love, like I love babies.
l'**ambiance** f [ãbjãs]	mood, atmosphere
l'**ami, e** m, f [ami]	friend

l'**amitié** *f* [amitje]   friendship

amoureux, -euse [amurø, z]   in love, enamored
Je suis amoureuse de Gérard   I'm in love with Gérard
Dépardieu.   Dépardieu.

le **camarade** [kamarad]   comrade

la **connaissance** [kɔnɛsɑ̃s]   acquaintance
J'ai fait la connaissance d'une   I've made the acquaintance of a
jolie fille.   pretty girl.

connaître [kɔnɛtr]   know, be acquainted with

le **contact** [kɔ̃takt]   contact
Je ne suis plus en contact avec   I'm no longer in contact with
Joëlle.   Joëlle.

le **copain**, la **copine**   pal, chum
[kɔpɛ̃, kɔpin]

détester [detɛste]   hate, detest

embrasser [ɑ̃brase]   embrace; kiss

l'**ennemi, e** *m, f* [ɛnmi]   enemy

être bien avec qqn   be on good terms with s.o.
[ɛtrəbjɛ̃navəkkɛlkɛ̃]
Je voudrais l'épouser, je suis bien   I'd like to marry him; we get
avec lui.   along well.

faire la cour [fɛrlakur]   court, woo

froid, e [frwa, d]   cool, cold

proche [prɔʃ]   near, neighboring

la **relation** [rəlɑsjɔ̃]   relation, connection

le **sentiment** [sɑ̃timɑ̃]   sentiment, feeling

sympa(thique) [sɛ̃pa tik]   likable, pleasant
C'est un type sympa.   He's a likable guy.

tomber amoureux, -euse de   fall in love with
[tɔ̃beamurø, zdə]

tutoyer [tytwaje]   address familiarly (with "tu")

le **voisin**, la **voisine** [vwazɛ̃, in]   neighbor

affectif, -ive [afɛktif, iv]	affective
amical, e, -aux [amikal, o]	amicable, friendly
chaleureux, -euse [ʃalœrø, z]	warm, cordial, animated
cordial, e, -aux [kɔrdjal, o]	cordial
Cordialement vôtre ...	Cordially Yours, Sincerely Yours ...
courir après qqn [kuriraprɛkɛlkɛ̃]	run after s.o.
Il court après toutes les filles.	He runs after all the girls.
faire la bise [fɛrlabiz]	give a little kiss
Fais la bise à la dame.	Give the lady a little kiss.
la **haine** ['ɛn]	hatred, hate
hostile [ɔstil]	hostile
Nous sommes hostiles à toute répression.	We are hostile to every form of repression.
l'**hostilité** *f* [ɔstilite]	hostility
la **liaison** [ljɛzɔ̃]	liaison, relationship
la **sympathie** [sɛ̃pati]	sympathy, fellow-feeling
vouvoyer [vuvwaje]	address politely (with "vous")

Positive Experiences

avoir confiance en qqn [avwarkɔ̃fjɑ̃sɑ̃kɛlkɛ̃]	trust s.o.
J'ai confiance en ma femme.	I trust my wife.
avoir de la chance [avwardlaʃɑ̃s]	be lucky, have good luck
avoir de la veine [avwardlavɛn]	be in luck
avoir du succès [avwardysyksɛ]	be successful, have success
avoir envie de [avwarɑ̃vidə]	want
Tu n'as pas envie de faire une belote?	Don't you want to play a game of "belote"?
avoir la chance de [avwarlaʃɑ̃sdə]	have the opportunity to
J'ai la chance de passer une semaine à Paris.	I have the opportunity to spend a week in Paris.

avoir pitié [avwarpitje]
Aie pitié de moi.

have pity
Have pity on me.

le **bonheur** [bɔnœr]

happiness

la **chance** [ʃãs]

chance; luck, good luck

la **confiance** [kɔ̃fjãs]

trust, confidence

désirer [dezire]
Que désirez-vous?
Elle désire qu'il vienne la voir.

wish, desire
What do you wish?
She wants him to come see her.

espérer [ɛspere]

hope

l'**espoir** *m* [ɛspwar]

hope

être dans la lune
[ɛtrədãlalyn]

be in a brown study, be
wool-gathering

faire fortune [fɛrfɔrtyn]

make a fortune

fidèle [fidɛl]

faithful

gai, e [gɛ]

gay, cheerful, lively

heureux, -euse [œrø, z]

happy

indépendant, e [ɛ̃depãdã, t]

independent

libre [libr]

free

la **patience** [pasjãs]

patience

patient, e [pasjã, t]

patient

le **plaisir** [plezir]
Avec plaisir.

pleasure
With pleasure!

la **responsabilité** [rɛspɔ̃sabilite]

responsibility

responsable [rɛspɔ̃sabl]
Tu es responsable de tout.

responsible
You're responsible for everything.

riche [riʃ]

rich

satisfait, e [satisfɛ, t]
Je suis satisfait de ton travail à
l'école.

satisfied
I'm satisfied with your
performance in school.

la **beauté** [bote]

beauty

le **bien-être** [bjɛ̃nɛtr]

well-being

épanouir (s') [sepanwir]

bloom; beam

être à l'aise [ɛtralɛz]

be at ease, be comfortable

la **gaieté** [gɛte]

gaiety, cheerfulness

161

la **joie** [ʒwa]	joy
l'**optimiste** *mf* [ɔptimist]	optimist
le **prestige** [prɛstiʒ]	prestige
la **richesse** [riʃɛs]	wealth; richness
la **vertu** [vɛrty]	virtue

▬▬▬ Negative Experiences ▬▬▬

avoir de la peine [avwardlapɛn]
J'ai eu de la peine à comprendre.

have trouble, have difficulty
I had trouble understanding.

avoir des histoires
[avwardezistwar]

have problems

avoir du mal à [avwardymala]
J'ai du mal à comprendre ça.

have a hard time, have difficulty in
I have a hard time understanding
that.

avoir honte [avwar'ɔt]

be ashamed

avoir peur [avwarpœr]
J'ai peur qu'il soit trop tard.

be afraid
I'm afraid it's too late.

le **chagrin** [ʃagrɛ̃]

grief, sorrow

la **charge** [ʃarʒ]

charge; load, burden

le **conflit** [kɔ̃fli]

conflict

être de mauvaise humeur
[ɛtrədəmovɛzymœr]
Je ne l'aime pas trop, il est souvent
de mauvaise humeur.

be in a bad humor

I don't like him much, he's often
in a bad humor.

la **déception** [desɛpsjɔ̃]

disappointment

décevoir [desəvwar]

disappoint

décourager [dekuraʒe]

discourage

désespéré, e [dezɛspere]

desperate, hopeless

l'**embarras** *m* [ãbara]

embarrassment; trouble

embarrassé, e [ãbarase]

embarrassed

énerver (s') [senɛrve]
Ça ne vaut pas la peine de s'énerver.
Ne t'énerve pas!

get nervous; be exasperated
It's not worth getting upset about.
Don't get excited!

l'**ennui** *m* [ãnɥi]	boredom; worry, trouble
ennuyer (s') [sãnɥije]	be bored
l'**épreuve** *f* [eprœv]	test; ordeal
être à plaindre [ɛtraplɛ̃dr]	be deplorable
fâcher (se) [səfaʃe]	get angry
Corinne s'est fâchée avec son ami.	Corinne got angry at her friend.
faire de la peine à qqn [fɛrdəlapɛnakɛlkɛ̃]	pain s.o.
faire des scènes [fɛrdesɛn]	create scenes, have tantrums
faire pitié à qqn [fɛrpitjeakɛlkɛ̃]	feel sorry, pity
faire une gaffe [fɛryngaf]	drop a brick, make a blunder
Jean a fait une gaffe et maintenant il a honte.	Jean made an awful blunder, and now he's ashamed.
furieux, -euse [fyrjø, z]	furious
inquiet, -iète [ɛ̃kjɛ, t]	anxious, worried, uneasy
jaloux, -ouse [ʒalu, z]	jealous
Je suis jaloux de Paul.	I'm jealous of Paul.
le **malheur** [malœr]	misfortune; bad luck
malheureux, -euse [malœrø, z]	unfortunate
mécontent, e [mekɔ̃tã, t]	dissatisfied, displeased
Je suis mécontent de ton travail à l'école.	I'm dissatisfied with your performance in school.
pauvre [povr]	poor
la **peur** [pœr]	fear
seul, e [sœl]	alone
le **souci** [susi]	care
triste [trist]	sad

bouleversé, e [bulvɛrse]	upset, distressed
le **désespoir** [dezɛspwar]	despair
l'**excès** *m* [ɛksɛ]	excess
la **faiblesse** [fɛblɛs]	weakness
imprudent, e [ɛ̃prydã, t]	imprudent
l'**inquiétude** *f* [ɛ̃kjetyd]	uneasiness, worry

la **jalousie** [ʒaluzi]	jealousy
maladroit, e [maladrwa, t]	clumsy, awkward
la **misère** [mizɛr]	misery, poverty
la **pauvreté** [povrəte]	poverty
le **regret** [rəgrɛ]	regret
Je te quitte sans regret.	I'm leaving you without regret.
la **solitude** [sɔlityd]	solitude, loneliness
Beaucoup de vieux vivent dans la solitude.	Many old people lead solitary lives.
la **terreur** [tɛrœr]	terror
tromper [trɔ̃pe]	deceive, cheat
Robert a trompé sa femme.	Robert was unfaithful to his wife.

General Circumstances of Life

la **conscience** [kɔ̃sjɑ̃s]	conscience; consciousness
J'ai bonne conscience.	I have a clear conscience.
courir un risque [kurirœ̃risk]	run a risk
l'**expérience** f [ɛksperjɑ̃s]	experience
l'**expression** f [ɛksprɛsjɔ̃]	expression
familier, -ère [familje, ɛr]	familiar
garder [garde]	guard; keep; maintain
Paul a gardé son sang froid.	Paul maintained his self-control.
Qui garde les enfants?	Who is baby-sitting the children?
l'**habitude** f [abityd]	habit, custom, use
J'ai l'habitude de faire la sieste.	It's my habit to take an afternoon nap.
D'habitude, c'est moi qui fait la vaisselle.	Usually I'm the one who does the dishes.
habituel, le [abitɥɛl]	habitual, customary, usual
jeune [ʒœn]	young
la **jeunesse** [ʒœnɛs]	youth
l'**obligation** f [ɔbligasjɔ̃]	obligation
l'**occasion** f [ɔkazjɔ̃]	occasion

s'occuper de [sɔkypedə]
Je m'occupe des enfants.

look after, see to, be busy with
I'm busy with the children.

prendre des risques
[prɑ̃drəderisk]

take risks, take the risk

privé, e [prive]
C'est ma vie privée, ça ne te
regarde pas.

private
That's my private life; it doesn't
concern you.

le **rêve** [rɛv]

dream

le **vieillard** [vjɛjar]

old man

la **vieillesse** [vjɛjɛs]

old age

vieillir [vjɛjir]

age, grow old

---

l'**adolescent, e** [adɔlɛsɑ̃, t]

adolescent

l'**attitude** *f* [atityd]

attitude

avoir des rapports
[avwarderapɔr]

have connections

la **carrière** [karjɛr]

career

le **comportement** [kɔ̃pɔrtəmɑ̃]

deportment, behavior

le **moral** [mɔral]
Je n'ai pas le moral.

moral, spirit, mental faculties
I'm disheartened.

particulier, -ère
[partikylje, ɛr]

particular; special; private

la **prise de conscience**
[prizdəkɔ̃sjɑ̃s]

awakening, awareness

propre [prɔpr]
Je n'aurais pas attendu ça de mes
propres enfants.

own
I wouldn't have expected that from
my own children.

le **rapport** [rapɔr]

connection

le **troisième âge** [trwazjɛmɑʒ]
Les gens du troisième âge sont de
plus en plus nombreux.

senior years
There are more and more senior
citizens.

General Terms

aller voir [alevwar]	visit, go see
attendre [atãdr]	wait
chercher [ʃɛrʃe]	look for, seek
choisir [ʃwazir]	choose
le **choix** [ʃwa]	choice
concerner [kɔsɛrne]	concern
Ça nous concerne.	That concerns us.
diriger [diriʒe]	direct; control; conduct
emmener [ãmǝne]	take away, lead away
inviter [ɛvite]	invite
montrer [mɔtre]	show
placer [plase]	place; seat
On était mal placés.	We had bad seats.
présenter [prezãte]	present; introduce
ramener [ramne]	bring back; take home
Tu me ramènes?	Are you taking me home?
recevoir [rǝsvwar]	receive
On a été bien reçus.	We were well received.
la **rencontre** [rãkɔtr]	encounter, meeting
rencontrer [rãkɔtre]	meet, encounter
le **rendez-vous** [rãdevu]	appointment; rendezvous
rendre qqc à qqn [rãdrkɛlkǝʃozakɛlkɛ̃]	return s.th. to s.o.
retenir [rǝtnir]	retain, hold back; detain
Je ne vous retiens pas plus longtemps.	I won't keep you any longer.
retrouver [rǝtruve]	find again, recover
sauver [sove]	save
supporter [sypɔrte]	support; endure; tolerate
la **surprise** [syrpriz]	surprise
tirer [tire]	pull
trouver [truve]	find; think; like
Comment tu trouves le nouveau prof?	How do you like the new teacher?

intéresser [ɛ̃terese]	interest
rattraper [ratrape]	catch again; overtake
rechercher [rəʃɛrʃe]	seek; investigate
réclamer [reklame]	demand; claim
réveiller [reveje]	awake, wake, wake up
revoir [rəvwar]	see again; meet again; review
le **sacrifice** [sakrifis]	sacrifice
surprendre [syrprɑ̃dr]	surprise
traiter [trete]	treat; call s.o. a name
On s'est fait traiter d'imbéciles.	They called us imbeciles.
Jean-Luc traite sa femme comme une bonne.	Jean-Luc treats his wife like a maid.

Positive Actions

aider [ede]	help
Il faut aider Marie Christine.	Marie Christine has to be helped.
aimer [eme]	love, like
cacher [kaʃe]	hide, conceal
calmer [kalme]	still, quiet, soothe
caresser [karese]	caress, stroke
couvrir [kuvrir]	cover
donner [dɔne]	give
donner un coup de main [dɔneɛ̃kudmɛ̃]	give a helping hand
embrasser [ɑ̃brase]	embrace; kiss
louer [lwe]	praise
protéger [prɔteʒe]	protect
serrer [sere]	press; clasp
Serre-moi dans les bras.	Put your arms around me.
serrer la main [serelamɛ̃]	shake hands
soutenir [sutnir]	support
tolérer [tɔlere]	tolerate, endure

adopter [adɔpte]	adopt; embrace
attirer [atire]	attract
Je me sens attiré par Nicole.	I feel attracted to Nicole.
délivrer [delivre]	deliver, set free; hand over
libérer [libere]	liberate
respecter [respɛkte]	respect

Negative Actions

battre [batr]	beat, thrash
le **coup** [ku]	blow, stroke, hit
Un coup de poing.	A blow with the fist.
Un coup de pied.	A kick.
enfermer [ɑ̃fɛrme]	shut in; enclose
faire du mal à qqn [fɛrdymalakɛlkɛ̃]	hurt s.o.
faire marcher [fɛrmarʃe]	take in, fool, take for a ride
Tu m'as fait marcher.	You took me for a ride.
frapper [frape]	strike, slap, hit
gêner [ʒene]	irk; annoy; trouble
la **gifle** [ʒifl]	slap in the face
imiter [imite]	imitate
lâcher [lɑʃe]	let go of
Lâche-moi.	Let go of me.
laisser [lese]	leave; let
mettre à la porte [mɛtralapɔrt]	turn out, eject
perdre de vue [pɛrdrədvy]	lose sight of
pousser [puse]	push
punir [pynir]	punish
quitter [kite]	leave
remplacer [rɑ̃plase]	replace
renvoyer [rɑ̃vwaje]	dismiss
J'ai été renvoyé.	I've been dismissed.
repousser [rəpuse]	push back, repel; repulse

salir [salir]   soil, dirty, stain

séparer [separe]   separate

tuer [tɥe]   kill

---

contraindre [kɔ̃trɛ̃dr]   constrain, compel; restrain
On m'a contraint à démissionner.   I was forced to resign.

la **contrainte** [kɔ̃trɛ̃t]   constraint, coercion; restraint

dominer [domine]   dominate, rule

humilier [ymilje]   humiliate, humble, abase

inquiéter [ɛ̃kjete]   worry, disturb; trouble

maltraiter [maltrete]   mistreat

négliger [negliʒe]   neglect

la **perte** [pɛrt]   loss

poursuivre [pursɥivr]   pursue

presser [prese]   press; crush; entreat

priver [prive]   deprive, bereave
Je vais te priver de dessert.   I'm not going to let you have
                                    dessert.

provoquer [prɔvɔke]   provoke

sacrifier [sakrifje]   sacrifice
Je t'ai sacrifié les meilleures années   I've sacrificed the best years of my
de ma vie.   life for you.

secouer [səkwe]   shake

tromper [trɔ̃pe]   cheat; betray

vexer [vɛkse]   vex, plague, annoy

La jeune fille a frappé le garçon
et il lui a donné un coup de pied.
*The girl hit the boy and he
kicked her.*

======== **Places of Work** ========

la **banque** [bãk]	bank
le **bureau, x** [byro]	office
Je travaille dans un bureau.	I work in an office.
les **chemins de fer** *mpl* [ʃmɛ̃dfɛr]	railroad
l'**école** *f* [ekɔl]	school
l'**hôpital, -aux** *m* [ɔpital, o]	hospital
l'**hôtel** *m* [ɔtɛl]	hotel
le **magasin** [magazɛ̃]	store, shop
la **poste** [pɔst]	post office
Je travaille à la poste.	I work at the post office.
le **restaurant** [rɛstɔrã]	restaurant
la **société** [sɔsjete]	company, firm; association
Je travaille pour une société commerciale.	I work for a commercial company.
l'**usine** *f* [yzin]	factory

l'**atelier** *m* [atəlje]	workshop, studio, atelier
le **chantier** [ʃãtje]	workshop, yard; site
l'**exploitation** *f* [ɛksplwatɑsjɔ̃]	undertaking; working, operation
Je travaille dans une exploitation agricole.	I work in an agricultural enterprise.
la **ferme** [fɛrm]	farm, farmhouse
la **grande surface** [grãdsyrfas]	shopping center
la **mine** [min]	mine
les **P.T.T.** *fpl* [petete]	French post office, telephone, and telegraph
la **S.N.C.F. (Société Nationale des Chemins de fer Français** [ɛsɛnseɛf]	French railroad

━━━━━━ **Fields of Work** ━━━━━━

le **bâtiment** [batimã]	building trade
Je travaille dans le bâtiment.	I work in the building trade.
le **commerce** [kɔmɛrs]	trade, commerce
l'**enseignement** m [ãsɛɲəmã]	teaching profession, education
l'**entreprise** f [ãtrəpriz]	enterprise; firm, business
l'**industrie** f [ɛ̃dystri]	industry
le **spectacle** [spɛktakl]	show business, entertainment industry

l'**administration** f [administrasjɔ̃]	administration
l'**agriculture** f [agrikyltyr]	agriculture
l'**hôtellerie** f [ɔtɛlri]	hotel trade
l'**informatique** f [ɛ̃fɔrmatik]	data processing, computer science
la **marine** [marin]	shipping; navy
les **services publics** mpl [sɛrvispyblik]	public service
le **textile** [tɛkstil]	textile industry
le **tourisme** [turism]	tourism, tourist industry
les **transports** mpl [trãspɔr]	transportation

━━━━━━ **In the Workplace** ━━━━━━

actif, -ive [aktif, iv]	active; engaged in work
l'**activité** f [aktivite]	activity
l'**affaire** f [afɛr]	business; transaction
le **chef** [ʃɛf]	boss
le **chômage** [ʃomaʒ]	unemployment
Je suis au chômage.	I'm unemployed.
le **concours** [kɔ̃kur]	competition

171

le **congé** [kɔ̃ʒe]	leave, vacation
Les congés payés existent depuis 50 ans.	Paid vacations have been in existence for 50 years.
Je suis en congé de maladie.	I'm on sick leave.
l'**emploi** *m* [ɑ̃plwa]	employment; occupation, situation
l'**employé, e** [ɑ̃plwaje]	employee
employer [ɑ̃plwaje]	employ
engager [ɑ̃gaʒe]	hire
être pris, e [ɛtrəpri, z]	be busy
Je suis pris toute l'après-midi.	I'm busy all afternoon.
être reçu, e [ɛtrərəsy]	have passed an exam
exporter [ɛkspɔrte]	export
la **fonction** [fɔ̃ksjɔ̃]	function, duty, employment, work
le, la **fonctionnaire** [fɔ̃ksjɔnɛr]	civil servant, official
gagner [gaɲe]	earn
gagner de l'argent [gaɲedlarʒɑ̃]	earn money
gagner sa vie [gaɲesavi]	earn one's living
l'**heure supplémentaire** *f* [œrsyplemɑ̃tɛr]	overtime
importer [ɛ̃pɔtə]	import
livrer [livre]	deliver
l'**ouvrier, -ère** [uvrije, ɛr]	workman, laborer
le **patron**, la **patronne** [patrɔ̃, ɔn]	boss, employer
le **personnel** [pɛrsɔnɛl]	personnel
le **poste** [pɔst]	place, employment, post
prendre [prɑ̃dr]	take
produire [prɔdɥir]	produce
le **produit** [prɔdɥi]	product
le **salaire** [salɛr]	salary
taper à la machine [tapealamaʃin]	type
le **travail, -aux** [travaj, o]	work
travailler [travaje]	work

le **travailleur immigré** [travajœrimigre] — immigrant worker

la **vente** [vãt] — sale

---

l'**apprentissage** *m* [aprãtisaʒ] — apprenticeship, training

le **boulot** [bulo] — work

le **cadre moyen** [kadrmwajɛ̃] — mid-level employee

le **cadre supérieur** [kadrəsyperjœr] — senior-level employee

le **chômeur**, la **chômeuse** [ʃomœr, øz] — unemployed person

le **contrat** [kɔ̃tra] — contract

le **curriculum vitae** [kyrikylɔmvitɛ] — resume of one's career

les **débouchés** *mpl* [debuʃe] — openings, prospects (for career or trade

Il n'y a pas de débouchés dans le bâtiment. — There are no openings in the building trade.

la **demande d'emploi** [dəmãddãplwa] — situation wanted

Il y a de plus en plus de demandes d'emploi. — There are more and more "job wanted" ads.

embaucher [ãboʃe] — hire, engage, sign on
On embauche. — Help wanted.; Now Hiring.

être au chômage [ɛtroʃomaʒ] — be unemployed

expérimenté, e [ɛksperimãte] — experienced

faire le pont [fɛrlpɔ̃] — take the intervening day(s) off
Vendredi, je ne viens pas, je fais le pont. — I'm not coming in on Friday, I'm taking an extended weekend.

le **jour de congé** [ʒurdəkɔ̃ʒe] — day of leave or vacation
Le lundi est mon jour de congé. — Monday is my day off.

la **main d'œuvre** [mɛ̃dœvr] — manpower, labor

la **qualification** [kalifikɑsjɔ̃] — qualification

qualifié, e [kalifje] — qualified

les **revenus** *mpl* [rəvny] — income, revenue

le **salarié**, la **salariée** [salarje] — wage-earner, salaried employee

le **siège social** [sjɛʒsɔsjal] — main office

le, la **spécialiste** [spesjalist]	specialist, expert
le **stage** [staʒ]	training course
le, la **stagiaire** [staʒjɛr]	trainee
le **travail manuel** [travajmanɥɛl]	manual labor

Labor Problems

l'**action** *f* [aksjɔ̃]	action, law-suit
assister [asiste]	help, assist
augmenter [ɔgmɑ̃te] Le taux de chômage a augmenté.	increase, rise The unemployment rate has risen.
automatique [ɔtɔmatik]	automatic
contester [kɔ̃tɛste] Les mesures du gouvernement sont très contestées.	dispute, contest; debate The government's measures are called into serious question.
la **difficulté** [difikylte]	difficulty
économique [ekɔnɔmik]	economic
économiser [ekɔnɔmize]	economize
être en rapport [ɛtrɑ̃rapɔr]	be in contact
être en réunion [ɛtrɑ̃reynjɔ̃] M. le directeur est en réunion.	be in a meeting The manager is in a meeting.
la **grève** [grɛv]	strike
licencier [lisɑ̃sje]	lay off
la **manifestation** [manifɛstasjɔ̃]	demonstration
mener [məne] Il faut mener une campagne contre les licenciements.	lead, conduct We have to conduct a campaign against lay-offs.
l'**organisation** *f* [ɔrganizasjɔ̃]	organization
responsable [rɛspɔ̃sabl] Je suis responsable de tout.	responsible I'm responsible for everything.
la **réunion** [reynjɔ̃]	meeting
la **revendication** [rəvɑ̃dikasjɔ̃]	demand, claim
social, e, -aux [sɔsjal, o]	social

le **syndicat** [sɛ̃dika]	trade union
le **tarif** [tarif]	tariff, rate, scale of prices

l'**accroissement** *m* [akrwasmã]	growth, increase
le **clochard**, la **clocharde** [klɔʃar, d]	beggar, tramp
la **démarche** [demarʃ] Il faut faire des démarches auprès du préfet.	step, move, action We have to take steps with the chief administrator.
l'**expansion** *f* [ɛkspãsjɔ̃]	expansion
la **faillite** [fajit] Cette banque privée a fait faillite.	bankruptcy, insolvency; failure This private bank has failed.
le **licenciement** [lisãsimã]	laying off
lutter [lyte]	struggle
le **niveau de vie** [nivodvi]	standard of living
le **pouvoir d'achat** [puwardaʃa]	purchasing power
les **ressources** *fpl* [rəsurs]	resources
revendiquer [rəvãdike]	claim; lay claim to
le **S.M.I.C.** [smik]	legal minimum wage
syndical, e, -aux [sɛ̃dikal, o]	pertaining to a trade union
le **taux de chômage** [todʃomaʒ] En 1986, le taux de chômage était de 11,25%.	unemployment rate In 1986 the unemployment rate was 11.25 percent.

Il est commun de voir des grèves en France.
Strikes are common in France.

175

Drivers and Vehicles

l'**assurance** *f* [asyrãs]	insurance
assurer [asyre]	insure
l'**autobus** *m* [ɔtɔbys]	bus
l'**avion** *m* [avjɔ̃]	airplane
Je suis allé en avion à Munich.	I flew to Munich.
le **bateau, x** [bato]	boat, ship
le **bus** [bys]	bus
Pour aller à la gare, il faut prendre le bus.	To go to the train station, you have to take the bus.
le **camion** [kamjɔ̃]	truck
le **car** [kar]	sightseeing bus, interurban bus
le **chauffeur** [ʃofœr]	driver, chauffeur
conduire [kɔ̃dɥir]	drive
Tu me laisses conduire la voiture?	Will you let me drive the car?
lent, e [lã, t]	slow
la **machine** [maʃin]	machine, engine
la **moto** [mɔto]	motorcycle
le **moyen de transport** [mwajɛ̃dətrãspɔr]	means of transportation
neuf, neuve [nœf, nœv]	new
Mais tu as une voiture toute neuve.	You have a brand-new car.
nouveau, -vel, -velle, x [nuvo, nuvɛl]	new
Voilà ma nouvelle voiture, elle n'a que 10.000 km.	That's my new car; it has only 10,000 km on it.
le **permis** [pɛrmi]	driver's license
rapide [rapid]	fast, rapid
le **taxi** [taksi]	taxi
le **train** [trɛ̃]	train
le **vélo** [velo]	bicycle
Je vais au travail en vélo.	I ride my bike to work.

la **voiture** [vwatyr]	car; railroad car
la **voiture d'occasion** [vwatyrdɔkazjɔ̃]	used car

l'**auto** *f* [ɔto]	auto, car
l'**automobiliste** *mf* [ɔtɔmɔbilist]	driver
la **bicyclette** [bisiklɛt]	bicycle
le **break** [brɛk]	station wagon
la **camionnette** [kamjɔnɛt]	van
la **caravane** [karavan]	camping trailer, house trailer
la **carte grise** [kartəgriz]	automobile registration
la **décapotable** [dekapɔtabl]	convertible
l'**hélicoptère** *m* [ɛlikɔptɛr]	helicopter
la **mobylette** [mɔbilɛt]	motor-assisted bicycle
le **T.G.V.** [teʒeve] Le T.G.V. roule à 270 km à l'heure.	high-speed train The T.G.V. travels 270 kilometers per hour.
le **tram** [tram]	streetcar
le **véhicule** [veikyl]	vehicle
le **vélomoteur** [velɔmɔtœr]	motorbike
le **wagon** [wagɔ̃]	railroad car; freight car
le **wagon-lit** [wagɔ̃li]	sleeping car
le **wagon-restaurant** [wagɔ̃rəstɔrɑ̃]	dining car

Traffic Routes and Signs

l'**agent** *m* [aʒɑ̃]	policeman
l'**autoroute** *f* [ɔtɔrut]	superhighway
le **carrefour** [karfur]	crossroads
le **chemin** [ʃmɛ̃]	way; road
le **code de la route** [kɔddəlarut]	traffic regulations
le **danger** [dɑ̃ʒe] Danger de mort	danger Grave danger

177

dangereux, -euse [dãʒrø, z] — dangerous

le **feu, x** [fø] — traffic light
Tournez au feu à droite. — Turn right at the traffic light.

limiter [limite] — limit, restrict

la **nationale** [nasjɔnal] — national highway

obligatoire [ɔbligatwar] — compulsory, obligatory
Sens obligatoire — Right way (traffic sign)

le **panneau, x** [pano] — sign

le **parking** [parkiŋ] — parking lot; parking garage

le **passage** [pɑsaʒ] — passage; crossing
Passage à niveau — Grade crossing
Passage interdit — Do not enter; No thoroughfare

la **priorité** [prijɔrite] — right-of-way
Vous n'avez pas la priorité — Yield right-of-way
Priorité à droite — Yield to right-hand traffic

le **règlement** [rɛgləmã] — rule, regulation

la **route** [rut] — road; route, itinerary
La route de Strasbourg passe par Saverne. — The road to Strassburg goes through Saverne.

la **rue** [ry] — street
J'habite rue de Strasbourg. — I live on Strassburg Street.

sens interdit [sãsɛ̃tɛrdi] — no entry

sens unique [sãsynik] — one-way street

la **sortie** [sɔrti] — exit, way out

le **stationnement** [stasjɔnmã] — parking
Stationnement réglementé — Alternating parking system

le **verglas** [vɛrgla] — ice, glazed frost
Verglas fréquent — Road ices over

le **virage** [viraʒ] — curve

le **chantier** [ʃãtje] — construction site

chaussée déformée [ʃosedefɔrme] — damaged road surface

la **déviation** [devjasjɔ̃] — detour

les **gravillons** *mpl* [gravijɔ̃] — fine gravel

la **limitation de vitesse** [limitɑsjɔ̃dvitɛs]	speed limit
le **parcomètre** [parkɔmɛtr]	parking meter
le **péage** [peaʒ]	toll road
sans issue [sɑ̃zisy]	dead end, no outlet
le **sentier** [sɑ̃tje]	path
stationnement interdit [stasjɔnmɑ̃ɛ̃tɛrdi]	no parking
la **voie rapide** [vwarapid]	expressway, speedway
la **zone bleue** [zonblø]	short-term parking zone

▬▬ In the Workshop and at the Gas Station ▬▬

arrêter le moteur [aretelmotœr]	turn off the motor, stop the motor
la **ceinture** [sɛ̃tyr]	belt
la **clé** [kle]	key
l'**essence** *f* [esɑ̃s]	gasoline
faire le plein [fɛrləplɛ̃]	fill it up
le **feu, x** [fø] Mon feu arrière ne marche pas.	light My rear light doesn't work.
le **frein** [frɛ̃]	brake
le **garage** [garaʒ]	garage
gonfler [gɔ̃fle]	pump up
l'**huile** *f* [ɥil] Vérifiez l'huile s.v.p.	oil Please check the oil.
la **marche arrière** [marʃarjɛr]	reverse gear
la **marche avant** [marʃavɑ̃]	forward gear
le **moteur** [mɔtœr]	motor
l'**ordinaire** *m* [ɔrdinɛr]	regular gasoline
la **panne** [pan] Je suis tombé en panne.	breakdown, trouble I had car trouble.
le **pneu** [pnø] J'ai changé de marque de pneus.	tire I've changed tire brands.
la **roue** [ru]	wheel

la **roue de secours** [rudsəkur]	spare wheel (with tire)
sans plomb [sãplɔ̃]	lead-free
la **station-service** [stasjɔ̃sɛrvis]	service station
le **super** [sypɛr]	super, extra (grade of gasoline)
vérifier [verifje]	check (out)
la **vitesse** [vitɛs]	speed; gear
Le nouveau modèle a cinq vitesses.	The new model has five speeds.
le **volant** [vɔlã]	steering wheel

la **banquette arrière** [bãkɛtariɛr]	back seat
la **boîte de vitesses** [bwatdəvitɛs]	transmission
la **bougie** [buʒi]	cylinder
le **capot** [kapo]	hood (of automobile)
le **carburateur** [karbyratœr]	carburetor
le **clignotant** [kliɲɔtã]	blinker
consommer [kɔ̃sɔme]	use, consume
le **démarreur** [demarœr]	starter
l'**essuie-glace** *m* [esɥiglas]	windshield-wiper
J'ai crevé. [ʒekrəve]	I have a flat.
le **lave-glace** [lavglas]	windshield washer
le **niveau d'huile** [nivodɥil]	oil level
le **pare-brise** [parbriz]	windshield
le **pare-chocs** [parʃɔk]	bumper
le **phare** [far]	headlight
le **pot d'échappement** [podeʃapmã]	muffler
la **précaution** [prekosjɔ̃]	precaution
le **radiateur** [radjatœr]	radiator
la **vidange** [vidãʒ]	oil change
Faites la vidange s.v.p.	Change the oil, please.

180

In Traffic

l'**accident** *m* [aksidā]	accident
arrêter (s') [sarete]	stop
attacher [ataʃe] Attachez vos ceintures.	fasten Fasten your seatbelts!
bloquer [blɔke] La route est complètement bloquée.	block The road is completely blocked.
le **bouchon** [buʃɔ̃] Sur la RN7, il y a un bouchon de 10 km.	traffic jam On the RN7 there's a traffic jam 10 km long.
la **circulation** [sirkylɑsjɔ̃]	traffic
circuler [sirkyle] Dans Paris, je circule prudemment.	drive In Paris I drive cautiously.
le **commissariat** [kɔmisarja]	police station
le **contrôle** [kɔ̃trol]	check, inspection
courir un risque [kurirɛ̃risk]	run a risk
démarrer [demare] Démarre.	start Start it up!
dépasser [depɑse]	pass, overtake
le **détour** [detur]	detour
doubler [duble]	pass
éclairer [eklere] Mes phares éclairent mal.	light, illuminate My headlights aren't bright enough.
l'**embouteillage** *m* [ābutɛjaʒ]	traffic jam, bottleneck
l'**énergie** *f* [enɛrʒi]	energy
être au volant [ɛtrovɔlā] Arrête! C'est moi qui suis au volant.	be at the wheel, steer Stop! I'm the one who's driving!
faire un détour [fɛrɛ̃detur]	make a detour
freiner [frene]	apply the brakes
garer [gare] Il vaut mieux garer la voiture dans un parking.	park It's better to park the car in a parking garage.
mettre en marche [mɛtrāmarʃ]	put in gear
passer [pɑse]	go past, drive past

le **plan** [plã]	city map
la **police** [pɔlis]	police
le **poste (de police)** [pɔst dəpɔlis]	police station; lock-up
prendre des risques [prãdrəderisk]	take risks
Tu prends trop de risques au volant.	You take too many risks at the wheel.
prendre le volant [prãdrəlvɔlã]	take the wheel
ralentir [ralãtir]	slow down
rouler [rule]	drive
Ma voiture roule à 160 km à l'heure.	My car does 160 kilometers per hour.
la **sécurité** [sekyrite]	safety
tenir la route [tənirlarut]	hold the road well, hug the road
tourner [turne]	turn
tourner à droite [turneadrwat]	turn right
tourner à gauche [turneagoʃ]	turn left
tout droit [tudrwa]	straight ahead
Continuez tout droit.	Keep on straight ahead.
le **transport** [trãspɔr]	transport, transportation
transporter [trãspɔrte]	transport
traverser [travɛrse]	cross
le **trou** [tru]	hole
la **victime** [viktim]	victim
Il y a trop de victimes de la circulation.	There are too many traffic victims.

accélérer [akselere]	accelerate
l'**amende** *f* [amãd]	fine
l'**avertissement** *m* [avɛrtismã]	warning
la **contravention** [kõtravãsjõ]	(traffic) ticket
donner un coup de frein [dɔneẽkudfrẽ]	hit the brakes
écraser [ekraze]	run over
Chaque matin, je vois un chat écrasé sur la route.	Every morning I see a cat that's been run over on the road.

182

l'**encombrement** *m* [ãkõbrəmã]	traffic jam, congestion
l'**excès de vitesse** *m* [ɛksɛdvitɛs]	exceeding the speed limit
J'ai eu une amende pour excès de vitesse.	I got a fine for exceeding the speed limit.
faire demi-tour [fɛrdəmitur]	make a U-turn, turn back
Faire demi-tour est dangereux.	Making a U-turn is dangerous.
le **procès verbal** [prɔsɛvɛrbal]	ticket
Alors l'agent m'a collé un P.V.	Then the policeman gave me a ticket.
rater le virage [ratelviraʒ]	fail to make the curve
serrer à droite [sereadrwat]	drive on the right
Véhicules lents, serrez à droite.	Slow vehicles, keep to the right.
stationner [stasjɔne]	park
tenir sa droite [tənirsadrwat]	drive on the right

Nonmotorized Road Users

l'**arrêt d'autobus** *m* [arɛdɔtɔbys]	bus stop
attendre [atãdr]	wait
le **carnet** [karnɛ]	book of tickets
changer [ʃãʒe]	transfer, change
Il faut changer à Châtelet.	You have to transfer at Châtelet.
descendre [desãdr]	get off, get out
Tous les voyageurs descendent du train.	All passengers get off the train here.
la **direction** [dirɛksjõ]	direction
Direction Mairie d'Issy	To Mairie d'Issy
la **gare** [gar]	train station
les **gens** *mpl* [ʒã]	people
la **ligne** [li]	line
le **métro** [metro]	metro, subway
monter [mõte]	get in, get on
Je suis monté dans le bus.	I got on the bus.
le **passager,** la **passagère** [pasaʒe, ɛr]	passenger

183

le **passant,** la **passante** [pɑsã, t]	passer-by
le **piéton** [pjetɔ̃]	pedestrian
presser (se) [səprese]	hurry
le **quai** [ke]	platform
rater [rate] J'ai raté le bus.	miss I've missed the bus.
la **station de métro** [stasjɔ̃dmetro]	subway station
le **ticket** [tikɛ]	ticket
le **trajet** [traʒɛ] Chaque matin j'ai une heure de trajet pour aller au travail.	distance, trip, passage Every morning I have an hour-long trip to get to work.
valable [valabl] En dehors de cette limite, les tickets ne sont plus valables.	valid Beyond this point tickets are no longer valid.
accès interdit *m* [aksɛɛ̃tɛrdi]	no entry, no access
composter [kɔ̃pɔste]	stamp (a ticket)
la **correspondance** [kɔrɛspɔ̃dɑ̃s]	connecting train
le **R.E.R.** [ɛrəɛr]	suburban (commuter) train
le **terminus** [tɛrminys]	terminal, end of the line
les **transports en commun** [trɑ̃spɔrɑ̃kɔmɛ̃]	public means of transportation

Les stations de métro à Paris sont plus propres que celles à New York.
The subway stations in Paris are cleaner than in New York.

■■■■■ **Post Office, Telephone, and Telegraph** ■■■■■

l'**adresse** *f* [adrɛs]
C'est à quelle adresse?

address
To what address is it going?

la **boîte aux lettres** [bwatolɛtr]

mailbox

la **cabine (téléphonique)**
[kabin telefɔnik]
Les nouvelles cabines fonctionnent
toutes par carte.

telephone booth

The new phone booths all are
card-operated.

le **cachet** [kaʃɛ]

postmark

la **carte postale** [kartpɔstal]

postcard

le **courrier** [kurje]
J'ai reçu un tas de courrier ce
matin.

mail
This morning I got a pile of mail.

écrire [ekrir]

write

l'**enveloppe** *f* [ãvlɔp]

envelope

envoyer [ãvwaje]

send

le **facteur**, la **factrice**
[faktœr, tris]

mailman, mail carrier

faire part [fɛrpar]
Claudine nous fait part de son
mariage.

announce
Claudine is announcing her
wedding to us.

le **guichet** [giʃɛ]
Adressez-vous au guichet trois.

window; counter
Go over to Window 3.

la **lettre** [lɛtr]

letter

Ne quittez pas. [nəkitepa]

Hold the line.

le **paquet** [pakɛ]

package, parcel

la **poste** [pɔst]
Le bureau de poste est fermé à six
heures.

post office
The post office closes at 6 P.M.

le **tarif** [tarif]

rate; list of rates

le **téléphone** [telefɔn]
J'ai reçu un coup de téléphone
de Paul.

telephone
I received a telephone call
from Paul.

185

téléphoner [telefɔne]	telephone
J'ai téléphoné à ta mère.	I phoned your mother.
le **timbre** [tɛ̃mbr]	stamp
On peut acheter des timbres au bureau de tabac.	Stamps can be purchased in a tobacco shop.
urgent, e [yrʒa, t]	urgent; rush
les **vœux** *mpl* [vø]	wishes
Meilleurs vœux	Best wishes!

la **boîte postale** [bwatpɔstal]	post-office box
le **colis** [kɔli]	package, parcel
le **compte chèque postal** [kɔ̃tʃɛkpɔstal]	postal checking account
l'**expéditeur** *m* [ɛkspeditœr]	sender
la **lettre expresse** [lɛtrɛksprɛs]	special-delivery (express) letter
le **mandat** [mãda]	transfer
poste restante [pɔstrɛstãt]	General Delivery
recommandé, e [rəkɔmãde]	registered
le **télégramme** [telegram]	telegram
télégraphier [telegrafje]	telegraph

Money Matters

l'**addition** *f* [adisjɔ̃]	check (for a meal)
L'addition s.v.p.	The check, please.
l'**argent** *m* [arʒã]	money
avoir de la monnaie [avwardlamonɛ]	have small change
Vous avez de la monnaie?	Do you have any small change?
la **banque** [bãk]	bank
le **billet** [bijɛ]	bill (currency)
Un billet de cent francs.	A 100 franc bill.
la **caisse** [kɛs]	cash register; cashier
Passez à la caisse.	Please go to the cash register.
le **centime** [sãtim]	smallest French coin

changer [ʃãʒe]   change
Je voudrais changer des marks en   I'd like to change marks to francs.
francs.

le **chèque** [ʃɛk]   check

le **compte** [kɔ̃t]   account
Vous avez un compte en banque?   Do you have a bank account?

compter [kɔ̃te]   count

coûter [kute]   cost
Ça coûte combien?   How much does it cost?

le **crédit** [kredi]   credit

dépenser [depãse]   spend

la **dette** [dɛt]   debt
Je n'aime pas faire des dettes.   I don't like incurring debts.

devoir [dəvwar]   owe
Combien je vous dois?   How much do I owe you?

emprunter [ãprɛ̃te]   borrow

faire des économies   save, economize
[fɛrdezekɔnɔmi]

la **fortune** [fɔrtyn]   fortune
J.R. a fait fortune dans le pétrole.   J.R. made a fortune in the oil
                                            business.

les **frais** *mpl* [frɛ]   expenses
Les frais de voyage.   Travel expenses.
On partage les frais?   Shall we share the expenses?

le **franc** [frã]   franc

gratuit, e [gratɥi, t]   free, gratis

la **monnaie** [mɔnɛ]   (small) change; money
L'ECU est la monnaie européenne.   The ECU is the European
                                            Currency Unit.

payer [peje]   pay

payer comptant [pejekɔ̃tã]   pay cash
Vous payez comptant?   You're paying cash?

la **pièce de monnaie**   coin
[pjɛsdəmɔnɛ]

le **portefeuille** [pɔrtəfœj]   wallet, billfold

le **porte-monnaie** [pɔrtmɔnɛ]   change purse, coin purse

prêter [prete]   lend
Tu me prêtes dix mille balles?   Will you lend me 10,000 francs?

187

le **prix** [pri]	price
rembourser [rãburse]	reimburse
la **somme** [sɔm]	sum
valable [valabl]	valid
la **valeur** [valœr]	value

la **carte de crédit** [kartdəkredi]	credit card
Vous acceptez les cartes de crédit?	Do you accept credit cards?
le **change** [ʃãʒ]	exchange
le **chèque de voyage** [ʃɛkdəvwajaʒ]	traveler's check
le **chéquier** [ʃekje]	checkbook
coûteux, -euse [kutø, z]	costly, expensive
les **devises** *fpl* [dəviz]	currencies; foreign currency
l'**eurochèque** *m* [ørɔʃɛk]	Eurocheque
Il y a des maisons qui n'acceptent pas les eurochèques.	There are firms that do not accept Eurocheques.
le **livret d'épargne** [livrɛdepar]	savings book
les **recettes** *fpl* [rəsɛt]	revenue
le **sou** [su]	sou; penny, farthing
Je n'ai pas de sous.	I haven't got a cent.
le **taux d'intérêt** [todɛ̃terɛ]	interest rate
la **tirelire** [tirlir]	piggy bank

The World of
Human Beings

Constitution

l'**Assemblée nationale** *f* [asãblenasjɔnal]	National Assembly
L'Assemblée nationale et le Sénat constituent le Parlement.	The National Assembly and the Senate constitute the Parliament.
central, e, -aux [sãtral, o]	central
le **conseil** [kɔsɛj]	advice; council, board
la **constitution** [kɔstitysjɔ̃]	constitution
la **déclaration** [deklarasjɔ̃]	declaration
démocratique [demokratik]	democratic
l'**élection** *f* [elɛksjɔ̃]	election
élire [elir]	elect
Le Président est élu au suffrage universel direct.	The President is elected by direct popular vote.
le **gouvernement** [guvɛrnmã]	government
l'**individu** *m* [ɛ̃dividy]	individual
légal, e, -aux [legal, o]	legal
la **liberté** [libɛrte]	liberty, freedom
la **loi** [lwa]	law
le **membre** [mãbr]	member
le **ministre** [ministr]	minister
Le ministre de l'Intérieur.	The secretary of the interior.
Le ministre des Finances.	The secretary of finance.
Le ministre de la Défense Nationale.	The secretary of defense.
Le ministre de la Santé Publique.	The secretary of public health.
Le ministre de l'Education Nationale.	The secretary of education.
la **nationalité** [nasjɔnalite]	nationality
le **Premier ministre** [prəmjeministr]	prime minister
le **président,** la **présidente** [prezidã, t]	president

la **république** [repyblik] republic

la **séance** [seãs] sitting, session
La séance publique. The public session.
La séance est ouverte. The session is open.

la **société** [sɔsjete] society

le **système** [sistɛm] system

la **voix** [vwa] voice

le **vote** [vɔt] vote
Les Françaises ont le droit de vote French women have had the right
depuis 1944. to vote since 1944.

voter [vɔte] vote

voter une loi [vɔteynlwa] pass a law

l'**autorité** f [ɔtɔrite] authority

le **chef d'Etat** [ʃɛfdeta] head of state, chief of state
Le chef d'Etat, c'est le Président. The head of state is the president.

le **citoyen**, la **citoyenne** citizen
[sitwajɛ̃, ɛn]

dissoudre [disudr] dissolve
Le Président peut dissoudre The president can dissolve the
l'Assemblée. National Assembly.

le **drapeau, x** [drapo] flag

l'**égalité** f [egalite] equality

les **élections législatives** fpl parliamentary elections
[elɛksjɔ̃leʒislativ]

l'**élection présidentielle** f presidential election
[elɛksjɔ̃prezidãsjɛl]

l'**indépendance** f [ɛ̃depãdãs] independence

la **législative** [leʒislativ] legislative

nommer [nɔme] name
M. Gross a été nommé ambassadeur Mr. Gross was named ambassador
à Paris. to Paris.

le **parlement** [parləmã] parliament

parlementaire [parləmãtɛr] parliamentary

le **pouvoir exécutif** executive power
[puvwarɛksekytif]

le **pouvoir judiciaire** [puvwarʒydisjɛr]	judiciary power
le **pouvoir législatif** [puvwarleʒislatif]	legislative power
proclamer [prɔklame] Charles de Gaulle a proclamé la Cinquième République.	proclaim Charles de Gaulle proclaimed the Fifth Republic.
ratifier [ratifje]	ratify
le **Sénat** [sena]	Senate
le **sénateur** [senatœr]	senator
le **siège** [sjɛʒ] Le Parti Communiste a obtenu 35 sièges.	seat The Communist Party obtained 35 seats.
le **suffrage universel** [syfraʒynivɛrsɛl] Le Président est élu au suffrage universel direct.	popular vote The president is elected by direct popular vote.

Le Parlement Français en session. *The French Parliament in session.*

Public Administration

la **capitale** [kapital]	capital
le **département** [departəmã]	department
l'**Etat** *m* [eta]	state
la **mairie** [meri]	town hall, city hall
officiel, le [ɔfisjɛl]	official
l'**organisation** *f* [ɔrganizɑsjɔ̃]	organization
le **pays** [pei]	country
le **règlement** [rɛgləmã]	regulation, rule

administratif, -ive [administratif, iv]	administrative
l'**administration** *f* [administrasjɔ̃]	administration
l'**arrondissement** *m* [arõdismã]	district
la **bureaucratie** [byrokrasi]	bureaucracy
bureaucratique [byrokratik]	bureaucratic
la **centralisation** [sãtralisɑsjɔ̃] La centralisation a diminuée depuis 1982.	centralization Since 1982 centralization has decreased.
la **collectivité** [kɔlɛktivite]	collectivity, community
communal, e, -aux [kɔmynal, o]	communal
la **commune** [kɔmyn]	commune (parish, township)
le **conseil municipal** [kõsɛjmynisipal]	town council
le **conseil régional** [kõsɛjreʒjɔnal]	regional council
la **décentralisation** [desãtralizɑsjɔ̃]	decentralization
décentraliser [desãtralize]	decentralize

les **D.O.M.-T.O.M.** *mpl* [dɔmtɔm]	overseas regions of France
La Nouvelle Calédonie est un territoire d'outre-mer.	New Caledonia is an overseas territory.
La Martinique est un département d'outre-mer.	Martinique is an overseas department.
l'**institution** *f* [ɛstitysjɔ̃]	institution
la **métropole** [metrɔpɔl]	metropolis; mother country
La France métropole	France (excluding Corsica and overseas regions)
le **ministère** [ministɛr]	ministry
municipal, e, -aux [mynisipal, o]	municipal, town, city
la **préfecture** [prefɛktyr]	prefecture
le **préfet** [prefɛ]	prefect; chief administrator of a department
Le préfet est nommé par le ministre de l'Intérieur.	The prefect is named by the secretary of the interior.
régional, e, -aux [reʒjɔnal, o]	regional
la **régionalisation** [reʒjɔnalɑsjɔ̃]	regionalization

━━━ Political Life ━━━

la **bourgeoisie** [burʒwazi]	middle class
La bourgeoisie est au pouvoir depuis la Révolution.	The middle class has been in power since the Revolution.
le **candidat**, la **candidate** [kãdida, t]	candidate
le **changement** [ʃãʒmã]	change; shift
le, la **communiste** [kɔmynist]	Communist
diriger [diriʒe]	direct
la **droite** [drwat]	the right
efficace [efikas]	effective, successful
être de droite [ɛtrədədrwat]	be on the political right
Le Figaro est de droite.	Le Figaro is on the political right.
être de gauche [ɛtrədgoʃ]	be on the political left
fonctionner [fɔksjɔne]	function

la **gauche** [goʃ]	the left
les **gens** *mpl* [ʒã]	people
le **groupe** [grup]	group
Le Front National est un groupe politique minoritaire.	The National Front is a political minority group.
l'**homme d'Etat** *m* [ɔmdeta]	statesman
indépendant, e [ɛ̃depãdã, t]	independent
industriel, le [ɛ̃dystrijɛl]	industrial
La France est un pays industriel.	France is an industrial nation.
l'**initiative** *f* [inisjativ]	initiative
la **majorité** [maʒɔrite]	majority
Au sein de la majorité.	Within the majority parliamentary groups.
la **minorité** [minɔrite]	minority
L'Assemblée a mis le gouvernement en minorité.	The National Assembly outvoted the government.
national, e, -aux [nasjɔnal, o]	national
l'**opposition** *f* [ɔpozisjɔ̃]	opposition
le **parti** [parti]	party
politique [pɔlitik]	political
le **programme** [prɔgram]	program
le **résultat** [rezylta]	result
la **réunion** [reynjɔ̃]	meeting
la **revendication** [rəvãdikɑsjo]	demand, claim
le, la **secrétaire** [səkretɛr]	secretary
Le secrétaire d'Etat.	The secretary of state.
le, la **socialiste** [sɔsjalist]	socialist
la **solution** [sɔlysjɔ̃]	solution
le **sujet** [syʒɛ]	subject
le **syndicat** [sɛ̃dika]	trade union
Les négociations avec les syndicats n'ont pas encore abouti.	The negotiations with the trade unions are not yet ended.
la **victoire** [viktwar]	victory

195

adhérer [adere]   join
J'ai adhéré au parti socialiste.   I've joined the Socialist Party.

adopter [adɔpte]   adopt; pass, carry (a bill)
L'Assemblée nationale a adopté   The National Assembly has passed
une loi importante.   an important law.

l'**adversaire** *mf* [advɛrsɛr]   adversary

analyser [analize]   analyze

assumer la responsabilité   assume the responsibility
[asymelarɛspɔ̃sabilite]

l'**autonomie** *f* [ɔtɔnɔmi]   autonomy

l'**autonomiste** *mf* [ɔtɔnɔmist]   proponent of autonomy

le **budget** [bydʒɛ]   budget
L'Assemblée a voté le budget.   The National Assembly has
                                             passed the budget.

le **capitalisme** [kapitalism]   capitalism

le, la **capitaliste** [kapitalist]   capitalist

consulter [kɔ̃sylte]   consult, advise

la **contestation** [kɔ̃tɛstasjɔ̃]   protest

le **débat** [deba]   debate

la **démission** [demisjɔ̃]   resignation

démissionner [demisjɔne]   resign

le **député** [depyte]   deputy, member of Parliament
M. Lecanuet, député-maire   Mr. Lecanuet, Deputy and Mayor
de Rouen.   of Rouen.

gouverner [guvɛrne]   govern

le **leader** [lidɛr]   party leader
M. Marchais est le leader du parti   Marchais is the leader of the
communiste.   Communist Party.

manifester [manifɛste]   demonstrate

le **message** [mesaʒ]   message
Il faut que le message passe.   The message has to arrive.

négocier [negɔsje]   negotiate
Le traité a été négocié avec soin.   The treaty was negotiated
                                             carefully.

le **patronat** [patrɔna]   management

la **population** [pɔpylɑsjɔ̃]	population
la **population active** [pɔpylɑsjɔ̃aktiv]	gainfully employed population
le **projet de loi** [prɔʒɛdlwa]	draft bill
le **racisme** [rasism]	racism
La lutte anti-racisme.	The struggle against racism.
le, la **raciste** [rasist]	racist
rassembler (se) [sərasɑ̃ble]	meet
la **subvention** [sybvɑ̃sjɔ̃]	subsidy, aid
succéder (se) [səsyksede]	succeed each other
le **sympathisant,** la **sympathisante** [sɛ̃patizɑ̃, t]	sympathizer

▬▬▬ International Relations ▬▬▬

l'**échange** *m* [eʃɑ̃ʒ]	exchange
On s'est contenté d'un échange de vues.	They were satisfied with an exchange of views.
les **Etats-Unis** *mpl* [etazyni]	United States
l'**étranger** *m* [etrɑ̃ʒe]	foreign countries
étranger, -ère [etrɑ̃ʒe, ɛr]	foreign
l'**Europe** *f* [ørɔp]	Europe
européen, ne [ørɔpeɛ̃, ɛn]	European
franco-allemand, e [frɑ̃kɔalmɑ̃, d]	Franco-German
international, e, -aux [ɛ̃tɛrnasjɔnal, o]	international
mondial, e, -aux [mɔ̃djal, o]	world; worldwide
la **paix** [pɛ]	peace
En temps de paix.	In peacetime.
La paix par le désarmement.	Peace through disarmament.
Le traité de paix.	The peace treaty.
la **puissance** [pɥisɑ̃s]	power
puissant, e [pɥisɑ̃, t]	powerful
le **régime** [reʒim]	regime

la **relation** [rəlɑsjɔ̃]	relation
Les relations internationales sont tendues.	International relations are tense.
la **réunion au sommet** [reynjɔ̃osɔmɛ]	summit meeting
le **tiers monde** [tjɛrmɔ̃d]	the Third World

l'**accord** *m* [akɔr]	accord
Les deux pays sont arrivés à un accord.	The two countries have reached an accord.
l'**ambassadeur,** l'**ambassadrice** [ãbasadœr, dris]	ambassador
l'**amélioration** *f* [ameljorɑsjɔ̃]	improvement
L'amélioration des relations est considérable.	The improvement in relations is considerable.
asiatique [azjatik]	Asiatic
l'**Asie** *f* [azi]	Asia
l'**Australie** *f* [ɔstrali]	Australia
australien, ne [ɔstraljɛ̃, ɛn]	Australian
avoir des rapports [avwarderapɔr]	have relations
la **C.E.E.** [seəə]	EC
Communauté économique européenne.	European Community.
la **Chine** [ʃin]	China
chinois, e [ʃinwa, z]	Chinese
la **coopération** [kɔɔperɑsjɔ̃]	cooperation
la **détente** [detɑ̃t]	detente, relaxation of tension
La politique de détente.	The policy of detente.
l'**évolution** *f* [evɔlysjɔ̃]	evolution
francophone [frãkɔfɔn]	French-speaking, Francophone
la **francophonie** [frãkɔfɔni]	French-speaking world
le **Marché Commun** [marʃekɔmɛ̃]	Common Market
l'**ONU** *f* [ɔny]	UN

l'**OTAN** f [ɔtā]	NATO
la **pression** [prɛsjɔ̃]	pressure
la **Russie** [rys]	Russia
l'**Allemagne** [almãɲ]	Germany
le **traité** [trete]	treaty
Le traité de Versailles.	The Treaty of Versailles.

Crises

le **conflit** [kɔ̃fli]	conflict
Un conflit a éclaté au Liban.	A conflict has broken out in Lebanon.
le **coup d'Etat** [kudeta]	coup d'etat
la **crise** [kriz]	crisis
le **danger** [dãʒe]	danger
la **dictature** [diktatyr]	dictatorship
la **difficulté** [difikylte]	difficulty
la **révolution** [revɔlysjɔ̃]	revolution
la **violence** [vjɔlãs]	violence

aggraver (s') [sagrave]	become more serious
l'**agitation** f [aʒitasjɔ̃]	agitation; disturbance; unrest
l'**attentat** m [atãta]	attempt, assault
intervenir [ɛ̃tɛrvənir]	intervene
la **provocation** [prɔvokɑsjɔ̃]	provocation
renverser [rãvɛrse]	overthrow
Renverser le gouvernement.	Overthrow the government.
répandre (se) [sərepãdr]	spread
la **révolte** [revɔlt]	revolt, rebellion
révolter [revɔlte]	revolt, rebel
la **terreur** [tɛrœr]	terror
le **terrorisme** [tɛrɔrism]	terrorism

Press

à suivre [asyivr]	to be continued
l'**affiche** *f* [afiʃ]	poster, bill
l'**annonce** *f* [anɔ̄s]	announcement; advertisement
annoncer [anɔ̄se]	advertise
l'**article** *m* [artikl]	article
assister à [asistea]	attend, be present at
l'**auteur** *m* [otœr]	author
le **concurrent,** la **concurrente** [kɔ̄kyrɑ̄, t]	competitor
critique [kritik] Le Canard Enchaîné est un journal critique.	critical Le Canard Enchaîné is a critical newspaper.
la **critique** [kritik]	criticism; review, critique
critiquer [kritike]	criticize
le **détail** [detaj] C'est expliqué en détail.	detail It is explained in detail.
l'**hebdomadaire** *m* [ɛbdɔmadɛr]	weekly (newspaper)
illustré, e [ilystre]	illustrated
l'**influence** *f* [ɛ̄flyɑ̄s]	influence
influencer [ɛ̄flyɑ̄se]	influence
l'**information** *f* [ɛ̄fɔrmasjɔ̄]	information
informer [ɛ̄fɔrme]	inform
le **journal, -aux** [ʒurnal, o]	newspaper; journal
le, la **journaliste** [ʒurnalist]	journalist
la **nouvelle** [nuvɛl]	piece of news
l'**opinion** *f* [ɔpinjɔ̄] L'opinion publique change vite.	opinion Public opinion changes quickly.
la **page** [paʒ] Un journal à la page.	page An up-to-date newspaper.

paraître [parɛtr]   appear
Le Monde paraît tous les soirs sauf   Le Monde appears every evening
le dimanche.   except Sunday.

le **point de vue** [pwɛ̃dvy]   point of view, standpoint

la **position** [pozisjɔ̃]   position

la **presse** [prɛs]   press

le **reportage** [rəpɔrtaʒ]   reporting

résumer [rezyme]   summarize

la **revue** [rəvy]   review; magazine

la **série** [seri]   series

la **suite** [sɥit]   continuation, sequel

le **sujet** [syʒɛ]   subject

le **texte** [tɛkst]   text

le **titre** [titr]   title

---

l'**agence de presse** *f*   press agency
[aʒɑ̃sdəprɛs]

l'**audace** *f* [odas]   audacity

le **correspondant,**   correspondent
la **correspondante** [kɔrɛspɔ̃dɑ̃, t]

l'**éditeur, -trice** [editœr, tris]   publisher; editor

l'**envoyé spécial** *m*   special reporter
[ɑ̃vwajespesjal]

les **faits divers** *mpl* [fɛdivɛr]   news items

fonder [fɔ̃de]   found

imprimer [ɛ̃prime]   print

l'**imprimerie** *f* [ɛ̃primri]   printing office, print shop

le **lecteur,** la **lectrice**   reader; proofreader
[lɛktœr, tris]

la **lecture** [lɛktyr]   reading

le **magazine** [magazin]   magazine

la **maison d'édition** [mɛzɔ̃dedisjɔ̃]   publishing house

le **mensuel** [mɑ̃sɥɛl]   monthly magazine

objectif, -ive [ɔbʒɛktif, iv]   objective

l'**objectivité** *f* [ɔbʒɛktivite]	objectivity
le **périodique** [perjɔdik]	periodical
le, la **photographe** [fɔtɔgraf]	photographer
la **publication** [pyblikɑsjɔ̃]	publication
publier [pyblije]	publish
le **quotidien** [kɔtidjɛ̃]	daily newspaper
le **rédacteur,** la **rédactrice** [redaktœr, tris]	editor
le **rédacteur en chef** [redaktœrɑ̃ʃɛf]	editor-in-chief
rédiger [rediʒe]	draft, write up; edit
la **rubrique** [rybrik]	head, heading, title
la **sensation** [sɑ̃sɑsjɔ̃]	sensation
le **tirage** [tiraʒ] Ouest-France a le plus grand tirage en France.	circulation Ouest-France has the highest circulation in France.

Radio and Television

l'**actualité** *f* [aktyalite]	current event
actuel, le [aktyɛl]	current
au courant [okurɑ̃]	informed
la **chaîne** [ʃɛn] Les Dossiers de l'Ecran, c'est sur quelle chaîne?	channel On what channel is Les Dossiers de l'Ecran?
l'**écran** *m* [ekrɑ̃] Sur le petit écran.	screen On television.
l'**émission** *f* [emisjɔ̃]	transmission, broadcast
enregistrer [ɑ̃rəʒistre]	record; transcribe
être au courant de [ɛtrokurɑ̃də]	be informed about
l'**interview** *f* [ɛ̃tɛrvju]	interview
la **météo** [meteo]	weather report; weather bureau
le **micro** [mikro] Léon Zitrone au micro.	microphone Leon Zitrone at the microphone.

202

le **programme** [prɔgram]	program
public, -ique [pyblik]	public
la **pub(licité)** [pyb lisite]	advertising
Je ne regarde que la pub.	I watch only the commercials.
le **son** [sɔ̃]	sound
le **studio** [stydjo]	studio
la **télé(vision)** [tele vizjɔ̃]	television, TV
la **voix** [vwa]	voice

l'**antenne** *f* [ãtɛn]	antenna; station
Je vous rends l'antenne.	Back to our studio.
l'**audience** *f* [odjãs]	audience
audio-visuel, le [odjovisɥɛl]	audiovisual
l'**auditeur, -trice** [oditœr, tris]	listener
le **débat** [deba]	debate
diffuser [difyze]	broadcast
l'**émetteur** *m* [emɛtœr]	broadcasting station; transmitter
L'émetteur pour la Bretagne est en panne.	The transmitter for Brittany is out of order.
le **feuilleton** [fœjtɔ̃]	newspaper serial; radio, TV series
Les Français raffolent des feuilletons comme Dallas.	The French are wild about series like Dallas.
l'**héroïne** *f* [erɔin]	heroine
le **héros** ['ero]	hero
publicitaire [pyblisitɛr]	advertising
Slogan publicitaire.	Advertising slogan.
la **réception** [resɛpsjɔ̃]	reception
le **téléspectateur,** la **téléspectatrice** [telespɛktatœr, tris]	(television) viewer
les **variétés** *fpl* [varjete]	variety show

On War and Military Affairs

l'**action** *f* [aksjɔ̃]	action
attaquer [atake]	attack
la **bataille** [bataj]	battle
bloquer [blɔke]	block
la **bombe** [bɔ̃b]	bomb
brutal, e, -aux [brytal, o]	brutal
le **chef** [ʃɛf]	leader
le **conflit** [kɔ̃fli]	conflict
la **conséquence** [kɔ̃sekãs]	consequence
le **coup de feu** [kudfø] Le coup de feu a tué un manifestant.	shot, gunshot The shot killed a demonstrator.
déclarer [deklare] Le gouvernement a déclaré la guerre au terrorisme.	declare The government has declared war on terrorism.
défendre [defãdr]	defend
la **défense** [defãs] Le ministre de la Défense Nationale.	defense The secretary of defense.
efficace [efikas]	effective, successful
l'**ennemi, e** [ɛnmi]	enemy
grave [grav] Un incident grave s'est produit à la frontière.	serious, grave A serious incident occurred at the border.
le **groupe** [grup]	group
la **guerre** [gɛr]	war
l'**incident** *m* [ɛ̃sidã]	incident
mener [məne]	lead
militaire [militɛr]	military
nucléaire [nykleɛr] La guerre nucléaire n'aura pas lieu.	nuclear Nuclear war will not take place.
l'**occupation** *f* [ɔkypasjɔ̃]	occupation

occuper [ɔkype]	occupy
l'**ordre** *m* [ɔrdr]	order
la **paix** [pɛ]	peace
le **pays** [pei]	country
le **plan** [plã]	plan
la **province** [prɔvɛ̃s]	province
la **région** [reʒjɔ̃]	region
rétablir [retablir]	restore
L'armée syrienne a rétabli l'ordre.	The Syrian Army has restored order.
le **soldat** [sɔlda]	soldier
tuer [tɥe]	kill
la **victime** [viktim]	victim
L'attentat de la rue de Rennes a fait de nombreuses victimes.	The attempt on the Rue de Rennes claimed many victims.
la **victoire** [viktwar]	victory

l'**adversaire** *mf* [advɛrsɛr]	adversary, opponent
l'**arme** *f* [arm]	arm; weapon
l'**armée** *f* [arme]	army
armer [arme]	arm
l'**armistice** *m* [armistis]	armistice
L'armistice a été respecté pendant trois jours.	The armistice was observed for three days.
l'**avertissement** *m* [avɛrtismã]	warning
les **blessés** *mpl* [blese]	injured persons; casualties
capituler [kapityle]	capitulate
la **défaite** [defɛt]	defeat
le **défilé** [defile]	parade
envahir [ãvair]	invade
l'**exécution** *f* [ɛgzekysjɔ̃]	execution
l'**expansion** *f* [ɛkspãsjɔ̃]	spread, expansion
la **force de frappe** [fɔrsdəfrap]	(nuclear) striking force (of France)
la **fuite** [fɥit]	flight

hostile [ɔstil]	hostile
l'**invasion** *f* [ɛvɑzjɔ̃]	invasion
les **morts** *mpl* [mɔr]	dead persons; corpses
l'**objecteur de conscience** *m* [ɔbʒɛktœrdkɔ̃sjɑ̃s]	conscientious objector
le **service militaire** [sɛrvismilitɛr] Guy a fait son service militaire en Allemagne.	military service Guy did his military service in Germany.
la **torture** [tɔrtyr] Le prisonnier a parlé sous la torture.	torture The prisoner talked under torture.
la **trahison** [traizɔ̃]	treason
le **traître**, la **traîtresse** [trɛtr, ɛs]	traitor
la **troupe** [trup]	troop
le **vainqueur** [vɛ̃kœr]	victor
volontaire [vɔlɔ̃tɛr] Jean s'est porté volontaire.	voluntary Jean volunteered.

On Justice

accuser [akyze] On vous accuse de vol.	accuse You are accused of theft.
la **bagarre** [bagar]	brawl, row, riot
le **cas** [kɑ]	case
compliqué, e [kɔ̃plike]	complicated
condamner [kɔ̃damne]	condemn
coupable [kupabl]	guilty
le **crime** [krim]	crime, offence
le **droit** [drwa]	law; right, justice
enlever [ɑ̃lve]	carry away; kidnap
l'**enquête** *f* [ɑ̃kɛt] La police mène l'enquête sur ce hold-up.	investigation, inquiry The police are investigating this holdup.
l'**injustice** *f* [ɛ̃ʒystis]	injustice

innocent, e [inɔsã, t]	innocent
interroger [ɛ̃tɛrɔʒe]	interrogate, question
le **juge** [ʒyʒ]	judge
jurer [ʒyre]	swear
juste [ʒyst]	just, righteous; accurate
la **justice** [ʒystis]	justice; courts of justice
Je demande justice.	I demand justice.
On m'a trainé en justice.	I was dragged before the court.
la **liberté** [libɛrte]	liberty, freedom
la **loi** [lwa]	law
Il a passé sa vie à violer la loi.	He spent his life breaking the law.
majeur, e [maʒœr]	of full age
la **police** [pɔlis]	police
le **poste (de police)** [pɔst dəpɔlis]	police station
la **preuve** [prœv]	proof
le **prison** [prizɔ̃]	prison
prouver [pruve]	prove
punir [pynir]	punish
la **question** [kɛstjɔ̃]	question
le **témoin** [temwɛ̃]	witness
la **violence** [vjɔlãs]	violence
violent, e [vjɔlã, t]	violent
le **vol** [vɔl]	theft
le **voleur**, la **voleuse** [vɔlœr, øz]	thief
l'**accusé, e** [akyze]	accused (person), defendant
l'**assassin** *m* [asasɛ̃]	murderer
la **bande** [bãd]	band
le **délit** [deli]	offense, wrong, crime
le **dossier** [dosje]	dossier, record; files
la **drogue** [drɔg]	drug

l'**escroc** *m* [ɛskro]	crook, swindler
le **gangster** [gãgstɛr]	gangster
l'**interrogatoire** *m* [ɛ̃tɛrɔgatwar]	examination
le **juge d'instruction** [ʒyʒdɛ̃stryksjɔ̃]	examining magistrate
le **meurtre** [mœrtr]	murder
le **mobile** [mɔbil]	motive
l'**otage** *m* [ɔtaʒ]	hostage
Les bandits ont pris un vendeur en otage.	The bandits took a salesman as a hostage.
le **paragraphe** [paragraf]	paragraph
la **piste** [pist]	track, trail
La police est sur la piste des malfaiteurs.	The police are on the trail of the offenders.
la **Police judiciaire** [pɔlisʒydisjɛr]	Criminal Investigation Department
le **procès** [prɔsɛ]	trial; lawsuit
On lui a fait le procès.	He was tried.
la **rafle** [rɑfl]	raid, mass arrest
rechercher [rəʃɛrʃe]	seek; investigate
suspect, e [syspɛ, ɛkt]	suspicious, suspect
la **trace** [tras]	trace
Le cambrioleur n'a pas laissé de traces.	The burglar left no traces.
le **tribunal, -aux** [tribynal, o]	court
le **verdict** [vɛ̃dikt]	verdict

On Politics

améliorer [ameljɔre]	improve
contester [kɔ̃tɛste]	contest
Les syndicats contestent ce projet de loi.	The trade unions are contesting this draft bill.
l'**équilibre** *m* [ekilibr]	balance, equilibrium
l'**étape** *f* [etap]	stage

l'**événement** m [evɛnmɑ̃]	event
il se passe [ilsəpas]	it happens
Il se passe des événements graves.	Serious events happen.
la **manif(estation)** [manif ɛstɑsjɔ̃]	demonstration
officiel, le [ɔfisjɛl]	official
le **progrès** [prɔgrɛ]	progress
la **radio** [radjo]	radio
le **résultat** [rezylta]	result
la **situation** [sityɑsjɔ̃]	situation
la **solution** [sɔlysjɔ̃]	solution
supprimer [syprime]	suppress, abolish
On a supprimé les plus grandes injustices.	The greatest injustices have been abolished.
l'**union** f [ynjɔ̃]	union

aggraver (s') [sagrave]	become more serious
La situation du tiers monde s'aggrave.	The situation of the Third World is becoming more serious.
l'**Hexagone** m [ɛkzagɔn]	France
l'**intrigue** f [ɛ̃trig]	intrigue
le **message** [mesaʒ]	message
le **militant**, la **militante** [militɑ̃, t]	militant; active member of a political party
occidental, e, -aux [ɔksidɑ̃tal, o]	western
opposé, e [ɔpoze]	opposed
provoquer [prɔvɔke]	provoke
le **scandale** [skɑ̃dal]	scandal
secret, -ète [səkrɛ, t]	secret
le **symbole** [sɛ̃bɔl]	symbol

On Catastrophes

l'**accident** *m* [aksidã]	accident
brûler [bryle]	burn
la **catastrophe** [katastrɔf]	catastrophe
la **chimie** [ʃimi]	chemistry
le **danger** [dãʒe]	danger
les **dégâts** *mpl* [degɑ]	damage, havoc
dramatique [dramatik]	dramatic
l'**élément** *m* [elemã]	element
l'**explosion** *f* [ɛksplozjõ]	explosion
inattendu, e [inatãdy]	unexpected
l'**incendie** *m* [ɛ̃sãdi]	fire
pollué, e [pɔlɥe]	polluted
la **pollution** [pɔlysjõ]	pollution
La pollution chimique du Rhin a tué tous les poissons.	The chemical pollution of the Rhine has killed all the fish.
prendre feu [prãdrəfø]	catch fire
tragique [traʒik]	tragic

l'**avalanche** *f* [avalãʃ]	avalanche
les **besoins** *mpl* [bəswɛ̃]	needs
la **centrale nucléaire** [sãtralnykleɛr]	nuclear power plant
le **choc** [ʃɔk]	shock
la **coulée de lave** [kuledlav]	outflow of lava
La coulée de lave a détruit St. Pierre.	The flow of lava destroyed St. Pierre.
le **désastre** [dezastr]	disaster
Le désastre de Lisbonne a coûté 60000 morts.	The Lisbon disaster cost 60,000 human lives.
la **dimension** [dimãsjõ]	dimension
distribuer [distribɥe]	distribute

la **distribution** [distribysjɔ̃]	distribution
l'**épidémie** f [epidemi]	epidemic
Le SIDA est en train de devenir une épidémie.	AIDS is in the process of becoming an epidemic.
l'**éruption** f [erypsjɔ̃]	eruption
héroïque [erɔik]	heroic
imprévu, e [ɛ̃prevy]	unforeseen
l'**inondation** f [inɔ̃dɑsjɔ̃]	flooding, inundation
intervenir [ɛ̃tɛrvənir]	intervene
la **marée noire** [marenwar]	oil spill, oil pollution
le **nuage radioactif** [nɥaʒradjɔaktif]	radioactive cloud
Le nuage radioactif de Tchernobyl a traversé toute l'Europe.	The radioactive cloud of Chernobyl crossed all of Europe.
le **nuage toxique** [nɥaʒtɔksik]	toxic cloud
la **précaution** [prekosjɔ̃]	precaution
la **radioactivité** [radjɔaktivite]	radioactivity
la **tempête** [tɑ̃pɛt]	storm, tempest
On annonce une tempête sur la Manche.	A storm on the English Channel is being forecast.
la **tornade** [tɔrnad]	tornado
le **tremblement de terre** [trɑ̃bləmɑ̃dtɛr]	earthquake

On Social Problems

le **chômage** [ʃomaʒ]	unemployment
Le taux de chômage ne cesse d'augmenter.	The unemployment rate keeps on climbing.
la **civilisation** [sivilizɑsjɔ̃]	civilization
la **difficulté** [difikylte]	difficulty
diminuer [diminɥe]	diminish, decrease
Le taux de croissance diminue.	The growth rate is decreasing.
l'**économie** f [ekɔnɔmi]	economy
économique [ekɔnɔmik]	economic

faire partie de [fɛrpartidə]
La France fait partie des pays riches.

belong to
France is one of the rich nations.

les **gens** *mpl* [ʒɑ̃]

people

l'**impôt** *m* [ɛpo]

tax

les **jeunes** *mpl* [ʒœn]

young people

la **jeunesse** [ʒœnɛs]

youth

mériter [merite]

earn

le **monde** [mɔ̃d]

world

le **mouvement** [muvmɑ̃]
Le mouvement ouvrier existe
depuis plus d'un siècle.

movement
The labor movement has been in
existence for over a century.

l'**ouvrier, -ère** [uvrije, ɛr]

worker, laborer

pauvre [povr]

poor

positif, -ive [pozitif, iv]

positive

la **possibilité** [pɔsibilite]

possibility

possible [pɔsibl]

possible

réaliste [realist]

realistic

la **réalité** [realite]
La réalité dépasse souvent la fiction.

reality
Reality is often worse than fiction.

la **réduction** [redyksjɔ̃]

reduction in price

la **réforme** [refɔrm]

reform

riche [riʃ]

rich

scandaleux, -euse [skɑ̃dalø, z]

scandalous

la **société** [sɔsjete]

society

soulever un problème
[sulveɛ̃prɔblɛm]

raise a problem

la **vieillesse** [vjɛjɛs]

old age

accroître [akrwatr]	grow, increase
les **conditions de vie** *fpl* [kɔ̃disjɔ̃dvi]	living conditions
dépeupler (se) [sədepœple] L'Allemagne se dépeuple rapidement.	lose population, depopulate Germany is losing population rapidly.
l'**exode rural** *m* [ɛgzɔdryral]	rural exodus
l'**exode urbain** *m* [ɛgzɔdyrbɛ̃]	urban exodus
immigré, e [imigre]	immigrant
la **lutte** [lyt]	struggle
lutter [lyte] Nous luttons pour un meilleur monde.	struggle, fight We're fighting for a better world.
le **milieu, x** [miljø]	environment; milieu
le **niveau, x** [nivo]	level
la **pauvreté** [povrəte]	poverty

Des nuages radioactifs, des mers polluées, le crime partout, et nous devons obéir aux grandes personnes!
Radioactive clouds, polluted seas, crime everywhere, and we should obey grown-ups!

People and Their Environment

General Terms

améliorer (s') [sameljɔre] — improve
Le temps s'améliore. — The weather is improving.

le **changement** [ʃãʒmã] — change
Je ne supporte pas le changement de temps. — I can't tolerate the change in the weather.

le **ciel** [sjɛl] — sky

le **climat** [klima] — climate

coucher (se) [səkuʃe] — set

le **degré** [dəgre] — degree
Il fait 25 degrés. — It is 25 degrees Centigrade.

diminuer [diminɥe] — decrease, diminish

faible [fɛbl] — weak

fort, e [fɔr, t] — strong

lever (se) [səlve] — rise
Le soleil se lève à six heures. — The sun rises at 6 A.M.
Le vent se lève. — The wind is rising.

la **météo** [meteo] — weather report

moyen, ne [mwajɛ̃, ɛn] — average

l'**ombre** *f* [ɔbr] — shadow; shade

prévoir [prevwar] — predict, forecast

souffler [sufle] — blow
Le vent souffle fort. — The wind is blowing hard.

la **température** [tãperatyr] — temperature

le **temps** [tã] — weather

le **vent** [vã] — wind

l'**anticyclone** *m* [ãtisiklon]	high(-pressure area)
l'**arc-en-ciel** *m* [arkãsjɛl]	rainbow
la **bourrasque** [burask]	squall, gust
la **brise** [briz]	breeze
la **dépression** [depresjõ]	low(-pressure area)
les **prévisions** *fpl* [previzjõ]	weather forecast

Warm, Good Weather

agréable [agreabl]	agreeable
beau, bel, belle, x [bo, bɛl]	good, fine
Il fait beau.	The weather is good.
briller [brije]	shine
Le soleil brille.	The sun is shining.
la **chaleur** [ʃalœr]	heat
clair, e [klɛr]	clear
doux, douce [du, dus]	mild
en plein soleil [ãplɛ̃sɔlɛj]	in full sun
favorable [favɔrabl]	favorable
Il fait chaud. [ilfɛʃo]	It is hot.
le **rayon** [rɛjõ]	ray, beam
sec, sèche [sɛk, sɛʃ]	dry
le **soleil** [sɔlɛj]	sun
Il fait du soleil.	It is sunny.
tiède [tjɛd]	lukewarm; mild

la **canicule** [kanikyl]	heat wave, dog days
l'**éclaircie** *f* [eklɛrsi]	clearing, break
éclaircir (s') [seklɛrsir]	clear up
Le soleil tape. [ləsɔlɛjtap]	The sun is scorching.

━━━━━━━━ **Cold, Bad Weather** ━━━━━━━━

baisser [bese]	sink, drop
La température baisse.	The temperature is dropping.
bas, se [bɑ, s]	low
le **courant d'air** [kurɑ̃dɛr]	air current
dur, e [dyr]	harsh
frais, fraîche [frɛ, frɛʃ]	cool; fresh
le **froid** [frwa]	cold
froid, e [frwa, d]	cold
geler [ʒle]	freeze
Il gèle.	It is freezing.
la **glace** [glas]	ice
Il fait du vent. [ilfɛdyvɑ̃]	It is windy.
Il fait frais. [ilfɛfrɛ]	It is cool.
Il fait froid. [ilfɛfrwa]	It is cold.
la **neige** [nɛʒ]	snow
neiger [neʒe]	snow
Il neige.	It is snowing.
le **verglas** [vɛrgla]	slick ice, glare ice

le **blizzard** [blizar]	blizzard, snowstorm
le **flocon de neige** [flɔkɔ̃dnɛʒ]	snowflake
fondre [fɔ̃dr]	melt
le **gel** [ʒɛl]	frost, freezing
la **gelée** [ʒle]	frost
la **givre** [ʒivr]	hoarfrost
la **grêle** [grɛl]	hail

Damp Weather

le **brouillard** [brujar]	fog
Il fait du brouillard.	It is foggy.
épais, se [epɛ, s]	dense, thick
Quel brouillard épais!	What dense fog!
la **goutte** [gut]	drop
humide [ymid]	humid
Il fait mauvais. [ilfɛmɔvɛ]	The weather is bad.
Il fait meilleur. [ilfɛmɛjœr]	The weather is better.
le **nuage** [nɥaʒ]	cloud
l'**orage** *m* [ɔraʒ]	storm
pleuvoir [plœvwar]	rain
Il pleut.	It is raining.
la **pluie** [plɥi]	rain
tomber [tɔ̃be]	fall
le **tonnerre** [tɔnɛr]	thunder
variable [varjabl]	variable

l'**averse** *f* [avɛrs]	shower
la **brume** [brym]	fog, mist
le **ciel couvert** [sjɛlkuvɛr]	overcast sky
le **crachin** [kraʃɛ̃]	light drizzle
l'**éclair** *m* [eklɛr]	lightning
être trempé, e [ɛtrətrɑ̃pe]	be soaked
la **foudre** [fudr]	lightning bolt
La foudre s'est abattue sur un arbre.	The bolt of lightning struck a tree.
la **tempête** [tɑ̃pɛt]	storm, tempest

Animals

l'**animal, -aux** *m* [animal, o]	animal
la **bête** [bɛt]	animal; beast
le **canard** [kanar]	duck
le **chat** [ʃa]	cat
le **cheval, -aux** [ʃval, o]	horse
le **chien** [ʃjɛ̃]	dog
le **cochon** [kɔʃɔ̃]	pig
l'**insecte** *m* [ɛ̃sɛkt]	insect
le **lapin** [lapɛ̃]	rabbit
le **lion** [ljɔ̃]	lion
le **loup** [lu]	wolf
la **mouche** [muʃ]	fly
le **mouton** [mutɔ̃]	sheep
l'**oiseau, x** *m* [wazo]	bird
le **papillon** [papijɔ̃]	butterfly
le **poisson** [pwasɔ̃]	fish
la **poule** [pul]	chicken
le **serpent** [sɛrpɑ̃]	snake
le **singe** [sɛ̃ʒ]	monkey
la **souris** [suri]	mouse
le **tigre** [tigr]	tiger
la **vache** [vaʃ]	cow
le **veau, x** [vo]	calf
l'**abeille** *f* [abɛj]	bee
l'**agneau, x** *m* [aɲo]	lamb
l'**aigle** *m* [ɛgl]	eagle
l'**alouette** *f* [alwɛt]	lark
l'**âne** *m* [ɑn]	ass, donkey

la **baleine** [balɛn]	whale
la **chèvre** [ʃɛvr]	goat
la **cigogne** [sigɔ]	stork
la **coccinelle** [kɔksinɛl]	ladybug
le **coq** [kɔk]	rooster
la **femelle** [fəmɛl]	female
la **fourmi** [furmi]	ant
la **guêpe** [gɛp]	wasp
le **hareng** ['arã]	herring
l'**hirondelle** f [irɔ̃dɛl]	swallow
le **mâle** [mɑl]	male
le **merle** [mɛrl]	blackbird
le **moustique** [mustik]	mosquito
l'**ours** m [urs]	bear
le **pigeon** [piʒɔ̃]	pigeon
la **queue** [kø]	tail
la **race** [ras]	breed
le **rat** [ra]	rat
le **renard** [rənar]	fox
le **requin** [rəkɛ̃]	shark
le **taureau, x** [tɔro]	bull
la **trace** [tras]	trace; track, trail; footprint
le **troupeau, x** [trupo]	herd
la **truite** [trɥit]	trout
la **vipère** [vipɛr]	viper

Plants

l'**arbre** m [arbr]	tree
le **blé** [ble]	wheat
le **bouton** [butɔ̃]	bud
la **branche** [brãʃ]	branch

la **cerise** [səriz]	cherry
le **champignon** [ʃɑ̃piɲɔ̃]	mushroom
la **feuille** [fœj]	leaf
la **fleur** [flœr]	flower
la **fraise** [frɛz]	strawberry
le **fruit** [frɥi]	fruit
l'**herbe** *f* [ɛrb]	herb; grass
mûr, e [myr]	ripe
la **plante** [plɑ̃t]	plant
la **poire** [pwar]	pear
la **pomme** [pɔm]	apple
la **pomme de terre** [pɔmdətɛr]	potato
la **prune** [pryn]	plum
la **rose** [roz]	rose
la **vigne** [vi]	vine; vineyard

l'**avoine** *f* [avwan]	oats
la **betterave** [bɛtrav]	beet
le **bouleau, x** [bulo]	birch
la **bruyère** [bryjɛr]	heather; heath
le **cassis** [kasis]	black currant
le **cerisier** [sərizjə]	cherry tree
le **chêne** [ʃɛn]	oak
le **colza** [kɔlza]	rape, rape-seed
le **coquelicot** [kɔkliko]	poppy
fâner [fɑne]	fade
fleurir [flœrir]	flower, bloom
la **framboise** [frɑ̃bwaz]	raspberry
le **froment** [frɔmɑ̃]	wheat
le **genêt** [ʒnɛ]	broom
le **glaïeul** [glajœl]	gladiola
la **groseille** [grosɛj]	red currant; gooseberry

le **hêtre** ['ɛtr]	beech
le **jonc** [ʒɔ̃]	rush
la **jonquille** [ʒɔ̃kij]	jonquil
le **lilas** [lila]	lilac
le **maïs** [mais]	corn
le **muguet** [mygɛ]	lily of the valley
la **mûre** [myr]	blackberry
la **noisette** [nwazɛt]	hazelnut
la **noix** [nwa]	walnut
l'**œillet** *m* [œjɛ]	carnation
l'**olivier** *m* [ɔlivje]	olive tree
l'**orge** *f* [ɔrʒ]	barley
l'**orme** *m* [ɔrm]	elm
le **palmier** [palmje]	palm tree
la **pâquerette** [pakrɛt]	white daisy
le **pêcher** [peʃe]	peach tree
le **peuplier** [pøplije]	poplar
le **pin** [pɛ̃]	pine
le **platane** [platan]	plane tree
le **pommier** [pɔmje]	apple tree
la **racine** [rasin]	root
la **ronce** [rɔ̃s]	bramble, blackberry bush
le **sapin** [sapɛ̃]	fir
le **seigle** [sɛgl]	rye
le **tilleul** [tijœl]	linden
le **tournesol** [turnəsɔl]	sunflower
la **tulipe** [tylip]	tulip
la **violette** [vjɔlɛt]	violet

Man and Nature

abandonner [abãdɔne]
Sur les terres abandonnées
poussent les ronces.

abandon
In abandoned fields, wild
blackberry bushes grow.

agricole [agrikɔl]

agricultural

le **champ** [ʃã]

field

cueillir [kœjir]

pick

la **culture** [kyltyr]
La culture du colza progresse.

culture; cultivation
The cultivation of cole seed is
increasing.

l'**élevage** *m* [ɛlvaʒ]

raising, breeding

élever [elve]

raise, breed

l'**environnement** *m* [ãvirɔnmã]
La protection de l'environnement
est primordiale.

environment
Protection of the environment is
fundamental.

le **jardin** [ʒardɛ̃]

garden

le **légume** [legym]

vegetable; legume

le **parc** [park]

park

le **paysan,** la **paysanne**
[peizã, an]

farmer

planter [plãte]

plant

pollué, e [pɔlɥe]

polluted

la **pollution** [pɔlysjɔ̃]
La pollution cause la mort des forêts.

pollution
Pollution causes the forests to die.

le, la **propriétaire** [prɔprijetɛr]

proprietor, owner; landowner

protéger [prɔteʒe]

protect

la **récolte** [rekɔlt]

harvest

semer [səme]

sow

le **bétail** [betaj]	livestock, grazing animals
les **céréales** *fpl* [sereal]	cereal
la **coopérative** [kɔɔperativ]	cooperative
Les coopératives agricoles sont très répandues en France.	Agricultural cooperatives are very common in France.
cultiver [kyltive]	cultivate
l'**écologie** *f* [ekɔlɔʒi]	ecology, environmental protection
l'**écologiste** *mf* [ekɔlɔʒist]	environmentalist
Les écologistes sont une minorité en France.	Environmentalists are a minority in France.
l'**engrais** *m* [ãgrɛ]	fertilizer; manure
irriguer [irige]	irrigate
la **protection de la nature** [prɔtɛksjɔ̃dlanatyr]	protection of nature
le **remembrement** [rəmãbrəmã]	reallocation (of arable land)
Le remembrement est la cause de beaucoup d'ennuis.	Reallocation of arable land is the cause of much trouble.
rural, e, -aux [ryral, o]	rural
Le nombre des exploitations rurales est en baisse.	The number of farms is on the decrease.
le **verger** [vɛrʒe]	orchard

Land

les **Alpes** *fpl* [alp]	Alps
l'**Amérique** *f* [amerik]	America
l'**Europe** *f* [ørɔp]	Europe
européen, ne [ørɔpeɛ̃, ɛn]	European
la **Forêt-Noire** [fɔrɛnwar]	Black Forest
le **Midi** [midi]	South of France
le **monde** [mɔ̃d]	world
le **pays** [pei]	country
la **province** [prɔvɛ̃s]	province
les **Pyrénées** *fpl* [pirene]	Pyrenees

la **région** [reʒjɔ̃]	region
le **sol** [sɔl]	soil
le **terrain** [terɛ̃]	terrain
la **terre** [tɛr]	earth, land
les **Vosges** *fpl* [voʒ]	Vosges

les **Ardennes** *fpl* [ardɛn]	Ardennes
le **continent** [kɔ̃tinɑ̃]	continent
le **Jura** [ʒyra]	Jura
le **Massif Central** [masifsɑ̃tral]	Massif Central
méridional, e, -aux [meridjɔnal, o]	southern
le **pôle Nord** [polnɔr]	North Pole
le **pôle Sud** [polsyd]	South Pole
terrestre [tɛrɛstr] La surface terrestre.	terrestrial; land The earth's surface.

━━━━━ Geological Formations ━━━━━

bas, se [bɑ, s]	low
le **col** [kɔl] Le plus haut col des Alpes est le col de Stelvio à 2757 m.	pass The highest pass in the Alps is the Stelvio Pass, at 2757 m.
la **colline** [kɔlin]	hill
la **côte** [kot]	coast
le **désert** [dezɛr]	desert
la **gorge** [gɔrʒ]	gorge
haut, e ['o, t] Le Mont Blanc est haut de 4807 m.	high Mont Blanc is 4807 m high.
la **hauteur** ['otœr]	height
l'**île** *f* [il] L'île de Sein est au large de la Pointe du Raz.	island The island of Sein is off the Pointe du Raz.
la **montagne** [mɔ̃ta]	mountain

la **pierre** [pjɛr]	stone
la **plage** [plaʒ]	beach
plat, e [pla, t]	flat
la **poussière** [pusjɛr]	dust
le **rocher** [rɔʃe]	rock; crag
le **sable** [sabl]	sand
le **sommet** [sɔmɛ]	summit, peak
la **vallée** [vale]	valley

aigu, aiguë [egy]	sharp
l'**altitude** f [altityd]	altitude
Il fait froid en altitude.	At high altitude it is cold.
le **bassin** [basɛ̃]	basin
la **chaîne de montagnes** [ʃɛndəmɔ̃ta]	range of mountains
la **dune** [dyn]	dune
l'**étendue** f [etãdy]	stretch; range, scope
la **falaise** [falɛz]	cliff, bluff
le **glacier** [glasje]	glacier
la **grotte** [grɔt]	grotto
le **littoral, -aux** [litɔral, o]	coast, coastline
Le littoral breton est très propre.	The Breton coast is very clean.
la **pente** [pãt]	slope
la **plaine** [plɛn]	plain
le **plateau, x** [plato]	plateau
la **superficie** [sypɛrfisi]	surface, area
le **volcan** [vɔlkã]	volcano

Water

couler [kule]	flow
le **Danube** [danyb]	Danube
l'**eau, x** *f* [o]	water
le **fleuve** [flœv]	river
le **lac** [lak]	lake
le **large** [larʒ] Le requin bleu est un poisson du large.	open sea The blue shark is a fish of the open sea.
la **Loire** [lwar]	Loire
la **mer** [mɛr]	ocean, sea
profond, e [prɔfɔ̃, d]	deep
le **Rhin** [rɛ̃]	Rhine
la **Rhône** [ron]	Rhone
la **rivière** [rivjɛr] L'Odet est une rivière qui se jette dans la mer.	river The Odet is a river that flows into the sea.
le **ruisseau, x** [rɥiso]	brook
la **Seine** [sɛn]	Seine
la **source** [surs]	spring, fountain
la **vague** [vag]	wave

l'**Atlantique** *m* [atlɑ̃tik]	Atlantic
la **baie** [bɛ]	bay
le **canal, -aux** [kanal, o]	canal
la **chute d'eau** [ʃytdo]	waterfall
le **courant** [kurɑ̃]	current
la **Dordogne** [dɔrdɔ]	Dordogne
l'**embouchure** *f* [ɑ̃buʃyr] Nantes se trouve à l'embouchure de la Loire.	mouth (of a river) Nantes is located at the mouth of the Loire.

en amont [ãnamɔ̃] Paris est en amont de Rouen.	upstream Paris lies upstream from Rouen.
en aval [ãnaval]	downstream
l'**Escaut** *m* [ɛsko]	Scheldt, Schelde
l'**étang** *m* [etã]	pond; lagoon
fondre [fɔ̃dr]	melt
la **Garonne** [garɔn]	Garonne
le **golfe** [gɔlf] Le golfe du Morbihan.	gulf, bay The Gulf of Morbihan.
maritime [maritim]	maritime
la **Marne** [marn]	Marne
la **Méditerranée** [mediterane]	Mediterranean
la **mer Baltique** [mɛrbaltik]	Baltic Sea
la **mer du Nord** [mɛrdynɔr]	North Sea
la **Meuse** [møz]	Meuse
la **Moselle** [mɔzɛl]	Moselle
l'**océan** *m* [ɔseã]	ocean
la **Saône** [son]	Saone
le **torrent** [tɔrã]	torrent

Sky

l'**air** *m* [ɛr]	air
le **ciel** [sjɛl]	sky
l'**étoile** *f* [etwal]	star
la **lune** [lyn]	moon
le **nuage** [nɥaʒ]	cloud
le **soleil** [sɔlɛj]	sun

l'**année-lumière** *f* [anelymjɛr]	light-year
la **comète** [kɔmɛt]	comet
l'**étoile filante** *f* [etwalfilãt]	falling star, shooting star
la **nébuleuse** [nebyløz]	nebula
la **planète** [planɛt]	planet
l'**univers** *m* [ynivɛr]	universe
la **voie lactée** [vwalakte]	Milky Way

Description of Nature

beau, bel, belle, x [bo, bɛl]	beautiful, pretty, lovely
le **bois** [bwa]	wood; woods
le **bruit** [brɥi]	noise
calme [kalm]	calm, quiet
la **campagne** [kãpa]	country
les **environs** *mpl* [ãvirõ]	surroundings, environs, vicinity
Les environs de Fontainebleau sont très boisés.	The surroundings of Fontainebleau are heavily wooded.
l'**équilibre** *m* [ekilibr]	equilibrium, balance
L'équilibre naturel est en danger.	The natural balance is in danger.
étendre (s') [setãdr]	stretch, spread, extend
La plaine s'étend sur une centaine de kilomètres.	The plain stretches over 100 kilometers.
la **forêt** [fɔrɛ]	forest
la **nature** [natyr]	nature
l'**odeur** *f* [ɔdœr]	odor, smell
l'**ombre** *f* [õbr]	shade; shadow
le **paysage** [peizaʒ]	landscape
pur, e [pyr]	pure, clean
le **silence** [silãs]	silence
la **surface** [syrfas]	surface
tranquille [trãkil]	tranquil, quiet
visible [vizibl]	visible

l'**arc-en-ciel** *m* [arkɑ̃sjɛl]	rainbow
l'**aube** *f* [ob]	dawn
la **beauté** [bote]	beauty
le **bocage** [bɔkaʒ]	grove; wooded region
brumeux , -euse [brymø, z]	foggy, misty
la **clairière** [klɛrjɛr]	clearing
le **coucher de soleil** [kuʃedsɔlɛj]	sunset
le **crépuscule** [krepyskyl]	dusk
désert, e [dezɛr, t]	deserted
étaler (s') [setale]	stretch out, sprawl
la **haie** ['ɛ]	hedge
la **lande** [lɑ̃d]	waste land, moor, heath
le **maquis** [maki]	scrub, bushy land
le **marais** [marɛ]	swamp, marsh, bog
pittoresque [pitɔrɛsk]	picturesque
la **rosée** [roze]	dew
sauvage [sovaʒ]	wild, savage
silencieux , -euse [silɑ̃sjø, z]	still, silent
le **site** [sit]	scenic site, beauty spot
la **solitude** [sɔlityd]	solitude

Ce tableau de Monet reflète le calme et la solitude.
This painting by Monet reflects calm and solitude.

The City

la **banlieue** [bɑ̃ljø]	suburb
J'habite en banlieue.	I live in the suburbs.
la **capitale** [kapital]	capital (city)
carré, e [kare]	square
J'ai 1000 mètres carrés de terrain.	I have 1000 square meters of land.
le **centre** [sɑ̃tr]	center
les **environs** *mpl* [ɑ̃virɔ̃]	environs, surroundings, vicinity
l'**espace** *m* [ɛspas]	space
étendre (s') [setɑ̃dr]	extend, stretch (out)
l'**industrie** *f* [ɛ̃dystri]	industry
industriel, le [ɛ̃dystrijɛl]	industrial
Lille est une ville industrielle.	Lille is an industrial town.
le **quartier** [kartje]	quarter; neighborhood; section
le **village** [vilaʒ]	village
la **ville** [vil]	town; city

l'**agglomération** *f* [aglɔmerɑsjɔ̃]	metropolitan area; built-up area
L'agglomération parisienne comprend 10 millions d'habitants.	The metropolitan area of Paris has 10 million inhabitants.
le **centre-ville** [sɑ̃trəvil]	center of town
la **cité-dortoir** [sitedɔrtwar]	dormitory suburb, bedroom town
Sarcelles est une affreuse cité-dortoir.	Sarcelles is an ugly bedroom town.
le **grand ensemble** [grɑ̃tɑ̃sɑ̃bl]	housing development
le **pâté de maisons** [pɑtedmezɔ̃]	block of houses
la **périphérie** [periferi]	periphery; outskirts
le **quartier populaire** [kartjepɔpylɛr]	working-class district
le **quartier résidentiel** [kartjerezidɑ̃sjɛl]	residential district
urbain, e [yrbɛ̃, ɛn]	urban, city

villageois, e [vilaʒwa, z]	village
la **ville nouvelle** [vilnuvεl]	new town
Evry-ville-nouvelle, au sud de Paris	Evry-ville-nouvelle, south of Paris

Buildings

le **bâtiment** [bɑtimã]	building
la **cathédrale** [katedral]	cathedral
le **château, x** [ʃato]	castle, palace
la **clinique** [klinik]	clinic; private hospital
le **collège** [kɔlεʒ]	high school
la **construction** [kõstryksjõ]	construction, building
l'**église** *f* [egliz]	church
le **garage** [garaʒ]	garage
la **gare** [gar]	railroad station
le **grand magasin** [grãmagazε̃]	department store
le **H.L.M.** [aʃεlεm]	low-rent apartment
J'ai droit à un H.L.M.	I have the right to a low-rent apartment.
Il y a beaucoup de H.L.M. en banlieue.	There are many low-rent apartments in the suburbs of Paris.
l'**hôpital, -aux** *m* [ɔpital, o]	hospital
l'**hôtel de ville** *m* [ɔtεldəvil]	city hall
l'**immeuble** *m* [imœbl]	building
le **lycée** [lise]	high school
le **magasin** [magazε̃]	store, shop
la **mairie** [meri]	town hall, city hall
la **maison** [mεzõ]	house
le **monument** [mɔnymã]	monument
Notre Dame est un monument historique.	Notre Dame is a historic monument.
le **mur** [myr]	wall
le **musée** [myze]	museum
la **poste** [pɔst]	post office

la **prison** [prizɔ̃]	prison
le **restaurant** [rɛstɔrã]	restaurant
les **ruines** [rɥin]	ruins
A Languidou il y a une chapelle en ruines.	In Languidou there is a chapel in ruins.
le **stade** [stad]	stadium
le **supermarché** [sypɛrmarʃe]	supermarket
la **tour** [tur]	tower
l'**université** *f* [ynivɛrsite]	university

l'**architecture** *f* [arʃitɛktyr]	architecture
la **centrale nucléaire** [sãtralnykleɛr]	nuclear power plant
le **centre commercial** [sãtrəkɔmɛrsial]	shopping district, shopping center
le **centre culturel** [sãtrəkyltyrɛl]	cultural center
l'**édifice** *m* [edifis]	building, edifice
la **grande surface** [grãdsyrfas]	shopping center
le **pavillon** [pavijɔ̃]	small single-family house
la **résidence** [rezidãs]	residence

━━━━━ Structures and Traffic Routes ━━━━━

l'**aéroport** *m* [aerɔpɔr]	airport
l'**autoroute** *f* [ɔtɔrut]	superhighway
l'**avenue** *f* [avəny]	avenue
le **boulevard** [bulvar]	boulevard
le **carrefour** [karfur]	crossroads
la **chaussée** [ʃose]	pavement, road
le **chemin** [ʃmɛ̃]	way; road
le **cimetière** [simtjɛr]	cemetery
la **cour** [kur]	court; courtyard
le **marché** [marʃe]	market

233

la **nationale** [nasjɔnal]	national highway
le **parking** [parkiŋ]	parking lot; parking garage
la **piscine** [pisin]	swimming pool
la **place** [plas]	place; city square
le **pont** [põ]	bridge
le **port** [pɔr]	port
le **quai** [ke]	quay, wharf; embankment
la **route** [rut]	road; route
la **rue** [ry]	street
le **terrain** [tɛrɛ̃]	terrain
le **trottoir** [trɔtwar]	sidewalk
la **voie** [vwa]	track; way; road

l'**échangeur** *m* [eʃãʒœr]	interchange
l'**égout** *m* [egu]	drainage; sewer
Le tout-à-l'égout parisien date de 1850.	The sewerage of Paris dates from 1850.
le **périphérique** [periferik]	circular highway around Paris
le **rail** [raj]	rail
le **tunnel** [tynɛl]	tunnel
la **voie piétonne** [vwapjetɔn]	pedestrian way
la **zone piétonne** [zonpjetɔn]	pedestrian zone

▬▬▬▬▬ Changes and Problems ▬▬▬▬▬

abandonner [abãdɔne]	abandon
affreux, -euse [afrø, z]	ugly, frightful
améliorer [ameljɔre]	improve
automatique [ɔtɔmatik]	automatic
beau, bel, belle, x [bo, bɛl]	pretty, beautiful, lovely
le **béton** [betõ]	concrete
le **bruit** [brɥi]	noise
bruyant, e [brɥijã, t]	noisy, loud

carré, e [kare]	square
central, e, -aux [sãtral, o]	central
le **changement** [ʃãʒmã]	change
le **charbon** [ʃarbõ]	coal
construire [kõstrɥir]	build, construct
démolir [demɔlir]	demolish, tear down
détruire [detrɥir]	destroy
l'**électricité** *f* [elɛktrisite]	electricity
électrique [elɛktrik]	electric(al)
l'**environnement** *m* [ãvirɔnmã]	environment
fonctionner [fõksjɔne]	function
la **fumée** [fyme]	smoke
gaspiller [gaspije]	waste
haut, e ['o, t]	high
la **hauteur** ['otœr]	height
l'**incendie** *m* [ɛ̃sãdi]	fire
moderne [mɔdɛrn]	modern
neuf, neuve [nœf, nœv]	new
J'habite un bâtiment tout neuf.	I live in a brand new building.
nouveau, -vel, -velle, x [nuvo, nuvɛl]	new
Mon nouvel appartement est plus grand.	My new apartment is bigger.
populaire [pɔpylɛr]	popular, common
profond, e [prɔfõ, d]	deep
le **projet** [prɔʒɛ]	project
la **technique** [tɛknik]	technique; engineering
transformer [trãsfɔrme]	transform

l'**aménagement** *m* [amenaʒmã]	arrangement; development
L'aménagement du Rhin a provoqué des problèmes.	The development of the Rhine has caused problems.
aménager [amenaʒe]	arrange; develop
l'**assainissement** *m* [asenismã]	draining

235

le **chantier** [ʃɑ̃tje]	construction site
les **déchets** *mpl* [deʃɛ]	loss, decrease
la **dégradation** [degradɑsjɔ̃]	degradation; decay, dilapidation
La dégradation des vieux quartiers.	The decay of the old sections of the city.
polluer [pɔlɥe]	pollute
le **taudis** [todi]	hovel
l'**urbanisation** *f* [yrbanizɑsjɔ̃]	urbanization
l'**urbanisme** *m* [yrbanism]	city planning

Cities in Europe

Aix-la-Chapelle [ɛkslaʃapɛl]	Aachen
Anvers [anvɛrs]	Antwerp
Athènes [atɛn]	Athens
Bâle [bɑl]	Basel, Basle
Berne [bɛrn]	Bern, Berne
Brême [brɛm]	Bremen
Bruges [bryʒ]	Bruges
Brunswick [brɛ̃svik]	Brunswick, Braunschweig
Bruxelles [brysɛl]	Brussels
Coblence [kɔblɑ̃s]	Coblenz, Koblenz
Cologne [kɔlɔ]	Cologne
Copenhague [kɔpɛn'ag]	Copenhagen
Cordoue [kɔrdu]	Cordoba
Cracovie [krakɔvi]	Cracow
Dresde [drɛsd]	Dresden
Francfort [frãkfɔr]	Frankfurt
Fribourg [fribur]	Fribourg
Gand [gɑ̃]	Ghent
Gênes [ʒɛn]	Genoa
Genève [ʒnɛv]	Geneva
Hambourg [ãbur]	Hamburg

Hanovre [anɔvr]	Hannover
La Haye [la'ɛ]	The Hague
Liège [ljɛʒ]	Liege
Lisbonne [lisbɔn]	Lisbon
Londres [lɔ̃dr]	London
Mayence [majɑ̃s]	Mainz
Milan [milɑ̃]	Milan
Moscou [mɔsku]	Moscow
Munich [mynik]	Munich
Naples [napl]	Naples
Nuremberg [nyrɑ̃bɛr]	Nuremberg
Prague [prag]	Prague
Ratisbonne [ratisbɔn]	Regensburg
Rome [rɔm]	Rome
Trèves [trɛv]	Trier
Varsovie [varsɔvi]	Warsaw
Venise [vəniz]	Venice
Vienne [vjɛn]	Vienna

▬▬▬ Divisions of Germany and Great Britain ▬▬▬

le **Bade-Wurtemberg** [badwyrtɑ̃bɛr]	Baden-Württemberg
la **Basse-Saxe** [bassaks]	Lower Saxony
la **Bavière** [bavjɛr]	Bavaria
le **Brandebourg** [brɑ̃dɛbur]	Brandenburg
la **Cornouaille** [kɔrnuaj]	Cornwall
l'**Ecosse** f [ekɔs]	Scotland
la **Hesse** ['ɛs]	Hesse
le **Mecklembourg-Poméranie** [meklɛ̃burpɔmerani]	Mecklenburg-Western Pomerania

le **Pays de Galles** [peidgal]	Wales
la **Rhénanie-Westphalie** [renanivɛstfali]	North Rhine-Westphalia
la **Rhénanie-Palatinat** [renanipalatina]	Rhineland-Palatinate
la **Sarre** [sar]	Saarland
la **Saxe** [saks]	Saxony
le **Saxe-Anhalt** [saks-ãnʒalt]	Saxony-Anhalt
le **Schleswig-Holstein** [ʃlɛswigɔlsten]	Schleswig-Holstein
la **Thuringe** [tyriŋ]	Thuringia

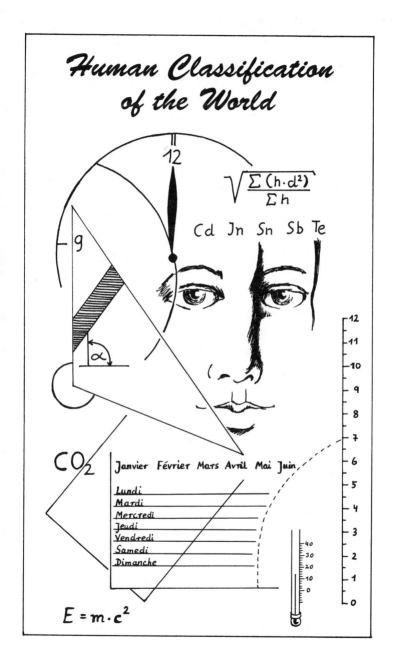

━━━━━━━━━━━━━━━━━━━━ **Colors** ━━━━━━━━━━━━━━━━━━━━

blanc, blanche [blɑ̃, blɑ̃ʃ] white

bleu, e [blø] blue
J'ai acheté une robe bleu ciel. I bought a sky-blue dress.

blond, e [blɔ̃, d] blond

brillant, e [brijɑ̃, t] brilliant, bright

brun, e [brœ̃, bryn] dark brown

clair, e [klɛr] light, pale

la **couleur** [kulœr] color
De quelle couleur sont ses yeux? What color are his eyes?

foncé, e [fɔ̃se] dark

gris, e [gri, z] gray

jaune [ʒon] yellow

marron *inv* [marɔ̃] brown

noir, e [nwar] black

orange *inv* [ɔrɑ̃ʒ] orange
Des chaussettes orange. Orange socks.

pâle [pɑl] pale

rose [roz] pink, rose

rouge [ruʒ] red

roux, rousse [ru, rus] auburn (hair)

sombre [sɔ̃br] dark

le **ton** [tɔ̃] shade, tone

uni, e [yni] solid (color)

vif, vive [vif, viv] lively; bright, intense

violet, te [vjɔlɛ, t] violet

---

blanc cassé *inv* [blɑ̃kase] off-white

châtain [ʃatɛ̃] chestnut, nut-brown
Marie-Louise est châtain. Marie-Louise is chestnut-haired.
Claire a des cheveux châtains. Claire has chestnut-colored hair.

d'argent [darʒɑ̃]	silver
d'or [dɔr]	golden
Elle a les cheveux d'or.	She has golden hair.
lilas *inv* [lila]	lilac
mauve [mov]	mauve
ocre *inv* [ɔkr]	ochre
paille *inv* [paj]	straw-colored

Shapes

aigu, aiguë [egy]	sharp; acute
le **carré** [kare]	square
carré, e [kare]	checked, checkered; squared
le **cercle** [sɛrkl]	circle
la **droite** [drwat]	straight line
en forme de [ɑ̃fɔrmdə]	in the shape of, shaped like
En forme de cœur.	Heart-shaped.
la **forme** [fɔrm]	form, shape
former [fɔrme]	form
la **ligne** [li]	line; figure
le **point** [pwɛ̃]	point
raide [rɛd]	stiff; steep
le **rectangle** [rɛktɑ̃gl]	rectangle
régulier, -ère [regylje, ɛr]	regular
rond, e [rɔ̃, d]	round
le **trait** [trɛ]	dash
le **triangle** [trijɑ̃gl]	triangle

la **courbe** [kurb]	curve
le **cube** [kyb]	cube
la **pyramide** [piramid]	pyramid
la **rangée** [rɑ̃ʒe]	row
la **sphère** [sfɛr]	sphere

241

General Terms

l'**énergie** *f* [enɛrʒi]	energy
fin, fine [fɛ̃, fin]	fine
fragile [fraʒil]	fragile, breakable
le **liquide** [likid]	liquid
le **matériel** [materjɛl]	material
la **matière** [matjɛr]	matter; material
nucléaire [nykleɛr]	nuclear
Energie nucléaire.	Nuclear energy.
solide [sɔlid]	solid
la **sorte** [sɔrt]	sort, kind

consister en [kɔ̃sисteā]	consist of
Le diamant consiste en carbone.	Diamonds consist of carbon.
inflammable [ɛ̃flamabl]	(in)flammable
la **matière première** [matjɛrprəmjɛr]	raw material
opaque [ɔpak]	opaque
l'**oxygène** *m* [ɔksiʒɛn]	oxygen
soluble [sɔlybl]	soluble
transparent, e [trɑ̃sparɑ̃, t]	transparent

Substances of Plant and Animal Origin

le **bois** [bwa]	wood
Ce jouet est en bois.	This toy is made of wood.
le **caoutchouc** [kautʃu]	rubber
le **carton** [kartɔ̃]	cardboard
le **charbon** [ʃarbɔ̃]	coal; charcoal
le **coton** [kɔtɔ̃]	cotton
le **cuir** [kɥir]	leather

la **ficelle** [fisɛl]	string
le **fil** [fil]	thread; wire
Fil à coudre.	Sewing thread.
la **fourrure** [furyr]	fur
la **laine** [lɛn]	wool
le **papier** [papje]	paper
le **tissu** [tisy]	cloth, fabric
la **toile** [twal]	cloth; linen

la **corde** [kɔrd]	rope, cord
le **duvet** [dyvɛ]	down
en osier [ɑ̃nozje]	wicker
la **fibre naturelle** [fibrənatyrɛl]	natural fiber
le **lin** [lɛ̃]	linen
le **parchemin** [parʃəmɛ̃]	parchment
la **soie** [swa]	silk
tissé, e [tise]	woven
tisser [tise]	weave

▬▬▬ Mineral and Chemical Substances ▬▬▬

l'**argent** *m* [arʒɑ̃]	silver
le **béton** [betɔ̃]	concrete
chimique [ʃimik]	chemical
la **colle** [kɔl]	glue
l'**essence** *f* [esɑ̃s]	gasoline
le **fer** [fɛr]	iron
L'âge du fer.	The Iron Age.
Le fil de fer.	The iron wire.
Le fil de fer barbelé.	The barbed wire.
Le fer blanc.	The tinplate.
le **gaz** [gaz]	gas
le **laiton** [lɛtɔ̃]	brass

243

le **métal, -aux** [metal, o]	metal
le **nylon** [nilɔ̃]	nylon
l'**or** *m* [ɔr]	gold
La médaille d'or.	The gold medal.
le **pétrole** [petrɔl]	petroleum
la **pierre** [pjɛr]	rock
le **plastique** [plastik]	plastic
le **verre** [vɛr]	glass

l'**acier** *m* [asje]	steel
l'**ardoise** *f* [ardwaz]	slate
Un toit d'ardoises.	A slate roof.
l'**argile** *m* [arʒil]	clay
l'**asphalte** *m* [asfalt]	asphalt
le **bronze** [brɔ̃z]	bronze
L'âge du bronze.	The Bronze Age.
le **carburant** [karbyrɑ̃]	motor fuel
la **céramique** [seramik]	ceramics; ceramic piece
la **craie** [krɛ]	chalk
le **cristal, -aux** [kristal, o]	crystal
le **cuivre** [kɥivr]	copper
l'**étain** *m* [etɛ̃]	pewter
la **fibre artificielle** [fibrartifisjɛl]	artificial fiber
la **fibre synthétique** [fibrsɛ̃tetik]	synthetic fiber
fondre [fɔ̃dr]	melt; smelt; cast
le **gas-oil,** le **gazole** [gazwal, gazɔl]	diesel fuel
le **goudron** [gudrɔ̃]	tar
le **grès** [grɛ]	sandstone
Le grès rouge des Vosges.	The red sandstone of the Vosges Mountains.
le **marbre** [marbr]	marble
le **mazout** [mazut]	fuel oil
métallique [metalik]	metallic
le **minerai** [minrɛ]	mineral

la **mousse** [mus]	foam rubber
le **plâtre** [plɑtr]	plaster
le **plomb** [plɔ̃]	lead
le **polystirène** [polistirɛn]	polystyrene plastic, Styrofoam
la **porcelaine** [pɔrsələn]	porcelain
le **produit pétrolier** [prodɥipetrɔlje]	petroleum product
souder [sude]	solder; weld
la **tôle** [tol]	sheet metal
La tôle ondulée.	The corrugated iron.
le **zinc** [zɛ̃g]	zinc

Je suis une source d'énergie dynamique, mais c'est mon devoir patriotique de la conserver.

I am a source of tremendous energy, but it is my patriotic duty to conserve it.

Cardinal Numbers

zéro [zero]	zero
un [ɛ̃]	one
deux [dø]	two
trois [trwa]	three
quatre [katr]	four
cinq [sɛ̃k]	five
six [sis]	six
sept [sɛt]	seven
huit [ɥit]	eight
neuf [nœf]	nine
dix [dis]	ten
onze [ɔ̃z]	eleven
douze [duz]	twelve
treize [trɛz]	thirteen
quatorze [katɔrz]	fourteen
quinze [kɛ̃z]	fifteen
seize [sɛz]	sixteen
dix-sept [disɛt]	seventeen
dix-huit [dizɥit]	eighteen
dix-neuf [diznœf]	nineteen
vingt [vɛ̃]	twenty
vingt et un [vɛ̃teɛ̃]	twenty-one
vingt-deux [vɛ̃tdø]	twenty-two
trente [trãt]	thirty
quarante [karãt]	forty
cinquante [sɛ̃kãt]	fifty
soixante [swasãt]	sixty
soixante-dix [swasãtdis]	seventy
soixante et onze [swasãteɔ̃z]	seventy-one
soixante-douze [swasãtduz]	seventy-two

quatre-vingts [katrəvɛ̃]	eighty
quatre-vingt-un [katrəvɛ̃ɛ̃]	eighty-one
quatre-vingt-dix [katrvɛ̃dis]	ninety
quatre-vingt-onze [katrəvɛ̃ɔ̃z]	ninety-one
cent [sɑ̃]	one hundred
mille [mil]	one thousand
Audierne a six mille habitants.	Audierne has six thousand inhabitants.
un million [ɛ̃ miljɔ̃]	one million
Paris a deux millions d'habitants.	Paris has two million inhabitants.
un milliard [ɛ̃ miljar]	one billion

▆▆▆▆▆ Expressions of Quantity ▆▆▆▆▆

demi, e [dəmi]	half
tiers [tjɛr]	third
quart [kar]	fourth
un cinquième [ɛ̃sɛ̃kjɛm]	one fifth
premier, -ère [prəmje, ɛr]	first
second, e [səgɔ̃, d]	second
troisième [trwazjɛm]	third
dizaine [dizɛn]	about ten; ten
douzaine [duzɛn]	dozen
J'ai acheté une douzaine d'œufs.	I bought a dozen eggs.
quinzaine [kɛ̃zɛn]	two weeks, fortnight
J'ai passé une quinzaine agréable à Paris.	I spent two pleasant weeks in Paris.
centaine [sɑ̃tɛn]	a hundred; a hundred or so
millier [milje]	about a thousand
milliers *mpl* [milje]	thousands
double [dubl]	double
Ça fait le double de ce qu'on a prévu.	That's double what we anticipated.
triple [tripl]	triple

General Terms

à peu près [apøprɛ]	about
au total [ototal]	in all
Ça fait combien au total?	How much is that in all?
le **chiffre** [ʃifr]	figure, number
comparer [kɔ̃pare]	compare
compter [kɔ̃te]	count
correspondre [kɔrɛspɔ̃dr]	correspond
Ça correspond à quoi?	To what does that correspond?
la **différence** [diferɑ̃s]	difference
diminuer [diminɥe]	diminish
la **division** [divizjɔ̃]	division
égal, e, -aux [egal, o]	equal
en moyenne [ɑ̃mwajɛn]	on average
entier, -ère [ɑ̃tje, ɛr]	entire, whole
Les nombres entiers.	The whole numbers.
environ [ɑ̃virɔ̃]	about, approximately
exact, e [ɛgzakt]	exact
fois [fwa]	time
Trois fois dix font trente.	Three times ten is thirty.
la **majorité** [maʒɔrite]	majority
le **maximum** [maksimɔm]	maximum
le **minimum** [minimɔm]	minimum
moins [mwɛ̃]	minus
Huit moins trois font cinq.	Eight minus three is five.
la **moitié** [mwatje]	half
La moitié des gens.	Half the people.
le **nombre** [nɔ̃br]	number
le **numéro** [nymero]	numeral
l'**ordre** *m* [ɔrdr]	order
Dans l'ordre alphabétique.	In alphabetical order.

pareil, le [parɛj]	identical, the same
C'est du pareil au même.	It's the same thing.
le **rang** [rɑ̃]	rank; ranking
la **somme** [sɔm]	sum
supérieur, e [syperjœr]	higher
total, e, -aux [tɔtal, o]	total
l'**unité** *f* [ynite]	unit

considérable [kɔ̃siderabl]	considerable
l'**égalité** *f* [egalite]	equality
faire ses comptes [fɛrsekɔ̃t]	add up
impair, e [ɛ̃pɛr]	uneven
Nombre impair.	Uneven number.
inférieur, e [ɛ̃ferjœr]	lower
pair, e [pɛr]	even
Nombre pair.	Even number.

◼◼◼ Measures and Weights ◼◼◼

le **bout** [bu]	end
le **carré** [kare]	square
carré, e [kare]	square, squared
le **centimètre** [sɑ̃timɛtr]	centimeter
court, e [kur, t]	short
le **degré** [dəgre]	degree
Il fait combien de degrés?	What's the temperature?
énorme [enɔrm]	enormous, gigantic
et demi [edmi]	one half
Un kilo et demi.	One and one half kilos.
le **gramme** [gram]	gram
grand, e [grɑ̃, d]	large, big
haut, e ['o, t]	high
immense [imɑ̃s]	immense
le **kilo** [kilo]	kilo

le **kilogramme** [kilogram]	kilogram
le **kilomètre** [kilomɛtr]	kilometer
km à l'heure [kilomɛtralœr]	kilometers per hour
Ma voiture roule à 160 km à l'heure.	My car does 160 kilometers per hour.
léger, -ère [leʒe, ɛr]	light
le **litre** [litr]	liter
J'ai bu un litre de jus de pommes.	I drank a liter of apple juice.
la **livre** [livr]	pound
J'ai pris une livre de tomates.	I bought a pound of tomatoes.
long, longue [lɔ̃, g]	long
la **longueur** [lɔ̃gœr]	length
La longueur d'ondes.	The wavelength.
lourd, e [lur, d]	heavy
la **mesure** [məzyr]	measure
le **mètre** [mɛtr]	meter
la **moyenne** [mwajɛn]	average
Je roule à 110 en moyenne.	I drive 110 on the average.
net, te [nɛt]	net
Poids net.	Net weight.
le **paquet** [pakɛ]	package
petit, e [pti, t]	small
le **poids** [pwa]	weight
la **taille** [taj]	size
le **volume** [vɔlym]	volume
le **mètre carré** [mɛtrkare]	square meter
le **mètre cube** [mɛtrkyb]	cubic meter
le **quintal, -aux** [kɛ̃tal, o]	one hundred kilograms
la **tonne** [tɔn]	ton

250

▬▬▬▬ Concepts of Quantity ▬▬▬▬

aucun de [okɛ̃də]
Aucun des deux n'a dit la vérité.

not one of, neither of
Neither of the two spoke the truth.

autant de [otɑ̃də]

as much, as many, so much,
so many

beaucoup [boku]
J'ai beaucoup d'amis.

much, many
I have many friends.

bien des [bjɛ̃de]

a great many

combien [kɔ̃bjɛ̃]

how much

doubler [duble]
J'ai doublé la mise.

double
I doubled the investment.

en plus [ɑ̃plys]

in addition

l'**ensemble** *m* [ɑ̃sɑ̃bl]

whole, mass

la **foule** [ful]
Tu as vu la foule devant le cinéma?

crowd
Did you see the crowd in front of
the movie theater?

le **groupe** [grup]

group

la **plupart** [plypar]
La plupart des gens vont tôt au lit.
La plupart du temps je suis occupée.

most
Most people go to bed early.
Most of the time I'm busy.

ne ... pas de [nə ... pàdə]
Je n'ai pas d'enfants.

no, none, not any
I don't have any children.

nombreux, -euse [nɔ̃brø, z]

numerous

pas grand-chose [pɑgrɑ̃ʃoz]
Je n'ai pas fait grand-chose.

nothing special; not much
I didn't do anything special.

pas un, une [pɑ z ɛ̃, pɑ z yn]
Pas une minute de plus.

not one, not a
Not a minute longer!

peu [pø]
Je dors peu.

little; not much
I don't sleep much.

peu de [pødə]

few; not much, not many

plein de [plɛ̃də]

full of

plus [plys]
Encore plus.

more
More and more.

plus de [plydə]	no more
Je n'ai plus d'essence.	I don't have any more gasoline.
plus du tout [plydytu]	no more at all
plusieurs [plyzjœr]	several
la **quantité** [kãtite]	quantity
rien de [rjẽdə]	nothing of
Rien de bien.	Nothing good.
rien du tout [rjẽdytu]	nothing at all
tant de [tãdə]	so much
Tant d'histoires pour rien du tout.	So much ado about nothing.
trop de [trodə]	too much, too many
un (tout petit) peu [ẽ tupti pø]	a (little) bit
un tas de [ẽtàsdə]	a lot of

contenir [kõtnir]	contain
en masse [ãmas]	in a body, in the mass, in bulk
en trop [ãtro]	too much, too many
Il y a un couvert en trop.	There's one place setting too many.
la **masse** [mas]	mass
la **part** [par]	part, share

Centimètres ou kilogrammes? Chiffres ou symboles? Pauvre garçon!
Centimeters or kilograms? Numbers or symbols? Poor boy!

Nouns

l'**arrière** *m* [arjɛr]
Je vais en arrière.

back part, rear
I'm going to the back.

le **bas** [bɑ]
Au bas de la page.

lower part, bottom, or foot (of s.th.)
At the foot of the page.

le **bout** [bu]

end

le **coin** [kwɛ̃]

corner

le **côté** [kote]

side

la **direction** [dirɛksjɔ̃]
Audierne, c'est quelle direction?

direction
In which direction is Audierne?

l'**endroit** *m* [ɑ̃drwa]
L'endroit me plaît.

place, spot
I like this place.

les **environs** *mpl* [ɑ̃virɔ̃]

surroundings

l'**est** *m* [ɛst]
J'habite à l'est de Paris.
J'habite dans l'est de Paris.

east
I live east of Paris.
I live in east Paris.

l'**étape** *f* [etap]

stage; stop; lap

le **fond** [fɔ̃]
Au fond d'une fontaine.

bottom
At the bottom of a well.

le **lieu, x** [ljø]
Ce n'est ni le temps ni le lieu pour
faire ça.

place
This is neither the time nor the
place for that.

la **longueur** [lɔ̃gœr]
Cinq mètres de longueur.

length
Five meters long.

le **mètre** [mɛtr]

meter

le **nord** [nɔr]

north

l'**ouest** *m* [wɛst]

west

la **place** [plas]

place

la **position** [pozisjɔ̃]

position

le **sens** [sɑ̃s]
Sens unique

direction, way
One-way street

le **sud** [syd]

south

le **tour** [tur]

circumference

253

la **distance** [distãs]	distance
l'**extérieur** *m* [ɛksterjœr]	exterior, outside
la **hauteur** ['otœr]	height
l'**intérieur** *m* [ɛ̃terjœr]	interior, inside
la **largeur** [larʒœr]	width, breadth
la **limite** [limit]	limit
le **milieu, x** [miljø]	middle

Adjectives

court, e [kur, t]	short
droit, e [drwa, t]	right
étroit, e [etrwa, t]	narrow
extérieur, e [ɛksterjœr]	exterior, outer
gauche [goʃ]	left
haut, e ['o, t]	high
intérieur, e [ɛ̃terjœr]	interior, inner
large [larʒ]	broad, wide; large
long, longue [lɔ̃, g]	long
mondial, e, -aux [mɔ̃djal, o]	world, world-wide
proche [prɔʃ]	near, close
supérieur, e [syperjœr]	higher; upper

inférieur, e [ɛ̃ferjœr]	lower
méridional, e, -aux [meridjɔnal, o]	southern
occidental, e, -aux [ɔksidãtal, o]	western, west; occidental
opposé, e [ɔpoze]	opposite
oriental, e, -aux [ɔrjãtal, o]	eastern, east; oriental
septentrional, e, -aux [sɛptãtrijɔnal, o]	northern

■■■■■■■■■■■■ **Prepositions** ■■■■■■■■■■■■

à côté de [akotedə]   by, near

à droite de [adrwatdə]   to or on the right of

à gauche de [agoʃdə]   to or on the left of

après [aprɛ]   after
Tournez à gauche après le pont.   Turn left after the bridge.

au bout de [obudə]   at the end of

au-dessous (de) [odsu də]   below

au-dessus (de) [odsy də]   above, beyond

autour de [oturdə]   around; about

avant [avā]   before
Dernière sortie avant la frontière.   Last exit before the border.

contre [kɔ̃tr]   against

dans [dā]   in, into
Je vais dans la cuisine.   I'm going into the kitchen.
Je suis dans la cuisine.   I'm in the kitchen.

derrière [dɛrjɛr]   behind
Le parking est derrière l'hôtel.   The parking lot is behind the hotel.

devant [dəvā]   before, in front of
Je me suis garée devant ton garage.   I parked in front of your garage.

en [ā]   in, into; to
J'habite en France.   I live in France.
Je vais en Russie.   I'm going to Russia.
Pierre est en prison.   Pierre is in prison.

en face de [āfasdə]   opposite, facing

entre [ātr]   between, among

jusqu'à [ʒyska]   as far as; until

loin de [lwɛ̄də]   far from
Loin des yeux, loin du cœur.   Out of sight, out of mind.

près de [prɛdə]   close to

sous [su]   under

sur [syr]   on

vers [vɛr]   toward; about
La route vers Dijon.   The road to Dijon.

à la hauteur de [alaˈotœrdə]	at a height of
à travers [atravɛr]	across, through
Je marche à travers champs.	I'm going across country.
d'ici à [disia]	from here to
Ça fait presque 600 km d'ici à Paris.	It's almost 600 km from here to Paris.
du côté de [dykotedə]	in the area of
On fait du camping du côté de Quimper.	We camp in the area of Quimper.
en dehors de [ãdəɔrdə]	outside of; beyond
En dehors des agglomérations la vitesse est limitée à 90 km/h.	Outside of built-up areas the speed limit is 90 km/h.
en travers de [ãtravɛrdə]	across
hors de [ˈɔrdə]	out of, outside of
le long de [ləlõdə]	along
Je me suis promené le long de la Seine.	I strolled along the Seine.
vis-à-vis de [vizavidə]	across from, facing

Adverbs

ailleurs [ajœr]	elsewhere
Je vais ailleurs.	I'm going somewhere else.
au premier plan [oprəmjeplã]	in the foreground
de côté [dəkote]	aside
Ma mémé a mis 50000 DM de côté.	My granny has put aside 50,000 DM.
de droite [dədrwat]	from the right
Qui est venu de droite?	Who came from the right?
de face [dəfas]	from the front
J'ai pris Notre Dame de face.	I photographed Notre Dame from the front.
de long [dəlõ]	lengthwise
Les Champs Elysées font trois kilomètres de long.	The Champs Elysées is three kilometers long.
de près [dəprɛ]	from close to, near
dedans [dədã]	within, in, inside

dehors [dəɔr]   out, without, outside

dessous [dsu]   under, underneath, below

dessus [dsy]   on, upon, over, above
Sens dessus dessous.   Upside down.
Bras dessus bras dessous.   Arm in arm.

en avant [ãnavã]   forward
Le joueur a joué la balle en avant.   The player moved the ball forward.

en ville [ãvil]   into town; in town
Tu viens avec nous en ville?   Are you coming with us into town?

ici [isi]   here

là [la]   there

là-bas [laba]   there, over there

là-dedans [laddã]   in there

là-dessous [ladsu]   under there

là-dessus [ladsy]   on that; thereupon; on top of that

là-haut [la'o]   up there; upstairs

nulle part [nylpar]   nowhere
Je ne vais nulle part.   I'm not going anywhere.

où [u]   where; whither
Où tu habites?   Where do you live?
Où tu vas?   Where are you going?

par terre [partɛr]   on the ground, on the floor

partout [partu]   everywhere

près [prɛ]   near
J'habite tout près.   I live very near.

quelque part [kɛlkəpar]   somewhere

tout droit [tudrwa]   straight ahead
Allez tout droit.   Drive straight ahead.

---

côte à côte [kotakot]   side by side

de haut en bas [də'otãbɑ]   from top to bottom

de long en large [dələ̃ãlarʒ]   far and wide

de travers [dətravɛr]   obliquely, diagonally
Elle m'a regardé de travers.   She looked at me askance.

en public [ãpyblik]   in public

━━━━━━━━━━━━━ **Year** ━━━━━━━━━━━━━

l'**an** *m* [ã]	year
En l'an deux mille.	In the year 2000.
l'**année** *f* [ane]	year (in its entirety)
L'année dernière.	Last year.
L'année prochaine.	Next year.
l'**automne** *m* [ɔtɔn]	fall, autumn
En automne.	In fall.
l'**été** *m* [ete]	summer
En été.	In summer.
l'**hiver** *m* [ivɛr]	winter
En hiver.	In winter.
le **printemps** [prɛ̃tã]	spring
Au printemps.	In spring.
la **saison** [sɛzɔ̃]	season

annuel, le [anɥɛl]	annual
le **trimestre** [trimɛstr]	quarter of a year

━━━━━━━━━━━━━ **Month** ━━━━━━━━━━━━━

janvier [ʒãvje]	January
Je suis né le 12 janvier 1946.	I was born on January 12, 1946.
février [fevrije]	February
mars [mars]	March
avril [avril]	April
mai [mɛ]	May
juin [ʒɥɛ̃]	June
juillet [ʒɥijɛ]	July
août [ut]	August
Au mois d'août.	In the month of August.
En août.	In August.
septembre [sɛptãbr]	September

octobre [ɔktɔbr]	October
novembre [nɔvãbr]	November
décembre [desãbr]	December
mois [mwa]	month
Le mois dernier.	Last month.
Le mois prochain.	Next month.

mensuel, le [mãsɥɛl]	monthly

━━━━━━━ Week ━━━━━━━

dimanche [dimãʃ]	Sunday
Dimanche dernier.	Last Sunday.
Jamais le dimanche.	Never on Sunday.
Dimanche prochain.	Next Sunday.
lundi [lɛ̃di]	Monday
mardi [mardi]	Tuesday
mercredi [mɛrkrədi]	Wednesday
jeudi [ʒødi]	Thursday
vendredi [vãdrədi]	Friday
samedi [samdi]	Saturday
hebdomadaire [ɛbdɔmadɛr]	weekly
la **semaine** [smɛn]	week
La semaine dernière.	Last week.
La semaine prochaine.	Next week.
le **week-end** [wikɛnd]	weekend

━━━━━━━ Day ━━━━━━━

après-demain [aprɛdmɛ̃]	day after tomorrow
l'**après-midi** *m or f* [apremidi]	afternoon
J'ai passé une après-midi agréable chez toi.	I spent a pleasant afternoon at your house.
L'après-midi, je ne travaille pas.	I don't work in the afternoon.
Cet après-midi je ne sors pas.	This afternoon I'm not going out.

259

aujourd'hui [oʒurdɥi] — today

avant-hier [avãtjɛr] — day before yesterday

demain [dəmɛ̃] — tomorrow

hier [jɛr] — yesterday

Il fait jour. [ilfɛʒur] — It is daylight.

Il fait noir. [ilfɛnwar] — It is dark.

le **jour** [ʒur] — day
Je fais mon footing tous les jours. — I jog every day.
Quel jour on est? — What day is today?

la **journée** [ʒurne] — day (in its entirety)
J'ai passé toute la journée chez Martine. — I was at Martine's all day.

le **matin** [matɛ̃] — morning
Tous les matins j'ai du mal à me lever. — Every morning I have trouble getting up.

la **matinée** [matine] — morning (duration)
Hier, j'ai fais la grasse matinée. — Yesterday morning I got up late.

midi [midi] — noon
Il est midi. — It is noon.
Je mange à midi. — I eat at noon.

minuit [minɥi] — midnight
Il est minuit. — It is midnight.
La messe commence à minuit. — The mass begins at midnight.

la **nuit** [nɥi] — night

le **soir** [swar] — evening
Je regarde la télé tous les soirs. — I watch TV every evening.

la **soirée** [sware] — evening (duration)
Je ne suis pas sorti de toute la soirée. — I didn't go out all evening.

---

de jour [dəʒur] — in the daytime

de nuit [dənɥi] — at night

le lendemain [ləlãdəmɛ̃] — the next day

quotidien, ne [kɔtidjɛ̃, ɛn] — daily

la **veille** [lavɛj] — the eve of; the day before
Il a dit qu'il était sorti la veille au soir. — He said that he went out the evening before.

Hour
---

demi, e [dəmi]
Il est dix heures et demie.
Il est midi et demi.

half
It is ten thirty.
It is twelve thirty.

l'**heure** *f* [œr]
C'est l'heure.
Il est quelle heure?
Il est trois heures.
Ça fait une heure que je t'attends.
Ça dure des heures et des heures.

hour; time (of day); o'clock
It is time.
What time is it?
It is three o'clock.
I've been waiting an hour for you.
That takes hours and hours.

la **minute** [minyt]

minute

précis, e [presi, z]
Rendez-vous à huit heures précises.

precise, exact
Meeting at eight o'clock on the dot.

quart [kar]
Il est neuf heures et quart.
Il est neuf heures moins le quart.

quarter
It is nine fifteen.
It is eight forty-five.

la **seconde** [səgɔ̃d]

second

Frequent Occurrences

à la fois [alafwa]
Je ne peux pas tout faire à la fois.

at the same time
I can't do everything at the same time.

de temps en temps [dətãzãtã]

from time to time

fois [fwa]
J'ai essayé trois fois de te téléphoner.
Je te l'ai dit 36 fois.

time
I tried three times to phone you.
I've told you that umpteen times.

jamais [ʒamɛ]
Je ne bois jamais.

never
I never drink.

la plupart du temps
[laplypardytã]

most of the time

peu à peu [pøapø]

little by little

quelquefois [kɛlkəfwa]

sometimes

recommencer [rəkɔmãse]

begin again

régulièrement [regyljɛrmã]	regularly
souvent [suvã]	often
toujours [tuʒur]	always
tout le temps [tultã]	all the time

de suite [dəsɥit]	in succession, in a row
J'ai appelé trois fois de suite.	I called three times in succession.
de temps à autre [dətãzaotr]	from time to time
des fois [defwa]	sometimes
fréquemment [frekamã]	frequently
fréquent, e [frekã, t]	frequent
permanent, e [pɛrmanã, t]	continuous, nonstop; permanent
sans arrêt [sãzarɛ]	without stopping
sans cesse [sãsɛs]	unceasingly, incessantly

Periods of Time

actuellement [aktɥɛlmã]	now, at the present time
Actuellement je suis stagiaire.	Now I'm an apprentice.
ancien, ne [ãsjɛ̃, ɛn]	former
au cours de [okurdə]	in the course of, during
Ce livre sortira au cours de l'année.	The book will appear in the course of the year.
avant [avã]	before, previously
Avant, j'allais au cinéma tous les soirs.	Previously, I went to the movies every evening.
Qu'est-ce que tu as dit avant?	What did you say before?
l'**avenir** *m* [avnir]	future
Je me suis trompé, mais à l'avenir je saurai comment faire.	I was wrong, but in future I'll know how it works.
court, e [kur, t]	short
de mon temps [dəmõtã]	in my day
depuis [dəpɥi]	since
la **durée** [dyre]	duration

durer [dyre]
Ça dure.

last, endure
That takes a long time!

en [ɑ̃]
En 1987.
Je lis ce bouquin en une heure.

in, within
In 1987.
I'll read this book in one hour.

entre [ɑ̃tr]

between, among

être en train de faire
[ɛtrɑ̃trɛ̃dfɛr]
Tu ne vois pas que je suis en train
de manger?

be in the act or process of doing

Don't you see that I'm in the
process of eating?

férié, e [ferje]
Fermé dimanche et jours fériés.

feast (day), holiday
Closed Sundays and holidays.

jusqu'à [ʒyska]

until

long, longue [lɔ̃, g]

long

longtemps [lɔ̃tɑ̃]

a long time

le **passé** [pɑse]

past

pendant [pɑ̃dɑ̃]
Tu ne fais rien pendant mon absence.

during
You do nothing during my absence.

pendant que [pɑ̃dɑ̃kə]
Tu ne fais rien pendant que je suis
parti.

while
You do nothing while I'm away.

présent, e [prezɑ̃, t]
A cause des circonstances
présentes.

present
Owing to the present
circumstances.

prochain, e [prɔʃɛ̃, ɛn]
A la prochaine.

next
Until next time!

quand [kɑ̃]
Quand tu voudras.
Tais-toi quand je parle.
J'ai respiré quand il est parti.

when, whenever; while
Whenever you like.
Be quiet while I'm talking!
I breathed a sigh of relief when he
went away.

le **séjour** [seʒur]

stay

le **siècle** [sjɛkl]
Au dix-neuvième siècle.

century
In the nineteenth century.

le **temps** [tɑ̃]
Le temps passe vite.

time
Time passes quickly.

les **vacances** *fpl* [vakɑ̃s]
Pendant les vacances.

vacation
During vacation.

autrefois [otrəfwa]	formerly, in former times, of old
contemporain, e [kõtãpɔrɛ̃, ɛn]	contemporary
dans le temps [dãltã]	formerly, of yore
le **délai** [delɛ]	delay; postponement, extension
en l'espace de [ãlɛspasdə]	within, in the space of
l'**époque** f [epɔk]	epoch
A l'époque, je travaillais chez Félix Potin.	At that time I was working at Felix Potin's.
L'année dernière à la même époque.	Last year at the same time.
la **période** [perjɔd]	period
pour le moment [purlmɔmã]	at the moment, at present
prolonger [prɔlõʒe]	prolong
tant que [tãkə]	as long as

Points in Time

à partir de [apartirdə]	from; from . . . on
A partir de maintenant.	From now on.
alors [alɔr]	then
Alors j'ai compris.	Then I understood.
après [aprɛ]	after, later
l'**arrivée** f [arive]	arrival
au bout de [obudə]	after
Au bout de trois heures.	After three hours.
au milieu de [omiljødə]	in the middle of
Au milieu de la nuit.	In the middle of the night.
avant de [avãdə]	before
bientôt [bjẽto]	soon
cesser [sese]	stop, cease
Il ne cesse de pleuvoir.	It doesn't stop raining.
le **commencement** [kɔmãsmã]	beginning, start
commencer [kɔmãse]	begin, start
Il commence à pleuvoir.	It is starting to rain.
Je commence la journée par faire de la gymnastique.	I begin the day by doing gymnastics.

d'abord [dabɔr]	at first
dans [dā]	in
Je reviens dans une heure.	I'll come back in an hour.
la **date** [dat]	date
le **début** [deby]	beginning; debut
le **départ** [depar]	departure
en ce moment [āsmɔmā]	at this moment, now
ensuite [āsɥit]	then
la **fin** [fɛ̃]	end
il est temps de [ilɛtādə]	it is time to
il y a [ilja]	ago
Je t'ai connu il y a quatre ans.	I met you four years ago.
le combien [ləkɔ̃bjɛ̃]	which one (in a series)
On est le combien?	What day of the month is it?
maintenant [mɛ̃tnā]	now
le **moment** [mɔmā]	moment
Noël *m* [nɔɛl]	Christmas
A Noël je reste à la maison.	I'm staying home at Christmas.
l'**origine** *f* [ɔriʒin]	origin
Pâques *fpl* [pɑk]	Easter
Il y a bal de noces le lundi de Pâques.	There's a wedding ball on Easter Monday.
la **Pentecôte** [pātkot]	Pentecost
la **rentrée** [rātre]	reopening of school in fall
La rentrée sera chère cette année.	Going back to school will be expensive this year.
se mettre à [səmɛtra]	start
Ne te mets pas à pleurer.	Don't start to cry.
tout à coup [tutaku]	suddenly
tout à l'heure [tutalœr]	in a little while; a little while ago
A tout à l'heure.	See you later.
Le facteur est passé toute à l'heure.	The mailman came by a little while ago.
tout de suite [tutsɥit]	right away
vers [vɛr]	toward, about

à ... près [a ... prɛ]	nearly, almost
à ce moment-là [asmɔmãla]	at that moment
à un moment donné [aɛ̃mɔmãdɔne]	at a certain time
après coup [aprɛku]	after the event, too late
après que [aprɛkə]	after
avant que [avãkə] Pars avant qu'il soit trop tard.	before Go before it's too late.
dès [dɛ] Je suis en forme dès le matin. Dès le début.	from ... on; since I'm in fine fettle from morning on. From the beginning.
dès que [dɛkə] Dès qu'il fait froid, je me sens mal à l'aise.	as soon as As soon as it gets cold, I feel uncomfortable.
immédiatement [imedjatmã]	immediately
l'**instant** *m* [ɛ̃stã]	instant, moment
sur le coup [syrlku]	on the spot, outright
la **Toussaint** [tusɛ̃]	All Saints' Day

▬▬▬▬ Subjective Assessments of Time ▬▬▬▬

à l'heure [alœr]	on time, punctual
à peine [apɛn]	hardly, scarcely
à temps [atã]	in time
au plus tard [oplytar]	at the latest
au plus tôt [oplyto]	at the earliest
avoir le temps (de) [avwarlətã də] Je n'ai pas le temps.	have time (to) I don't have time.
bref, brève [brɛf, brɛv] Sois bref.	brief, short Be brief.
de bonne heure [dəbɔnœr] Je me lève de bonne heure.	early I get up early.
déjà [deʒa]	already
dernier, -ère [dɛrnje, ɛr]	last

266

finir [finir]	finish, end
J'ai fini de travailler.	I've finished working.
J'ai fini par céder.	I ended up giving in.
Jamais de la vie. [ʒamɛdlavi]	Not on your life!
par la suite [parlasɥit]	later on
perdre son temps à [pɛrdrəsɔ̃tãa]	waste one's time (by)
J'ai perdu mon temps à faire la queue.	I wasted my time standing in line.
prêt, e [prɛ, t]	ready
récent, e [resã, t]	recent
le **retard** [rətar]	delay
Je suis en retard.	I'm late.
retarder [rətarde]	delay; be behind
tard [tar]	late
terminer [tɛrmine]	terminate
tôt [ṭo]	early; soon
vite [vit]	fast

à première vue [aprəmjɛrvy]	at first sight
d'avance [davãs]	in advance
la **limite** [limit]	limit

Nous étions en retard, alors nous avons couru bien vite chez nous.
We were late, so we ran home very fast.

Verbs

arriver à [arivea]
Je n'arrive pas à me concentrer.
J'y suis arrivé.

arrive at, attain, get to; succeed
I can't concentrate.
I succeeded in doing so.

avoir [avwar]

have

c'est [sɛ]

it is

devenir [dəvnir]

become

devoir [dəvwar]

must, be obliged to

être [ɛtr]

be

faire faire qqc [fɛrfɛrkɛlkəʃoz]
Je te fais travailler.

make do s.th.
I'll make you work.

il arrive (de/que) [ilariṽ də/kə]
Il m'arrive de rater mon bus.
Il arrive que je rate mon bus.

it happens (that)
I happened to miss the bus.
It sometimes happens that I miss
my bus.

il faut que [ilfokə]
Il faut que tu partes.

one must
You have to leave.

il paraît que [ilparɛkə]
Il paraît que le périf est fermé.

it seems that
It seems that the Peripherique
is closed.

il s'agit de [ilsaʒidə]
Il s'agit d'un meurtre.

it is a question of
It is a question of murder.

il y a [ilja]

there is, there are

laisser [lese]

let; leave

laisser faire [lesefɛr]
Laisse-moi partir.

allow to be done
Allow me to leave.

pouvoir [puvwar]
Je ne peux pas venir.

be able, can
I can't come.

savoir faire qqc
[savwarfɛrkɛlkəʃoz]
Je ne sais pas nager.

know how to do s.th.

I don't know how to swim.

sembler [sãble]

seem

venir de faire qqc
[vənirdfɛrkɛlkəʃoz]
Je viens de penser à toi.

have just done s.th.

I was just thinking of you.

Pronouns

au, aux, du, des [o, dy, de]
Je parle au patron.
Je mange du pain.

of the, to the
I'm speaking to the boss.
I'm eating bread.

dont [dɔ̃]
C'est le seul personnage dont je
me souviens.

whose; of whom/which
That's the only person whom
I remember.

elle, elles [ɛl]
Elle est malade.

she
She is ill.

en [ã]
J'en reprends.

of it, of them; some
I'll take some more.

eux [ø]
Je discuterai avec eux.

they, them
I'll debate with them.

il, ils [il]
Il est malade.

he, they
He is ill.

je [ʒə]
J'arrive.

I
I'm coming.

le, la, les [lə, la, le]
Je ne la connais pas.

him, it, her
I don't know her.

leur [lœr]
Je leur parle.

to them, their
I speak to them.

leurs [lœr]
Leurs photos me plaisent.

their
I like their photos.

lui [lɥi]
Je lui parle.
Lui, il est insupportable.

he, himself; to him, to her; him
I talk to him/her.
He is unbearable.

me [mə]
Tu me connais.

me, to me
You know me.

moi [mwa]
Tu viens chez moi?

I, me, to me
Are you coming to my place?

mon, ma, mes [mɔ̃, ma, me]
Mon oncle est malade.

my
My uncle is ill.

notre, nos [nɔtr, no]
Tu connais notre histoire.

our
You know our history.

nous [nu]
Non, pas nous.

we, us, to us
No, not us.

on [ɔ̃]
On s'en va.
On ne dit pas ça.

we, one
We're going.
One doesn't say that.

que [kə]
C'est la marque que je préfère.

that
It's the brand that I prefer.

qui [ki]
C'est toi qui as commencé.

who
It's you who began.

se [sə]

Il se lave.

himself, herself, oneself, itself,
themselves
He is washing himself.

soi [swa]
On est bien chez soi.

oneself
It's nice to be in one's own home.

son, sa, ses [sɔ̃, sa, se]
C'est dans son caractère.

his, her, its, one's
It's in his nature.

te [tə]
Je te connais.

you, to you
I know you.

toi [twa]
Dépêche-toi.

you
Hurry up.

ton, ta, tes [tɔ̃, ta, te]
Ton charme m'a saisi.

your
I'm overcome by your charm.

tu [ty]
Tu vois.

you
You see.

votre, vos [vɔtr, vo]
Votre maison me plaît.

your
I like your house.

vous [vu]
Je vous connais.
Je vous parle.
Si vous voulez.

you, to you
I know you.
I speak to you.
If you want.

y [i]
J'y pense.
J'y vais.

there; to it, to them
I'm thinking about it.
I'm going there.

▬▬▬ Interrogative Words ▬▬▬

combien [kɔ̃bjɛ̃]	how much
comment [kɔmɑ̃]	how
d'où [du]	from where
est-ce que [ɛskə]	Makes declarative statement into question
Est-ce que tu viens aussi?	Are you coming too?
où [u]	where
pourquoi [purkwa]	why
qu'est-ce que [kɛskə]	what
quand [kɑ̃]	when
quel, quelle [kɛl]	what; which

▬▬▬ Conjunctions ▬▬▬

au cas où [okau]	in the event that
c'est pourquoi [sɛpurkwa]	that's why; therefore
c'est un fait que [sɛtɛ̃fɛtkə]	it's a fact that
car [kar]	for, because
donc [dɔ̃k]	thus; therefore
et [e]	and
étant donné que [etɑ̃dɔnekə]	whereas, since
jusqu'à ce que [ʒyskaskə]	until
Je te casse les pieds jusqu'à ce que tu sortes avec moi.	I won't let you alone until you go out with me.
le fait que [ləfɛtkə]	the fact that
mais [mɛ]	but
ou [u]	or
ou bien [ubjɛ̃]	or
parce que [parskə]	because

pour que [purkə] Je vais vous garder les enfants pour que vous puissiez sortir.	so that I'm going to watch your children, so that you can go out.
puis [pɥi]	then
puisque [pɥiskə]	since, as, seeing that
sans que [sɑ̃kə] Je suis sorti sans que ma mère le sache.	without I went out without my mother's knowing it.
sauf que [sofkə]	except that
si [si] Je me demande s'il viendra. Si vous êtes libre, venez nous voir.	if; whether I wonder whether he will come. If you have time, come see us.
sinon [sinɔ̃]	otherwise; or else; unless
tandis que [tɑ̃dikə]	while; whereas

après que [aprɛkə]	after
avant que [avɑ̃kə] Je dois lui parler avant qu'il s'en aille.	before I have to talk to him before he goes.
bien que [bjɛ̃kə] Je sors bien qu'il pleuve. Je suis sorti bien qu'il pleuvait.	although I'm going out although it's raining. I went out although it was raining.
de manière que [dəmanjɛrkə]	so that
lorsque [lɔrskə]	when

Mais s'ils le font, c'est parce qu'ils s'aiment.
But if they do it, it is because they love each other.

━━━━━━━━━━━━━━━ **Negations** ━━━━━━━━━━━━━━━

ne ... aucun, e [nə ... okɛ̃, yn]   no, none, not any
Je n'ai aucune envie de sortir.   I have no wish to go out.

ne ... ni ... ni [nə ... ni ... ni]   neither ... nor
Je n'ai ni faim ni soif.   I'm neither hungry nor thirsty.

ne ... pas [nə ... pà]   not

ne ... pas du tout   not at all
[nə ... pàdytu]
Ça ne me plaît pas du tout.   I don't like that at all.

ne ... plus [nə ... ply]   no more, no longer
Je n'en peux plus.   I can't any more.

ne ... rien [nə ... rjɛ̃]   nothing, not anything
Je n'en crois rien.   I don't believe any of it.

ne ... ni l'un ni l'autre   neither, neither one
[nə ... nilɛ̃nilotr]
Je ne connais ni l'un ni l'autre.   I don't know either one.

ne ... personne [nə ... pɛrsɔn]   no one
Il n'y a personne ici.   There's no one here.

━━━━━━━━━━━━━━━ **Adverbs** ━━━━━━━━━━━━━━━

ainsi [ɛ̃si]   thus

assez [ase]   enough

aussi [osi]   also, too

c'est-à-dire [sɛtadir]   that is

comme [kɔm]   as

encore [ãkɔr]   still

etc. [ɛtsetera]   and so forth, etc.

juste [ʒyst]   correctly, exactly

même [mɛm]   even
Il a même osé me demander de   He even dared to ask me
l'argent.   for money.

moins [mwɛ̃]   less; fewer

273

par conséquent [parkɔsekã]	consequently
par contre [parkɔ̃tr]	against; by contrast
par exemple [parɛksãpl]	for example
peut-être [pøtɛtr]	perhaps
plus (...que) [plys ...kə]	more (...than)
presque [prɛskə]	almost
quand même [kãmɛm] J'y vais quand même.	just the same I'm going there just the same.
seulement [sœlmã]	but; only; solely, merely
surtout [syrtu]	above all, chiefly
très [trɛ]	very

cependant [səpãdã]	meanwhile; however, but, still
dans ce cas [dãska]	in this case
dans ces conditions [dãsekɔ̃disjɔ̃]	under these conditions
dans le fond [dãlfɔ̃]	actually, really, basically
en ce qui concerne [ãskikɔ̃sɛrn]	concerning
et ainsi de suite [eɛ̃sidsɥit]	and so on
n'importe [nɛ̃pɔrt] Tu dis n'importe quoi. N'importe comment.	no matter, never mind You're talking nonsense. No matter how.
pourtant [purtã]	however, nevertheless, yet
y compris [ikɔ̃pri]	including

Prepositions

à cause de [akozdə]	on account of, because of
à condition de [akɔ̃disjɔ̃də]	on condition
à force de [afɔrsdə]	by dint of
à l'aide de [alɛddə]	with the help of
à l'exception de [alɛksɛpsjɔ̃də]	with the exception of
au lieu de [oljødə]	instead of, in lieu of

au sujet de [osyʒɛdə]	about, concerning
avec [avɛk]	with
chez [ʃe]	to/at the house, home, office, etc. of
Je suis chez moi.	I'm at home.
Je vais chez le docteur.	I'm going to the doctor's office.
contre [kɔ̃tr]	against
d'après [daprɛ]	according to
D'après Michelin, c'est un bon restaurant.	According to Michelin, it's a good restaurant.
de [də]	of; from
grâce à [grɑsa]	thanks to
par [par]	by; through; out of
pour [pur]	for
sans [sɑ̃]	without
sauf [sof]	except
selon [səlɔ̃]	according to
sur [syr]	on

malgré [malgre]	despite
quant à [kɑ̃ta]	as for, as to, as far as
Quant à moi, je reste.	As for me, I'm staying.

▬▬ Indefinite and Demonstrative Constructions ▬▬

autre [otr]	other
ça [sa]	that
ce, cet, cette, ces [sə, sɛt, se]	this
Ce garçon m'étonnera toujours.	This boy will always amaze me.
ceci [səsi]	this, this thing, this matter
Ceci dit...	This having been said.
cela [səla]	that, that thing, that matter
celui, celle [səlɥi, sɛl]	the one
Celui qui finira le premier aura gagné.	The one who finishes first will have won.
ceux, celles [sø, sɛl]	the ones, those

chacun, e [ʃakɛ̃, yn]   each, each one
Chacun à son goût.   Each to his own taste.

chaque [ʃak]   each, every
C'est chaque fois la même chose.   It's the same thing every time.

la **chose** [ʃoz]   thing

entre autres [ãtrotr]   among other things

le **fait** [fɛt]   fact

l'un l'autre [lɛ̃lotr]   each other

le **machin** [maʃɛ̃]   thing, gadget; what's-his-name
Qui a fait ça? — Machinchose.   Who did that? — Oh, what's-his-
                                           name!

quelconque [kɛlkɔ̃k]   some, some sort of

quelqu'un [kɛlkɛ̃]   someone

quelque chose [kɛlkəʃoz]   something
On va leur offrir quelque chose   We're going to give you
de joli.   something pretty.

quelques [kɛlkə]   some, any; a few
Dans quelques instants, la suite de   In a few moments, our program
notre programme.   will continue.

quelques-uns, -unes   some
[kɛlkəzɛ̃, yn]
Je crois qu'il nous en reste   I believe we still have some left.
quelques-uns.

tel, telle [tɛl]   such

tout le monde [tulmɔ̃d]   everyone, everybody
Salut tout le monde.   Hello, everybody.

tout, toute, tous, toutes   all; whole; quite
[tu, tut, tus, tut]
Tu as mangé tout le gâteau.   You've eaten the whole cake.
On sort tous.   We're all going out.
Elle est toute contente.   She is quite content.
Je connais toutes les plages   I know all the beaches
de Bretagne.   of Brittany.

le **truc** [tryk]   gadget, device; thing
Comment on appelle ce truc?   What's this thing called?

La civilisation française est rapporteé dans des milliers de bibliothèques.
French civilization is recorded in thousands of libraries.

1 Interrogative Constructions

1. Questions without an Interrogative Pronoun (General Questions)

Tu viens? Vous restez?	Est-ce que tu viens? Est-ce que vous restez?	Viens-tu? Restez-vous?	Ton frère vient-il aussi? Le maire reste-t-il encore?
Intonation	Circumlocution	Inverted form	Double-subject construction
Spoken language	→		Written language

2. Questions with an Interrogative Pronoun (Selective Questions)

Intonation	Vous partez quand? –	Pourquoi tu pleures?
Circumlocution	Quand est-ce que vous partez?	Pourquoi est-ce que tu pleures?
Inverted form	Quand partez-vous? Quand part ton chef?	Pourquoi pleures-tu? –
Double-subject construction	Quand ton chef part-il?	Pourquoi ton frère pleure-t-il?

2 Formation of Noun Plurals

Phonetically the plural forms are identical with the corresponding singular forms. Exceptions: Nouns under 3 (below).

In *writing*, plurals are formed in the following ways:

1. Plural Ending in "-s"

un restaurant	des restaurants	une femme	des femmes	un ami	des_amis
[rɛstɔrɑ̃]		[fam]		[ɛnami]	[dezami]

Most nouns form their plural according to this pattern.

2. Plural Indicated Only by the Accompanying Word

un/des repas	un/des fils	un/des prix	un/des rendez-vous
[rəpa]	[fis]	[pri]	[rɑ̃devu]

Also: avis, cas, hors-d'œuvre, mois, pays, permis de conduire, printemps, temps, tennis

3. Other Plural Forms

un œuf	des œufs
[œf]	[ø]

3 Words That Accompany Nouns

	Initial sound	Singular — masculine	Singular — feminine	Plural — masculine	Plural — feminine
Definite article	Consonant	le thé au café du père de Paul	la bière à la boucherie de la mère de Paul	les parents aux vacances des parents de Paul	
	Vowel	l'épicier à l'arrêt de l'ami de Paul	l'épicerie à l'épicerie de l'amie de Sylvia	les_épiceries aux_amis des_amis de Sylvia	
Indefinite article	Consonant	un disque	une photo	des disques des_oranges	
	Vowel	un ami	une orange		
Partitive	Consonant	du sucre	de la confiture	—	
	Vowel	de l'argent	de l'eau		
Interrogative accompaniment	Consonant	quel disque?	quelle nuit?	quels disques?	quelles nuits?
	Vowel	quel ami?	quelle idée?	quels_enfants?	quelles_idées?
Demonstrative accompaniment	Consonant	ce disque	cette femme	ces disques ces_idées	
	Vowel	cet_appareil	cette eau		

Possessive accompaniment	Consonant	mon père ton frère son disque notre thé votre thé leur bus	ma mère ta sœur sa voiture notre fille votre photo leur bouteille	mes parents tes frères et sœurs ses disques nos vacances vos fils leurs filles
	Vowel	mon_oncle ton_ami son_argent notre ami votre argent leur oncle	mon_idée ton_amie son_huile notre épicerie votre orange leur eau	mes_oranges tes_oncles ses_amis nos_enfants vos_idées leurs_amies
Indefine accompaniment		tout le fromage	toute la crème	tous les jours toutes les nuits
Accompaniment for terms of quantity		un kilo de fromage une tasse de thé		un kilo d'abricots beaucoup de tomates

281

4 Noun Substitutes: The Personal Pronouns

1. Form and Function

| | | Disjunctive pronoun | Subject | Direct object | | Indirect object | | | Reflexive pronoun |
				Definite	Indefinite	with *à* Animate	Inanimate	with *de*	
Person speaking	Singular	moi	je	me		me			me
	Plural	nous	on	nous		nous			se
	Plural	nous	nous	nous		nous			nous
Person spoken to	Singular	toi	tu	te		te			te
	Plural	vous	vous	vous		vous			vous
	Polite form	vous	vous	vous		vous			vous
Person/thing spoken about	Sing masc	lui	il	le	en	lui	y	en	se
	Sing fem	elle	elle	la	en	lui	y	en	se
	Plur masc	eux	ils	les	en	leur	y	en	se
	Plur fem	elles	elles	les	en	leur	y	en	se

2. Position

	Subject	ne	Pron.	Verb/Auxiliary verb	pas		Participle
Present	Moi, Elle	ne	me	plaît		beaucoup,	cette robe.
	je	ne	l'	aime	pas	trop.	
Passé Composé	Non, Je	ne	t'	ai		déjà	montré le catalogue?
	je	ne	l'	ai	pas	encore	vu.

	Subject	ne	Auxiliary verb	pas	Pron.	Infinitive
Futur Composé	Tu	ne	vas	pas	la	commander, cette robe.
	Si, je		vais		la	commander.

5 Derived Adverbs

The Forms of the Derived Adverb

Unlike English, French adverbs are formed by attaching an adverbial ending to the corresponding adjective.

C'est une publicité Oui, elle influence	dangereuse. dangereusement	les enfants.	Usually *-ment* is attached to the feminine form of the adjective.
Enfin un slogan En tout cas, il est	intelligent! intelligemment	présenté.	Adjectives ending in *-ent* form adverbs by adding *-emment*.
Il n'est pas Si, si, il est	courant, couramment	ce modèle? utilisé.	Adjectives ending in *-ant* form adverbs by adding *-amment*.

Special forms: absolument, désespérément, énormément, profondément, vraiment.

6 Tenses

1. The Present Indicative

parler	ouvrir	finir	partir	attendre
je parle	j' ouvre	je finis	je pars	j' attends
tu parles	tu ouvres	tu finis	tu pars	tu attends
il parle	il ouvre	il finit	il part	il attend
nous parl**ons**	nous ouvr**ons**	nous finiss**ons**	nous part**ons**	nous attend**ons**
vous parl**ez**	vous ouvr**ez**	vous finiss**ez**	vous part**ez**	vous attend**ez**
ils parl**ent**	ils ouvr**ent**	ils finiss**ent**	ils part**ent**	ils attend**ent**

Special features of written French: nous mangeons, nous commençons. *Also:*changer, forcer

2. The «imparfait»

nous parlons	nous finissons
je parl**ais**	je finiss**ais**
tu parl**ais**	tu finiss**ais**
il parl**ait**	il finiss**ait**
nous parl**ions**	nous finiss**ions**
vous parl**iez**	vous finiss**iez**
ils parl**aient**	ils finiss**aient**

3. The «conditionnel»

je parle	attendre
je parler**ais**	j' attendr**ais**
tu parler**ais**	tu attendr**ais**
il parler**ait**	il attendr**ait**
nous parler**ions**	nous attendr**ions**
vous parler**iez**	vous attendr**iez**
ils parler**aient**	ils attendr**aient**

285

4. The «futur composé»

aller + Infinitive	je vais tu vas il va nous **allons** vous **allez** ils **vont**	demander finir attendre savoir écrire parler

5. The «futur simple»

je parle	attendre
je parlerai tu parleras il parlera nous parlerons vous parlerez ils parleront	j' attendrai tu attendras il attendra nous attendrons vous attendrez ils attend**ront**

6. The «passé composé»

with *avoir*		For reflexive verbs		with *être*	
j' ai tu as il a nous **avons** vous **avez** ils **ont**	mangé attendu fini **compris** écrit **ouvert**	je me tu t' il s' nous nous vous vous ils se	**suis** es est **sommes** **êtes** **sont**	lavé(e) lavé(e) lavé lavé(e)s lavé(e)(s) lavés	je **suis** tu **es** elle **est** nous **sommes** vous **êtes** ils **sont**	tombé(e) venu(e) sortie parti(e)s allé(e)(s) arrivés

7. The «plus-que-parfait»

	with *avoir*		For reflexive verbs			with *être*
j' avais	mangé	je m'	étais	lavé(e)	je étais	tombé(e)
tu avais	attendu	tu t'	étais	lavé(e)	tu étais	venu(e)
il avait	fini	il s'	était	lavé	elle était	sortie
nous avions	compris	nous nous	étions	lavé(e)s	nous étions	parti(e)s
vous aviez	écrit	vous vous	étiez	lavé(e)(s)	vous étiez	allé(e)(s)
ils avaient	ouvert	ils s'	étaient	lavés	ils étaient	arrivés

8. The «subjonctif»

parler	finir	boire
je parle	je finisse	je boive
tu parles	tu finisses	tu boives
il parle	il finisse	il boive
nous parlions	nous finissions	nous buvions
vous parliez	vous finissiez	vous buviez
ils parlent	ils finissent	ils boivent

9. The «passé immédiat»

venir de + Infinitive	je viens	de demander
	tu viens	de finir
	il vient	d' attendre
	nous venons	de savoir
	vous venez	d' écrire
	ils viennent de parler	

287

7 Verb Conjugations

Infinitive	Present Singular	Present Plural	imparfait	gérondif	présent du subjonctif	futur simple	participe passé
acheter	j'achète	nous achetons ils achètent	j'achetais	en achetant	que nous achetions que j'achète qu'ils achètent	j'achèterai	acheté
	Also:	crever, élever, s'élever*, emmener, enlever, se lever*, mener, se promener*, ramener, semer					
aller*	je vais tu vas il va	nous allons ils vont	j'allais	en allant	que nous allions que j'aille qu'ils aillent	j'irai	allé
appeler	j'appelle	nous appelons ils appellent	j'appelais	en appelant	que nous appelions que j'appelle qu'ils appellent	j'appellerai	appelé
	Also:	jeter, rappeler, se rappeler*					
s'asseoir*	je m'assois	ils s'assoient nous nous asseyons	je m'asseyais	en s'asseyant	que je m'asseye	je m'assiérai	assis

		nous attendons ils attendent	j'attendais	en attendant	que j'attende	j'attendrai	attendu
attendre	j'attends						
	Also: dépendre, descendre*, se détendre*, entendre, s'entendre*, s'étendre*, pendre, rendre, se rendre*, répondre, tondre, vendre						
avoir	j'ai tu as il a	nous avons ils ont	j'avais	en ayant	que j'aie qu'il ait que nous ayons qu'ils aient	j'aurai	eu [y]
battre	je bats	nous battons ils battent	je battais	en battant	que je batte	je battrai	battu
boire	je bois	nous buvons ils boivent	je buvais	en buvant	que nous buvions que je boive qu'ils boivent	je boirai	bu
conduire	je conduis	nous conduisons ils conduisent	je conduisais	en conduisant	que je conduise	je conduirai	conduit
	Also: construire, détruire, produire						

* These verbs form the *passé composé* with *être*.

Infinitive	Present		imparfait	gérondif	présent du subjonctif	futur simple	participe passé
	Singular	Plural					
connaître	je connais il connaît	nous connaissons ils connaissent	je connaissais	en connaissant	que je connaisse	je connaîtrai	connu
	Also:	disparaître, paraître, reconnaître					
convaincre	je convaincs il convainc	nous convainquons ils convainquent	je convainquais	en convainquant	que je convainque	je convaincrai	convaincu
croire	je crois	ils croient nous croyons	je croyais	en croyant	que je croie qu'ils croient que nous croyions	je croirai	cru
devoir	je dois	nous devons ils doivent	je devais	en devant	que nous devions que je doive qu'ils doivent	je devrai	dû
dire	je dis	nous disons vous dites ils disent	je disais	en disant	que je dise	je dirai	dit
	Also:	interdire					

Verbe	Présent	Imparfait	Participe présent	Subjonctif	Futur	Participe passé
se distraire*	je me distrais nous nous distrayons ils se distraient	je me distrayais	en se distrayant	que je me distraie qu'ils se distraient que nous nous distrayions	je me distrairai	distrait
écrire	j'écris nous écrivons ils écrivent Also: décrire	j'écrivais	en écrivant	que j'écrive	j'écrirai	écrit
envoyer	j'envoie nous envoyons ils envoient Also: renvoyer	j'envoyais	en envoyant	que j'envoie qu'ils envoient que nous envoyions	j'enverrai	envoyé
être	je suis tu es il est nous sommes vous êtes ils sont	j'étais	en étant	que je sois que nous soyons qu'ils soient	je serai	été
faire	je fais nous faisons vous faites ils font	je faisais	en faisant	que je fasse	je ferai	fait

* These verbs form the *passé composé* with *être.*

Infinitive	Present		imparfait	gérondif	présent du subjonctif	futur simple	participe passé
	Singular	Plural					
falloir							fallu
	il faut		il fallait		qu'il faille	il faudra	
finir	je finis					je finirai	fini
		nous finissons ils finissent	je finissais	en finissant	que je finisse		
	Also:	applaudir, avertir, choisir, définir, élargir, fleurir, garantir, nourrir, obéir, punir, réagir, réfléchir, remplir, répartir, rétablir, rétrécir, réunir, réussir, subir					
lire	je lis					je lirai	lu
		nous lisons ils lisent	je lisais	en lisant	que je lise		
	Also:	élire					
mettre		nous mettons ils mettent	je mettais	en mettant	que je mette	je mettrai	
	je mets						mis
	Also:	permettre, promettre, se remettre*					
mourir*		nous mourons ils meurent	il mourait	en mourant	que nous mourions	il mourra	mort
	je meurs				que je meure qu'ils meurent		

naître*	je nais il naît	nous naissons ils naissent	je naissais	en naissant	que je naisse	je naîtrai	né
ouvrir	j'ouvre	nous ouvrons ils ouvrent	j'ouvrais	en ouvrant	que j'ouvre	j'ouvrirai	ouvert
	Also: découvrir, offrir, souffrir						
partir*	je pars	nous partons ils partent	je partais	en partant	que je parte	je partirai	parti
	Also: dormir, mentir, répartir, sentir, servir, sortir*						
se plaindre*	je me plains	nous nous plaignons ils se plaignent	je me plaignais	en se plaignant	que je me plaigne	je me plaindrai	plaint
	Also: éteindre, peindre						
plaire	je plais il plaît	nous plaisons ils plaisent	je plaisais	en plaisant	que je plaise	je plairai	plu

*These verbs form the *passé composé* with *être*.

Infinitive	Present Singular	Present Plural	imparfait	gérondif	présent du subjonctif	futur simple	participe passé
pleuvoir	il pleut		il pleuvait		qu'il pleuve	il pleuvra	plu
pouvoir	je peux	nous pouvons ils peuvent	je pouvais	en pouvant	que je puisse	je pourrai	pu
préférer	je préfère	nous préférons ils préfèrent	je préférais	en préférant	que nous préférions que je préfère qu'ils préfèrent	je préférerai [ʒə prefɛrre]	préféré
Also:	accélérer, céder, considérer, espérer, exagérer, s'inquiéter*, protéger, répéter						
prendre	je prends	nous prenons ils prennent	je prenais	en prenant	que nous prenions que je prenne qu'ils prennent	je prendrai	pris
Also:	apprendre, comprendre, reprendre						
recevoir	je reçois	nous recevons ils reçoivent	je recevais	en recevant	que nous recevions que je reçoive qu'ils reçoivent	je recevrai	reçu
Also:	s'apercevoir*						

	je ris	nous rions ils rient	je riais	en riant	que je rie	je rirai	ri
rire							
	Also:	sourire					
savoir	je sais	nous savons ils savent	je savais	en sachant	que je sache	je saurai	su
suffire	je suffis	nous suffisons ils suffisent	je suffisais	en suffisant	que je suffise	je suffirai	suffi
suivre	je suis il suit	nous suivons ils suivent	je suivais	en suivant	que je suive	je suivrai	suivi
	Also:	poursuivre					
tenir	je tiens	nous tenons ils tiennent	je tenais	en tenant	que nous tenions que je tienne qu'ils tiennent	je tiendrai	tenu
	Also:	retenir					
valoir	il vaut	ils valent	il valait	en valant	qu'il vaille	il vaudra	valu

* These verbs form the *passé composé* with *être*.

Infinitive	Present		imparfait	gérondif	présent du subjonctif	futur simple	participe passé
	Singular	Plural					
venir*	je viens	nous venons ils viennent	je venais	en venant	que nous venions que je vienne qu'ils viennent	je viendrai	venu
	Also: convenir, devenir*, prévenir, revenir*						
vivre	je vis	nous vivons ils vivent	je vivais	en vivant	que je vive	je vivrai	vécu
voir	je vois	ils voient nous voyons	je voyais	en voyant	que je voie qu'ils voient que nous voyions	je verrai	vu
vouloir	je veux	nous voulons ils veulent	je voulais	en voulant	que nous voulions que je veuille qu'ils veuillent	je voudrai	voulu

* These verbs form the *passé composé* with *être*.

Index of all French Entries

All the basic vocabulary words appear in **boldface letters.** The more advanced terms are set in normal-type letters.

K

kilo 249
kilogramme 250
kilomètre 250
km à l'heure 250

L

la 269
la 143
là 257
La ferme! 53
La Haye 237
La paix! 53
La vache! 54
là-bas 257
lac 227
lâcher 24, 168
là-dedans 257
là-dessous 257
là-dessus 257
là-haut 257
laid, e 16, 45, 138
laine 84, 243
laisser 24, 168, 268
laisser faire 268
lait 73
laiton 243
laitue 75
lame à raser 110
lampe 92
lancer 24, 116
lande 230
langage 132
langue 74, 98, 128
langue étrangère 128
langue maternelle 128
lapin 74, 219
la plupart 251
la plupart du temps 261
laque 110
large 84, 227, 254
largement 60
largeur 254
lavabo 90, 124
lave-glace 180
laver 87, 96, 109
laver (se) 109
lave-vaisselle 95
le 269
le cas échéant 64

le combien 265
le fait que 271
le lendemain 260
le long de 256
Le soleil tape. 216
leader 196
leçon 132
lecteur, lectrice 201
lecture 36, 133, 201
légal, e 190
léger, -ère 84, 250
légion 150
législative 191
légume 75, 223
lent, e 14, 176
les 269
lessive 96
lettre 132, 140, 185
lettre expresse 186
leur 269
leurs 269
lever 24
lever (se) 19, 215
lever du soleil 230
lèvre 98
levure 70
lexique 130
liaison 160
libérer 152, 168
liberté 138, 150, 190, 207
librairie 66
libre 161
libre-service 73
licenciement 175
licencier 174
lied 143
Liège 237
lieu 253
lieu de naissance 3
ligne 109, 114, 183, 241
lilas 222, 241
lime à ongles 110
limer 22
limitation de vitesse 179
limite 254, 267
limiter 178
limonade 77
lin 243
linge 94
linguistique 130
lion 219
liquide 242
lire 34, 132

P

332

T

U

un 246
un cinquième 247
un milliard 247
un million 247
un (tout petit) peu 252
un tas de 252
uni, e 84, 157, 240
union 209
Union soviétique 8
unique 45
uniquement 64
unité 249
univers 229
université 137, 233
urbain, e 231
urbanisation 236
urbanisme 236
urgent, e 102, 186
usage 129
usé, e 85
usine 170
ut 143
utile 49
utiliser 26, 97

V

vacances 118, 263
vacancier, vacancière 119
vacciner 108
vache 219
vague 51, 227
vain, e 148
vainqueur 115, 206
vaisselle 70, 94
valable 49, 184, 188
valeur 139, 188
valise 118
vallée 226
vanter (se) 43
variable 218
varicelle 103
varié, e 79
varier 26
variétés 203
Varsovie 237
vase 93
veau 75, 219
vedette 145
véhicule 177

veille 260
veine 100
vélo 116, 176
vélomoteur 177
vendeur, vendeuse 5, 68, 81
vendre 68, 81
vendredi 259
venger (se) 35
venir 18
venir de faire 268
Venise 237
vent 215
vente 173
ventre 99
verbe 135
verdict 208
verger 224
verglas 178, 217
vérifier 35, 180
véritable 85
vérité 49, 148
vernis à ongles 110
verre 70, 244
vers 255, 265
vers 141
verser des larmes 30
vert, e 79
vertu 162
veste 83
vêtement 82
veuf, veuve 3
vexer 169
viande 75
victime 182, 205
victoire 114, 195, 205
victorieux, -euse 152
vidange 180
vide 79, 95
vide-ordures 95
vider 23
vie 21, 107
vieillard 165
vieillesse 165, 212
vieillir 165
Vienne 237
vieux, vieil, vieille 16
vif, vive 13, 240
vigne 221
villa 89
village 231
villageois, e 232
ville 231
ville nouvelle 232